# 13+ Science

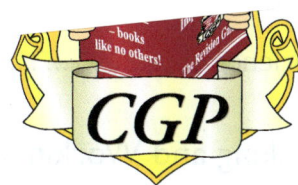

## For the Common Entrance exams

OK, so there's a lot going on in 13+ Science... but that's where this CGP Revision Guide comes in. It's full of everything you need for exam success.

There are study notes and examples for every topic, followed by plenty of practice questions. The practicals are covered too and you'll find fully worked answers at the back.

It's all totally up-to-date for the latest exams, and we've even included handy tips and tricks to help with your revision. Enjoy!

**How to access your free Online Edition**

This book includes a free Online Edition to read on your PC, Mac or tablet. You'll just need to go to **cgpbooks.co.uk/extras** and enter this code:

1577 9928 6625 4528

By the way, this code only works for one person. If somebody else has used this book before you, they might have already claimed the Online Edition.

# Revision Guide

# Contents

## Section C3 — Purity, Mixtures and Separating Mixtures



## Section C4 — Combustion and Thermal Decomposition



## Section C5 — Oxidation Reactions, Acids and Alkalis



## Section P1 — Energy and Resources



## Section P2 — Speed and Forces



## Section P3 — Pressure and Density



## Section P4 — Sound and Light



## Section P5 — Circuits and Magnets



## Section P6 — Space

Published by CGP

Editors:
Eleanor Crabtree, Luke Molloy, Georgina Paxman, Rachael Rogers, Camilla Sheridan, Tamara Sinivassen

With thanks to Ellen Burton, Barrie Crowther, Katie Fernandez, Emily Forsberg and George Wright for the proofreading.

With thanks to Jan Greenway for the copyright research.



ISBN: 978 1 78908 793 2

Printed by Elanders Ltd, Newcastle upon Tyne.
Clipart from Corel®
Illustrations by: Sandy Gardner Artist, email sandy@sandygardner.co.uk

# 13+ Science

Like it or not, you're going to be tested on 13+ Science at some point.
At least this page should shed some light on what to expect come exam day...

## There are Two Levels in the 13+ Science Exams

1) You can either do Foundation Level or Level 2 exams for Common Entrance 13+ Science (the Level 2 exams are a bit harder).
2) The exam papers are structured differently for each level.
3) There's only one paper for the Foundation exam, and it tests you on all three science subjects (Biology, Chemistry and Physics).
4) There are three separate papers for the Level 2 exam — one for each of the three sciences.
5) The number of marks and the amount of time you get is different for each level, as shown in these handy diagrams:

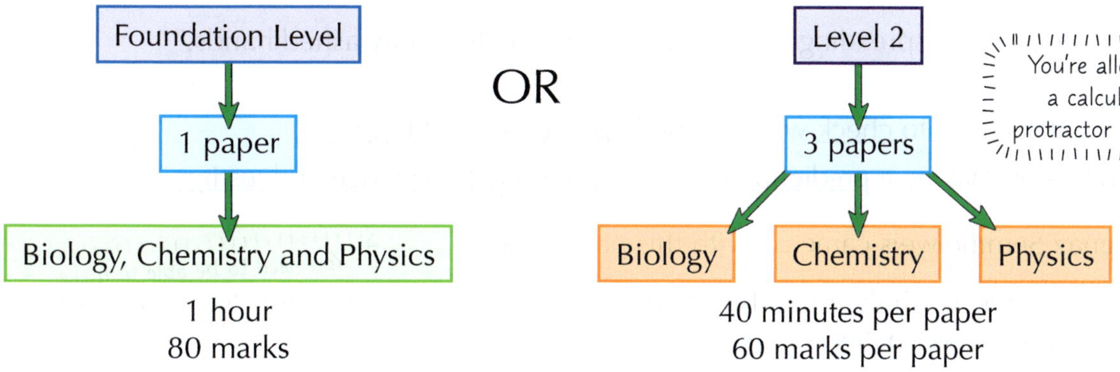


You're allowed to take a calculator and a protractor into all exams.

## All the Exams Test Your Thinking and Working as a Scientist Skills

1) Whichever exam you're doing, some of the questions on the paper will test your Thinking and Working as a Scientist (TWAS) skills.
2) You'll learn a lot about this from the practical activities you do in class, plus there's a whole section about Thinking and Working as a Scientist coming up next (see pages 2-10).
3) There are loads of ways the examiners could test your knowledge of this stuff. For example, you might be asked to calculate a mean, draw a graph of some results, analyse some data, or maybe draw a conclusion.

In each paper, at least 25% of the exam will test you on Thinking and Working as a Scientist skills.

**Level 2 Only Skills**

Some TWAS skills will only be tested on the Level 2 exams — these are:

- Understanding what might cause random and systematic errors (p.7).
- Rearranging formulae for appropriate calculations (p.9).
- Converting between units (p.9).

### Testing, testing, one two, one two...

This book is up and running and hopefully you're hearing me loud and clear. There's lots on Thinking and Working as a Scientist over the next few pages. Make sure you learn this as well the 'regular science'.

# The Scientific Method

Scientists work scientifically — it's their job. It means they can plan awesome investigations, get useful results and draw scientific conclusions from them. You need to be able to do all that too.

## A Hypothesis is an Explanation of Something

1) Scientists observe (look at) things they don't understand and ask questions about what they see.
2) They then use their knowledge and experience to come up with a possible explanation for what they've observed. This explanation is called a hypothesis.

**Example**

In a hospital in Vienna in the 1840s, lots of women were dying from a fever disease after giving birth. A doctor called Ignaz Semmelweis wondered why. He observed that lots of doctors were coming to the ward from other parts of the hospital and treating patients without washing their hands first.

Semmelweis came up with this hypothesis to explain his observation:

"Doctors are spreading diseases to patients on their unwashed hands."

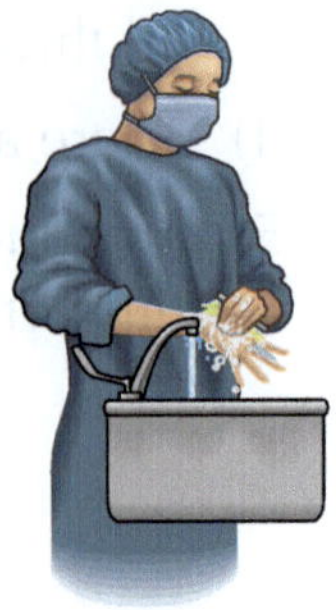

3) Next, scientists need to check whether the hypothesis is right or not.
4) They do this by making a prediction based on scientific knowledge and testing it.

**Example**

Ignaz Semmelweis came up with this prediction:

"If doctors wash their hands before seeing patients, fewer patients will die."

You need to be able to make predictions too — see page 4.

5) If tests show that the prediction is right, then there's evidence (signs) that the hypothesis is right too.
6) If tests show that the prediction is wrong, then the hypothesis is probably wrong as well.

## Other Scientists Test the Hypothesis

1) It's not enough for one scientist to do tests to see if the hypothesis is right or not.
2) That's why scientists publish their results — so other scientists can find out about the hypothesis and do the tests for themselves. Results are published in peer-reviewed journals.
3) Sometimes other scientists will find more evidence that the hypothesis is right.
4) When this happens, the hypothesis is accepted and goes into books for people to learn. An accepted hypothesis is often called a theory.

A journal is a collection of scientific papers. 'Peer-reviewed' means other scientists have checked the results and scientific explanations before the journal is published.

5) Sometimes they will come up with new ideas or find evidence that shows the hypothesis is wrong.
6) When this happens, the hypothesis has to change (or the scientist has to come up with a new one).
7) Sometimes new evidence will be found that means an accepted theory needs to change. This is how theories develop.

> 1) After a hypothesis has been accepted, the theory can be used to make a model.
> 2) A model is a simple description or picture of something that happens in real life. E.g. the particle model is a simple description of how particles move — see page 52.

8) Theories, models and scientific explanations are then used to develop further hypotheses.

# Issues Created by Science

Scientific developments can be great, but they can sometimes raise more questions than they answer...

## Science Affects Society and the World Around Us

1) Scientific knowledge is increased by scientists doing more experiments.
2) This knowledge leads to scientific developments, e.g. new technologies and new advice.
3) Scientific developments provide several advantages to society and our planet. For example, they can help save lives, improve people's health and quality of life, restore the natural environment and make everyday processes more efficient.
4) However, these developments are not without disadvantages — they can create issues and lead to debates. For example:

Scientists might recommend expensive changes — e.g. spending money on protecting wildlife habitats. Some people might think that it would be better to spend this money on other things, e.g. on schools or health services.

Wind turbines have been developed, which allow us to generate electricity from renewable resources rather than fossil fuels. But people might not want wind turbines built next to their houses.

Scientists have developed chemical pesticides, which kill pests that would damage crops. This increases the amount of food farmers can grow — so we can feed more people for less money. But some people think we shouldn't use pesticides, because many of them harm other species living in the area (e.g. by killing other insects that are not damaging the crops).

## Scientific Evidence can be Presented in a Biased Way

1) People who want to make a point can sometimes present data in a biased (unfair) way. For example, a company trying to sell a product might show you all the evidence that suggests it works better than other products, without showing you any of the evidence that suggests it doesn't.
2) It's the responsibility of scientists to make sure that their work is objective. This means making sure that they don't let other people influence their work or present their data in a biased way.

## Science Can't Answer Every Question — Especially Ethical Ones

1) We're always finding more answers, but we'll never know all the answers to everything.
2) Some scientific questions can't be answered yet. This is because there isn't enough data to support the scientists' hypotheses.
3) Eventually, we will be able to answer some of the questions when there is more evidence.
4) But science can't tell us whether something is ethically right or wrong. We have to decide for ourselves whether we are doing the right thing...

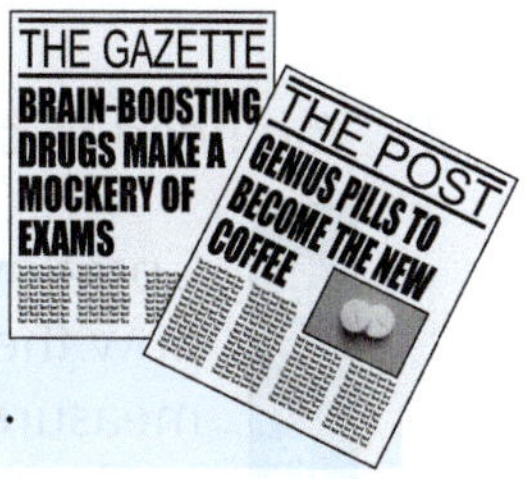


**E.g. New drugs can be taken to boost your 'brain power':**

Some people think they're good as they could improve concentration or memory. Other people say they're bad — they could give you an unfair advantage in exams.

# Planning Investigations

Scientists do investigations to find things out. You need to be able to do investigations too...

## Investigations Give Us Evidence

1) Scientists observe things and come up with hypotheses to explain them (see p.2).
You need to be able to do the same. For example:

Observation: People have big feet and spots. Hypothesis: Having big feet causes spots.

2) To determine whether or not a hypothesis is right, you need to do an investigation to gather evidence. To do this, you need to use your hypothesis to make a prediction — something you think will happen that you can test. E.g. people who have bigger feet will have more spots.
3) You can do investigations in a lab (laboratory) or somewhere else. For example:
   - A lab is the best place to study most chemical reactions.
   - But if you want to know how many rabbits there are in a wood, you'll need to go outside. This is called fieldwork... although it doesn't always have to be done in a field.

## Investigations Have to be Fair Tests

1) Before you start an investigation, you need to plan what you're going to do.
2) You must plan an investigation that will produce valid results. Valid results are results that are reliable (see page 6) AND answer the question (i.e. they show if your prediction is right or not).
3) For your results to be valid, your investigation must be a fair test. This means you must...

Only change one thing. Everything else must be kept the same.

4) The thing that you change is called the INDEPENDENT variable.
5) The things that you keep the same are called CONTROL variables.
6) The effect that's measured is called the DEPENDENT variable.

**Example: Investigation to see how changing the temperature of water changes how much salt dissolves in the water.**

Change the temperature of the water in each beaker...

...but keep everything else the same.

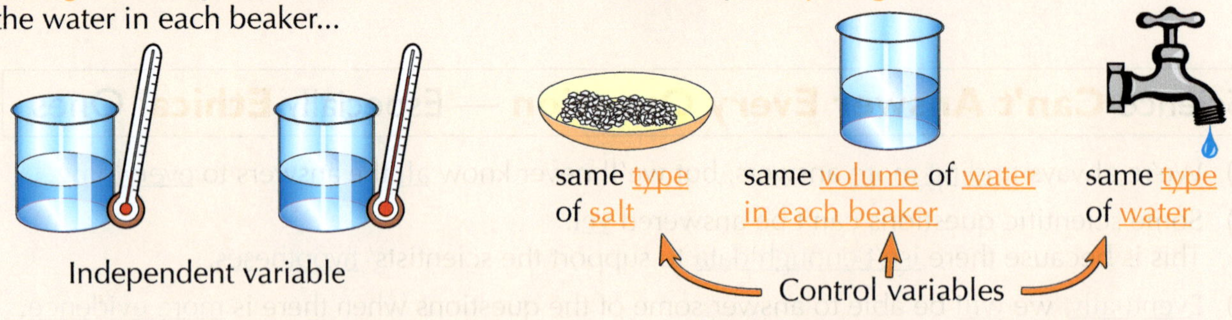


The dependent variable is how much salt dissolves — that's what you're measuring.

7) You need to consider how things that you can't control could affect your investigation too.

**Example**

Cornflowers grow best in sunny spots with alkaline soils. If you wanted to know how the number of cornflowers in an area was affected by light levels, you could measure the pH of the soil at your test spots too. Then you could comment in your evaluation (see p.10) on how the pH of the soil might have affected your results.

# Experimental Techniques and Risks

So you know what you want your experiment to do and what to measure. Next it's time to choose your method and think about any risks that might be involved with the experiment.

## Use Appropriate Techniques for the Work You're Doing

1) When you're planning an investigation, you'll need to make sure that you use appropriate methods for the work that you're doing. This applies whether you're working in a lab or in the field.
2) Here is an example of a technique that you'll need to know how to use in practical work.

### Choosing Samples

1) Sample size is how many things are in the group you're testing. For example, how many plants you test or how many people.
2) The bigger the sample size the better — it means you get more reliable results.
3) But scientists have to be sensible when choosing how big their sample should be. If it's too small, their results might not be very accurate. If it's too big the investigation might take ages to do.
4) It's best to choose your samples at random.

**Example: Random sampling in a field**

1) If you're investigating the types of plant found in a field, divide the field into a grid and take samples from random squares, all over the field.
2) If you just take samples from one corner, your results might not represent the types of plant found in the whole field.

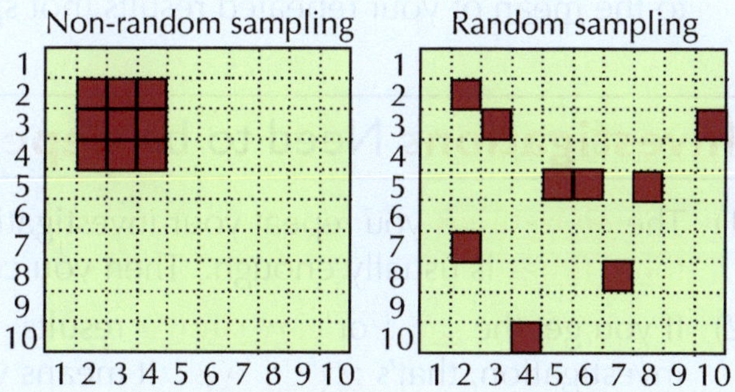


## Investigations Can be Hazardous

1) A hazard is something that could cause harm — e.g. bacteria, chemicals, electricity and fire.
2) All hazards have a risk attached to them — this is the chance that the hazard will cause harm.
3) You need to manage the risk of hazards by doing things to reduce them.

For example, if you're working with sulfuric acid, always wear gloves and goggles. This will reduce the risk of the acid coming into contact with your skin and eyes.

4) You also need to evaluate the risks associated with an experiment — if the risks are too big or too difficult to manage safely, you might need to ditch that method and come up with a different plan.

# Collecting Data

No matter what method you use, you need to think about the things on this page.

## Your Data Should be Accurate and Precise

1) Your data (results) needs to be accurate. Accurate results are really close to the true answer.
2) The accuracy of your results usually depends on your method — you need to make sure you're measuring the right thing.
3) You also need to make sure you don't miss anything that should be included in the measurements.

**Example**

If you want to measure the amount of gas produced by a water plant, you could count the bubbles given off. However, this isn't very accurate — you might miss some of the bubbles, or the bubbles might have different volumes.
You could make your results more accurate by measuring the volume of gas using a measuring cylinder instead.

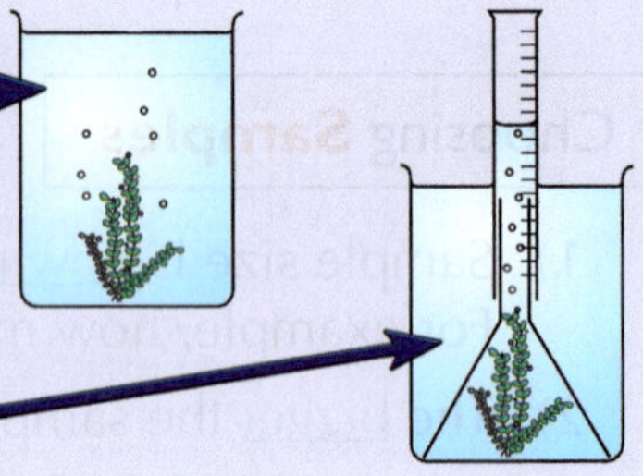

4) Collecting lots of results and calculating a mean (average) can also improve accuracy. It will also make your results more reliable (see below).
5) Your data also needs to be precise.
6) Precise results are ones where the data is all really close to the mean of your repeated results (not spread out).

| Repeat | Data set 1 ($cm^3$) | Data set 2 ($cm^3$) |
|---|---|---|
| 1 | 12 | 11 |
| 2 | 14 | 17 |
| 3 | 13 | 14 |
| Mean | 13 | 14 |

Data set 1 is more precise than data set 2.

## Investigations Need to be Repeated

1) The more times you repeat your investigation the better — but three times is usually enough. Then you can work out the mean.
2) If you get the same or very similar results each time you repeat your investigation, that's good news. It means your results are repeatable.
3) It also means they're more likely to be reproducible by other scientists. If other scientists can reproduce your results, it's more likely that your hypothesis is right (see p.2).
4) Results that are both repeatable and reproducible are said to be reliable.

You need to think about using appropriate materials for your experiment too.

## Your Equipment has to be Right for the Job

1) You need to choose the right equipment for your investigation.
2) For example, choose measuring equipment that will let you measure stuff accurately.

If you need to measure out 11 $cm^3$, this measuring cylinder would be great. It's the right size and you can see where 11 $cm^3$ is.

This measuring cylinder isn't as good. It's too big and you can't really see where 11 $cm^3$ is.

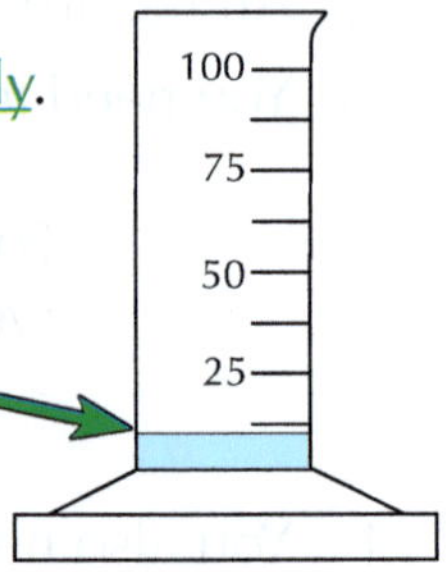


3) If you find that when you start the experiment the apparatus you're using isn't sensible, then you should change your apparatus or method. For example, if you're collecting gas given off in photosynthesis and find the vessel used to collect the gas is too big, either change the vessel or measure over a longer period of time (to collect more gas).

# Organising and Processing Data

Data you collect should be clear and useful — this may mean you need to do some calculations with it.

## Data Needs to be Organised so it can be Processed Later On

1) Tables are dead useful for organising data.
2) You should always make sure that each column has a heading and that you've included the units.

| Test tube | Volume of gas produced ($cm^3$) | | |
|---|---|---|---|
| | Repeat 1 | Repeat 2 | Repeat 3 |
| A | 28 | 37 | 32 |
| B | 47 | 51 | 60 |
| C | 68 | 72 | 70 |

## You Might Have to Process Your Data

1) When you've done repeats of an experiment you should always calculate the mean (a type of average). To do this, add together all the data values, then divide by the total number of data values.

| Repeat 1 ($cm^3$) | Repeat 2 ($cm^3$) | Repeat 3 ($cm^3$) | Mean ($cm^3$) | Range ($cm^3$) |
|---|---|---|---|---|
| 28 | 37 | 32 | (28 + 37 + 32) ÷ 3 = **32** | 37 – 28 = **9** |

2) You might also need to calculate the range (how spread out the data is). To do this find the largest number and subtract the smallest number from it. You want your results to be as precise (close to the mean) as possible — so the smaller the range, the better your results.
3) You may need to calculate the median or mode (two more types of average). To calculate the median, put all your data in numerical order — the median is the middle value. The number that appears most often in a data set is the mode.

If you have an even number of values, the median is halfway between the middle two values.

**Example**

**What is the median and mode for the data set: 1 2 1 1 3 4 2?**
The median is: 1 1 1 2 2 3 4. The mode is 1 because 1 appears most often.

4) You might need to calculate percentages. For example, if you want to give the amount X as a percentage of total amount Y, you do it like this:

$$\% = \frac{X}{Y} \times 100$$

**Example**

**240 g of a salt contains 60 g of sodium. What percentage of the salt is sodium?**
60 ÷ 240 = 0.25     0.25 x 100 = 25% of the salt is sodium.

## You Need to Watch Out for Errors in Your Results

1) The results of your experiment will always vary a bit because of random errors — tiny differences caused by things like making a mistake when you're measuring data. For example, you have to estimate the measurement if it's between two marks on a scale — sometimes your figure will be a bit above the real one, and sometimes it will be a bit below.
2) You can reduce the effect of random errors by taking repeat readings and finding the mean. This will make your results more precise.
3) If the same error is made every time, it's a systematic error. E.g. if you measure from the very end of your ruler instead of from the 0 cm mark every time, all your measurements would be a bit small.
4) You can fix some systematic errors in your results if you know about them. E.g. if your mass balance always reads 1 gram before you put anything on it you can subtract 1 gram from all your results.
5) Sometimes you get a result that doesn't fit in with the rest at all. This is called an anomalous result. You should investigate anomalous results and try to work out what happened.

# Presenting Data

Once you've processed your data, you need to present it. Behold, a page on just that...

## The Chart or Graph You Use Depends on the Type of Data You Have

1) Presenting your results in a chart or graph will help you to spot any patterns in your data.
2) Make sure axes on your charts and graphs have a sensible scale, are labelled and include the units.

### Bar Charts

Bar charts can be used to display:

1) Categoric data — data that comes in distinct categories, e.g. nutrients, metals.
2) Discrete (discontinuous) data — data that can be counted in chunks, where there's no in-between value, e.g. number of people is discrete because you can't have half a person.
3) Continuous data — numerical data that can have any value within a range, e.g. length or temperature.

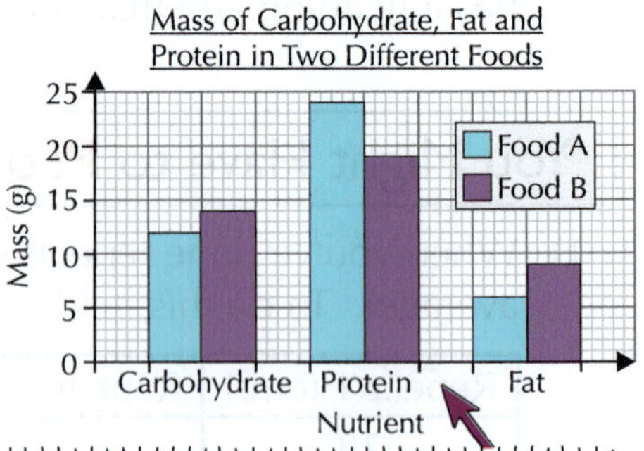


Leave a gap between different categories for categoric or discrete data. For continuous data, the bars should be touching.

### Scatter or Line Graphs

1) If both variables are continuous you can use a scatter graph to show if there is a relationship between them.
2) The dependent variable (the thing you measure) goes on the y-axis and the independent variable (the thing you change) goes on the x-axis.
3) You can draw a line of best fit (or a curve of best fit if your points make a curve) — a line that goes through or as near to as many of the points as possible.
4) You can use a line of best fit to estimate values for readings you didn't take during the experiment. This value might not be accurate if you extend the line beyond your data points.

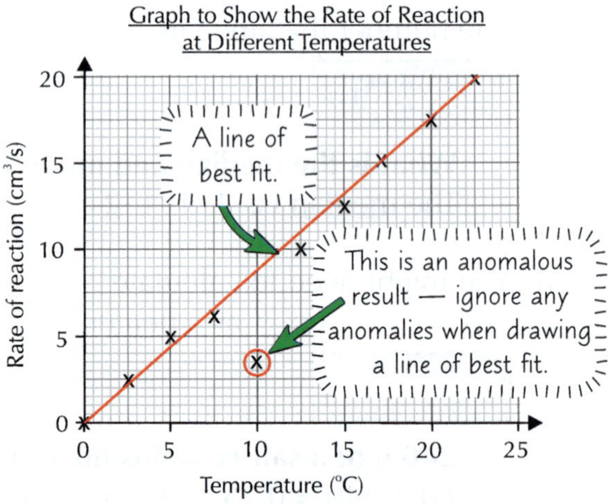


5) A line graph is normally used if you're plotting how a variable changes with time. The only difference between a line and scatter graph is that in a line graph the points are normally joined up by a line or curve.

### Distance-Time Graphs

1) A distance-time graph shows the distance travelled by an object over time.
2) The slope of the line (gradient) shows the speed at which the object is moving.
3) The steeper the graph, the faster the object is going.
4) Flat sections are where it's stopped.
5) Downhill sections mean it's moving back toward its starting point.
6) Curves represent a changing speed. A steepening curve means the object is speeding up. A curve levelling off means the object is slowing down.

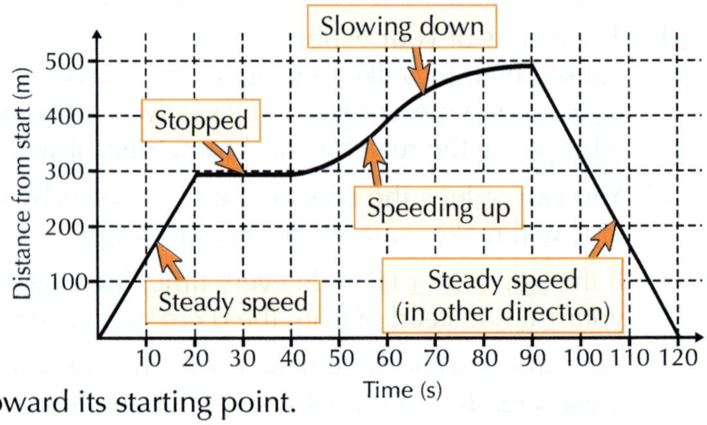

# Units and Equations

Sometimes you need to do some calculations to analyse your results.
If you do, you'd better make sure you get your units right...

## Scientists Use Standard Names and Units

1) There are lots of chemicals in the world, and a lot of them can be known by more than one name.
2) Scientists have a set of rules for naming molecules and compounds.
   This is so that when they talk about a chemical, they all know exactly which one they mean.
3) This set of rules is called IUPAC nomenclature.
4) Scientists have also come up with a set of standard units, called SI units.
5) This is because if different people used their own way of measuring, scientists wouldn't be able to compare any data.
6) All scientists use SI units to measure their data.
7) Here are some SI units you might see:

| Quantity | SI Base Unit |
|---|---|
| mass | kilogram, kg |
| length | metre, m |
| time | second, s |

## You Need to Know How to Convert Between Units

1) Here are some conversions you need to know:

   Time: 1 hour = 60 min, 1 min = 60 s
   Mass: 1 kg = 1000 g, 1 g = 1000 mg
   Length: 1 km = 1000 m, 1 m = 100 cm, 1 cm = 10 mm
   Area: 1 $m^2$ = 10 000 $cm^2$
   Volume: 1 $m^3$ = 1 000 000 $cm^3$

2) To convert (change) between units, you need to know the conversion factor.
   This is how many times bigger or smaller one unit is from the other.

   E.g. a kilogram (kg) is 1000 times bigger than a gram (g), so the conversion factor is 1000.

3) To convert from a larger unit to a smaller unit, multiply the amount of the larger unit by the conversion factor.

   E.g. 0.5 kg = (0.5 × 1000) g = 500 g

4) To convert from a smaller unit to a larger unit, divide the amount of the smaller unit by the conversion factor.

   E.g. 2500 g = (2500 ÷ 1000) kg = 2.5 kg

## Make Sure You Can Use Formulae

1) Formulae show relationships between variables.
2) To use a formula, you need to know the values of all but one of the variables.
3) Just stick the values you know into the formula, and do the calculation to find the final variable.
4) Always make sure the values you put into a formula have the right units.
5) If they don't have the right units, you'll have to convert them before you put them into the formula.

   E.g. if you want to calculate a speed in m/s (see page 101), you need to know the distance in metres and time in seconds. If you have measured the distance in centimetres, you need to convert it before you can put it in the formula.

6) If you need to rearrange a formula, you can use a formula triangle to help — there's more on these on page 160.

☐ ☐ ☐

# Concluding and Evaluating Data

Drawing a conclusion is all about finding patterns in your data.

## Graphs Show the **Relationship** Between **Two Variables**

When you're carrying out an investigation it's not enough to just present your data — you've also got to find any patterns or trends in the data. Graphs are great for this:

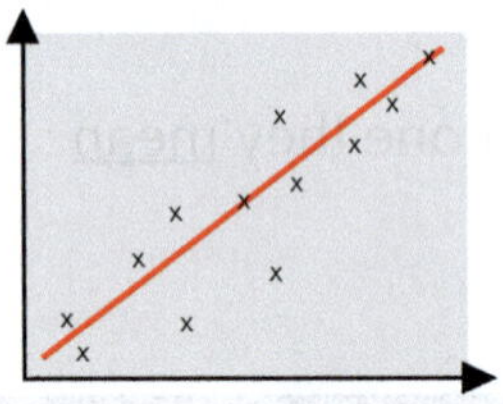

You can see here that as one variable increases the other increases too.

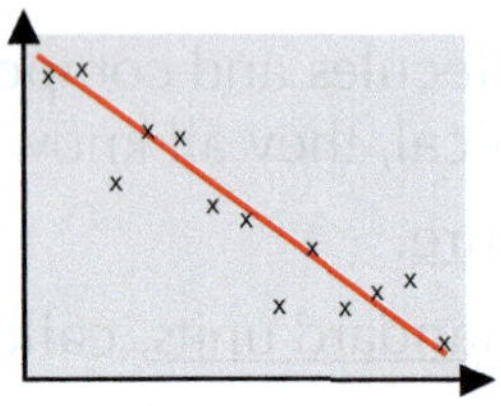

Here, as one variable increases the other decreases.

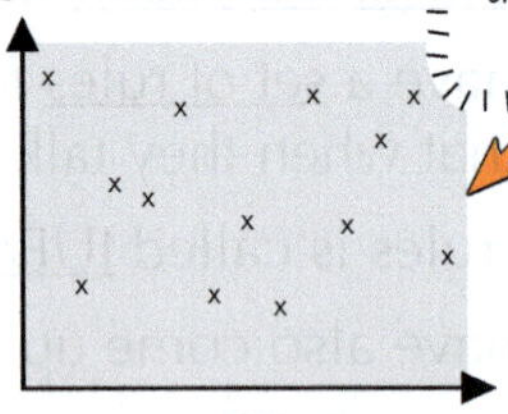

There's absolutely no pattern to be seen here...

This graph shows random distribution of the data — there's no relationship between the x and y values of the data points.

## A **Conclusion** is a **Summary** of What You've **Learnt**

1) Once you've organised and presented your data, you need to analyse it and come to a conclusion.
2) You just have to look at your data and say what pattern or trends you see.

**Example**

The table shows how tall pea plants grew with different fertilisers.

| Fertiliser | Mean growth / mm |
|---|---|
| A | 13.5 |
| B | 19.5 |
| C | 5.5 |

CONCLUSION:
Fertiliser B makes pea plants grow taller than fertiliser A or fertiliser C.

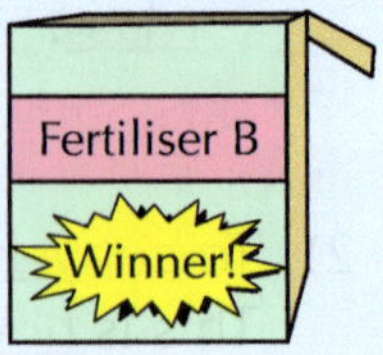


3) You also need to use the data that's been collected to justify the conclusion (back it up).

**Example (continued)**

Pea plants grown with fertiliser B grew 6 mm taller than the plants grown with fertiliser A and 14 mm taller than those grown with fertiliser C.

4) You should also use your own scientific knowledge (the stuff you've learnt in class) to try to explain the conclusion.
5) Finally, say whether or not your results back up your original hypothesis — or say whether your original prediction was right or wrong.

You could give your conclusion as a written report or as an electronic presentation.

## **Evaluation** — Describe **How** It Could be **Improved**

1) In an evaluation you look back over the whole investigation. You should comment on:
   1) The method — why did you choose it? Did it produce reliable results? If not, why not?
   2) Any potential sources of random error or systematic error (see p.7).
   3) The quality of the results — were they repeatable and accurate?
2) Then you can suggest any changes that would improve the three things above. For example, you might suggest changing the way you controlled a variable.
3) Your results might give you ideas for further investigations too. For example, you might come up with a new question that needs answering. Then the whole scientific process starts again...

There's more about reliable results on p.6.

# Cells

This page is about what living things are made of. Prepare to find out that you're quite similar to a plant.

## Living Things are Made of Cells

1) Another word for a living thing is an organism.
2) All organisms are made up of tiny building blocks known as cells.
   The fancy way to say this is that cells are the fundamental units of all living things.
3) You need to know the different components that make up animal cells and plant cells.

## Animal and Plant Cells Have Similarities and Differences

### An Animal Cell

An animal cell has the following cell structures:

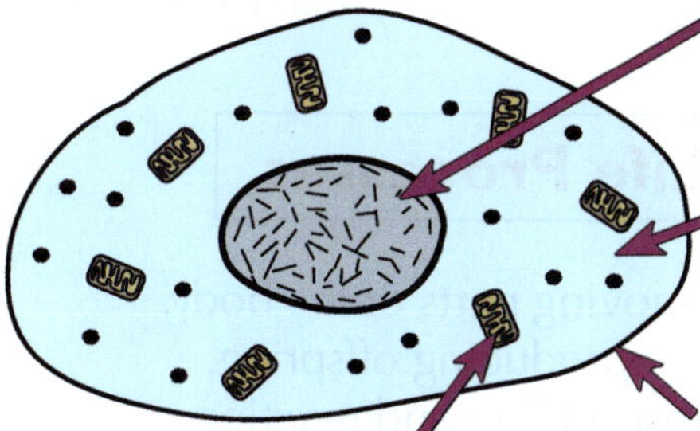

1) A nucleus:
   This controls what the cell does.
2) Cytoplasm:
   This is a jelly-like substance where most chemical reactions happen.
3) A cell surface membrane:
   This is a thin skin around the cell. It holds the cell together and controls what goes in and out.
4) Mitochondria:
   These are tiny structures inside the cell where most of the reactions for aerobic respiration (see p.36) take place. Respiration releases energy for the cell.

### A Plant Cell

Plant cells have a nucleus, cytoplasm, a cell membrane and mitochondria. But they also have:

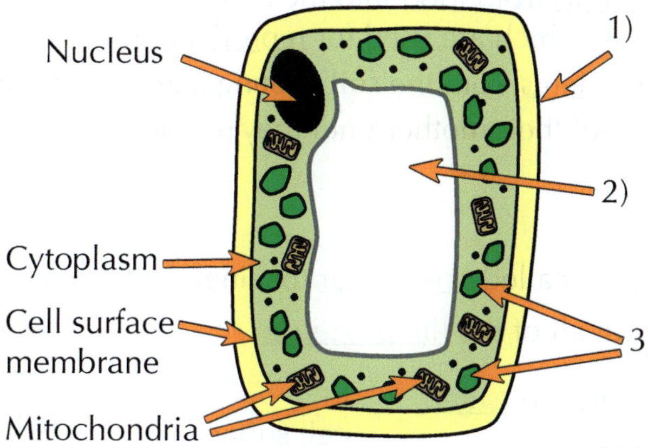


1) A cell wall:
   A rigid outer coating made of cellulose — it gives support to the cell.
2) A permanent fluid-filled vacuole:
   This is filled with cell sap — a weak solution of sugar and salts.
3) Chloroplasts:
   These contain chlorophyll used for photosynthesis (see p.33). Photosynthesis makes food for the plant.

REVISION TASK

**Cells — they're great for locking things up...**

You need to learn all the parts of an animal cell and a plant cell and what they do. Try covering the page then drawing and labelling the cells above — keep at it until it's all stuck in your head.

# More on Cells

Some organisms are made up of loads of cells, others are made up of just one single cell. Crikey.

## Learn How Cells are Organised

1) Animals and plants are made up of lots of cells — they're multicellular organisms.
2) In organisms with lots of cells, the cells are organised into groups. Here's how:

A group of similar cells come together to make a tissue.
A group of different tissues work together to make an organ.
A group of organs work together to make an organ system.
A multicellular organism is usually made up of several organ systems.

3) Human organisms have lots of organ systems, e.g. the gaseous exchange system (see p.23), the reproductive system (see p.25) and the digestive system.
4) Plants have organ systems too, e.g. the root system and shoot system.

**EXAMPLE**

Muscle cells make up muscle tissue... ...which, with other tissues, makes up the heart (an organ)... ...which, with other organs, makes up the cardiovascular system... ...which is one of the organ systems that makes up a human.

## All Organisms Need to Carry out the Seven Life Processes

1) However many cells an organism is made of, it needs to be able to carry out the seven life processes:
2) Each of the different levels of organisation have a role to play in carrying out the life processes. Here are some examples:

Movement — moving parts of the body.
Reproduction — producing offspring.
Sensitivity — responding and reacting.
Nutrition — getting food to stay alive.
Excretion — getting rid of waste.
Respiration — turning food into energy.
Growth — getting to adult size.

CELLS — all cells carry out respiration and can excrete waste products (e.g. carbon dioxide). Cells divide to produce new cells, which enables an organism to grow.

TISSUES — muscle tissue is able to move. Nervous tissue is able to sense changes in the environment and respond.

ORGANS — the small intestine is able to absorb nutrients from food into the blood. Anthers (in flowers) contain pollen grains, which are used for reproduction.

ORGAN SYSTEMS — a plant's root system absorbs nutrients from the soil. Young mammals grow within the reproductive systems of their mother until they're born.

## Some Living Things are Single-Celled

1) Living things that are made up of only one cell are called unicellular (or single-celled) organisms.
2) The single cell has adaptations so it can carry out all of the life processes.

**EXAMPLE**

1) Euglena are unicellular organisms that live in water.
2) They have a tail-like structure to help them move.
3) They have a moist surface membrane so they can absorb oxygen for respiration, and excrete waste gases.
4) They have chloroplasts so they can make their own food using photosynthesis.

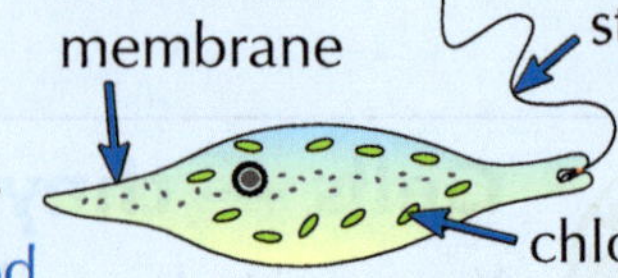

# The Light Microscope

PRACTICAL

A microscope makes really tiny objects look a lot bigger so you can see them. Clever stuff. You need to know how to use a microscope to look at plant and animal cells.

## You Might Need to Prepare a Microscope Slide

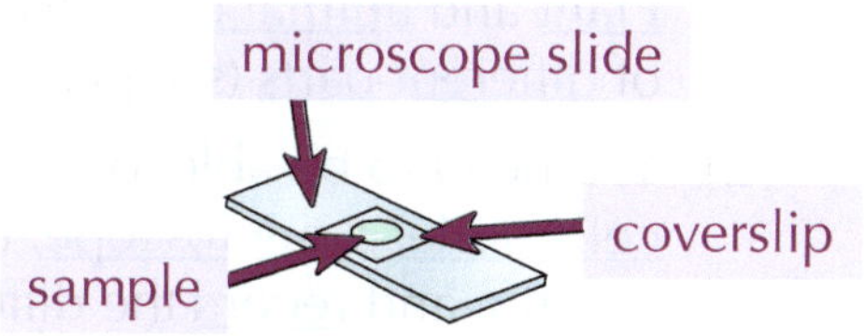


1) A microscope slide is a strip of thin clear glass or plastic with the material that you want to look at (e.g. cells) stuck to it.
2) To prepare a temporary microscope slide, take a small sample of the cells you want to look at. Place it in the middle of a clean microscope slide.
3) Use a pipette (dropper) to add a drop of water or a stain (see below) to the sample.
4) Carefully put a clean coverslip (a small, thin piece of plastic or glass) over the top. Then you're ready to look at your cells under the microscope.

Adding a stain (dye) to cells on a microscope slide makes it easier to see the cell parts. You need to use different stains depending on which bits of the cells you want to see. For example:
- methylene blue stains the nuclei of animal cells blue.
- iodine stains starch molecules (e.g. in plant cells) blue-black.
- eosin Y stains the cytoplasm in all cells pink.

## You Can Use a Microscope to Look at Cells

Here are the main parts of a light microscope — make sure you can identify them.

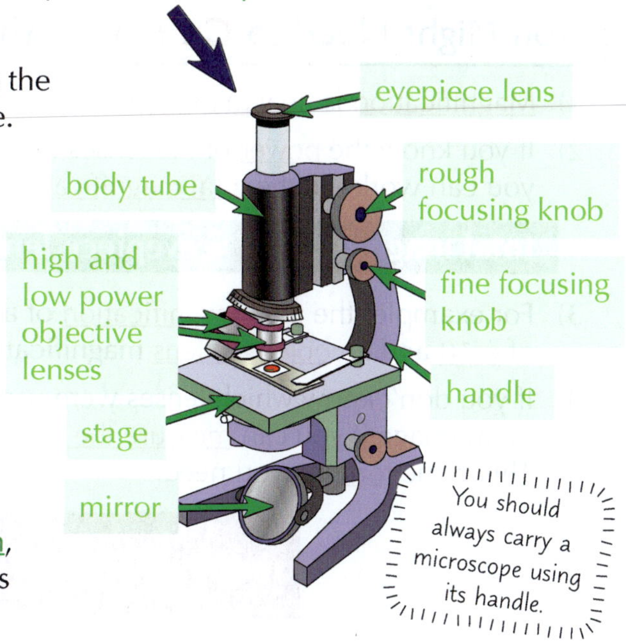


To use a light microscope to look at cells:
1) Place the microscope near a lamp or window. Angle the mirror so light shines up through the hole in the stage. (Don't reflect direct sunlight into the microscope — it could damage your eyes.)
2) Clip the slide you've prepared onto the stage.
3) Select the lowest powered objective lens.
4) Turn the rough focusing knob to move the objective lens down to just above the slide.
5) Look down the eyepiece lens and adjust the focus using the fine focusing knob. Keep adjusting until you get a clear image of the cells on the slide.
6) If you need to see the cells with greater magnification, switch to a higher powered objective lens and refocus the microscope (repeat steps 4 and 5).

### A stage and a bright light and those cells are ready to perform...

...well actually, they won't do a lot. But you'll be able to see some of their structures, which is pretty cool. Remember to always start with the lowest powered objective lens (the shortest one) and then swap onto a higher powered objective lens (a longer one) if you want the cells to look bigger.

# More on The Light Microscope

When you've finally got things in focus, you need to figure out what all those blobs and lines are...

## You Need to be Able to **Record** What You Can **See**

PRACTICAL

1) Plant and animal cells have lots of different parts (see page 11).
2) You need to be able to look at cells under a microscope, then identify and record the different parts you can see — this might mean drawing pictures of them...

Onion cells under a microscope:

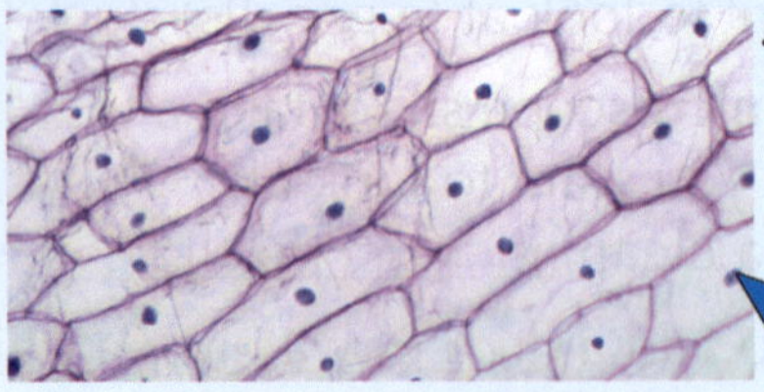

When you see lots of similar cells together like this, you're looking at part of a tissue (see p.12).

nucleus

- Using a sharp pencil, draw outlines of the main features using clear, unbroken lines. Don't include any colouring or shading.
- Make sure that your drawing takes up at least half of the space available and keep all the parts in proportion.
- Label the important features with straight lines which don't cross over each other, and include the magnification used (see below).

Onion cells, × 400 magnification

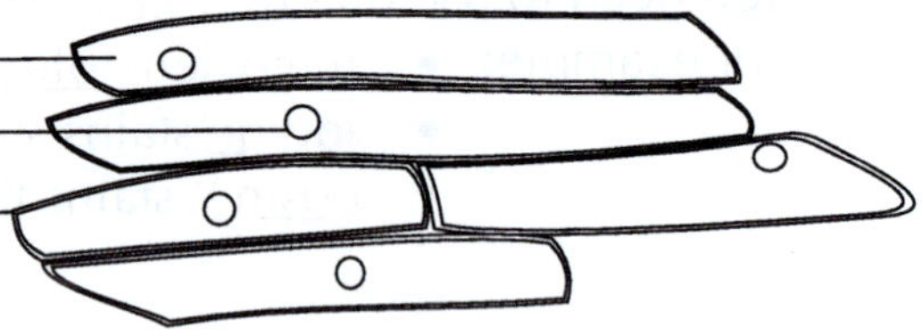


## You Might Need to **Calculate** the **Magnification**

1) Magnification is how many times bigger the image you can see is compared to the real object.
2) If you know the power of the lenses used by a microscope to view an image, you can work out the total magnification of the image using this simple formula:

**total magnification = eyepiece lens magnification × objective lens magnification**

3) For example, the total magnification of an image viewed with an eyepiece lens magnification of × 10 and an objective lens magnification of × 40 would be 10 × 40 = × 400.
4) If you don't know which lenses were used, you can still work out the magnification of an image if you can measure the image and know the real size of the object. This is the formula you need:

$$\text{magnification} = \frac{\text{image size}}{\text{real size}}$$

Both measurements should have the same units, e.g. mm. If they don't, you'll need to convert them first (see p.9).

REVISION TIP

### Microscopes — useful for looking at onions...

When you're revising it can be tempting to skip through some of the 'hands-on' science that you do in class, like drawing what you see through a microscope. But remember, in the exams there'll be questions on practical activities too, so it's important that you revise everything.

# Nutrition

Nutrition is all about getting the food and drink you need to stay healthy. For humans, a balanced diet will have the right amount of the five nutrients listed below, as well as fibre and water.
We get all the materials we need to build new cells from our food — so this is pretty important stuff.

## 1) Carbohydrates

These are like fuel for your body — your body uses glucose molecules in respiration to release all the energy you need to keep going (see page 36). Different foods contain different amounts of energy.

## 2) Proteins

Proteins are the raw materials for growth and the repair of damaged tissue.

## 3) Lipids

Lipids (fats and oils) act as a store of energy, which you use if your body runs out of carbohydrates. Stored lipids also act as insulation to keep you warm.

## 4) Vitamins

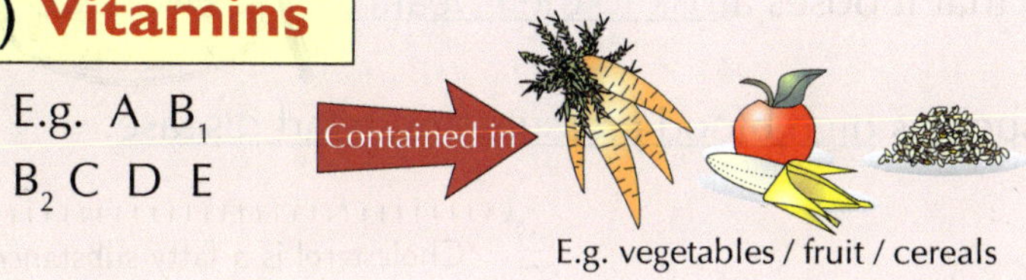


Vitamins are only needed in very small amounts. They keep many vital processes happening.

## 5) Minerals

| | | | |
|---|---|---|---|
| E.g. — | Iron | Calcium salts | Sodium |
| Found in — | | | |
| Needed for — | Blood | Teeth/Bones | Nerve cells |

A food diary (a log where you write down everything you eat and drink for a number of days or weeks) can give you an idea of how nutritious your diet is.

## Fibre

Dietary fibre helps food move through your digestive system. This helps to prevent constipation (when you're unable to pass 'poo').

## Water

Up to 60% of your body is water and all chemical reactions (e.g. digestion), take place in water – it's well important.

# Staying Healthy

Making sure you have a balanced diet (and enough exercise) is really important for keeping you healthy.

## An Unbalanced Diet Can Cause Health Problems

1) Some people don't get enough vitamins or minerals — this can cause deficiency diseases. E.g.:

   LACK OF VITAMIN C — Vitamin C is found in loads of fruits and vegetables such as oranges, strawberries, peppers and broccoli. A lack of vitamin C can cause scurvy, a disease that causes problems with the skin, joints and gums.

   LACK OF CALCIUM — Calcium is found in foods such as dairy products and leafy green vegetables. A lack of calcium in the diet can contribute to the development of osteoporosis — a disease in which the bones become less dense and are more likely to fracture. A lack of calcium can also lead to rickets in children — a disease that can lead to weak and soft bones.

2) Not eating enough food can also cause problems:
   1) If the body doesn't get all the energy it needs from food, it will start to use up its lipid stores.
   2) A person that doesn't eat enough will lose weight and may feel tired and weak.
   3) Not getting enough energy for a long time leads to starvation.

3) Problems can also be caused by getting too much of something, for example:

**Too much energy**

1) If you take in more energy from your diet than you use up, your body will store the extra energy as fat — so you will put on weight.
2) If a person develops so much body fat that it poses a risk to their health, then they are classed as obese.
3) Obesity can lead to health problems such as high blood pressure and heart disease.

**Too much saturated fat**

1) Products that contain animal fats (e.g. cheese, cream, butter) tend to have a high proportion of saturated fat.
2) Having too much saturated fat in your diet can increase your blood cholesterol level.
3) Having a high blood cholesterol level increases the risk of heart disease.

Cholesterol is a fatty substance that's essential for good health — it's found in every cell in the body.

## Understanding Food Labels can Help You Stay Healthy

Food labels give you information about the nutritional content of a food product. There are different ways the information can be displayed. Here's an example:

Energy, sugar, fat, saturated fat and salt are often highlighted — here they're colour-coded to indicate whether their levels are high (red), medium (orange) or low (green).

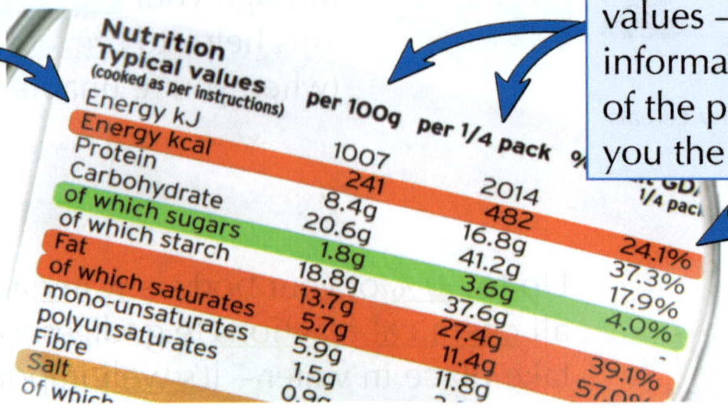

Nutrition
Typical values
(cooked as per instructions)
per 100g
per 1/4 pack
Energy kJ 1007 2014
Energy kcal 241 482
Protein 8.4g 16.8g
Carbohydrate 20.6g 41.2g
of which sugars 1.8g 3.6g
of which starch 18.8g 37.6g
Fat 13.7g 27.4g
of which saturates 5.7g 11.4g
mono-unsaturates 5.9g 11.8g
polyunsaturates 1.5g
Fibre
Salt
24.1%
37.3%
17.9%
4.0%
39.1%


There are often two sets of values — one to show you information for 100 g or 100 ml of the product, and one to show you the information per portion.

The amount of each nutrient in the food is often displayed as a percentage of the recommended amount an adult should have in a day.

# Food Tests

PRACTICAL

There are tests you can do to find out what a food sample contains. Test tubes at the ready...

## Start by Preparing Your Food Sample

1) Get a piece of food and break it up using a pestle and mortar.
2) Transfer the ground up food to a beaker and add some distilled water.
3) Give the mixture a good stir with a glass rod to dissolve some of the food.
4) Filter the solution using a funnel lined with filter paper to get rid of the solid bits of food.

## Use the Benedict's Test to Test for Sugar

1) Add Benedict's solution (which is blue) to the sample you want to test.
2) Heat the mixture in a hot water bath.
3) If there is sugar in the sample, the solution will change colour from blue to green, yellow or red.
4) The final colour depends on how much sugar is in the sample — the higher the concentration of sugar, the further the colour change goes.

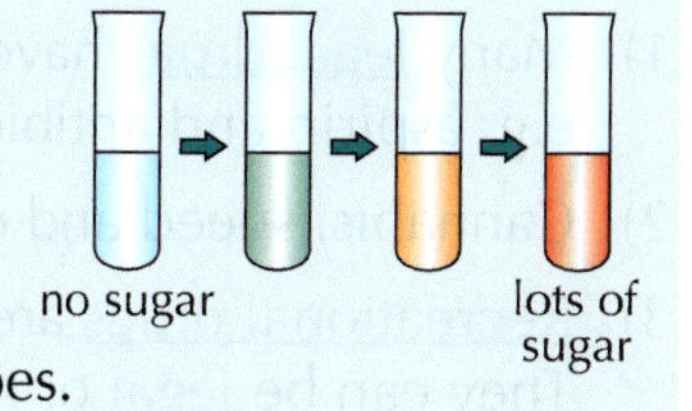


## Use Iodine Solution to Test for Starch

1) Just add iodine solution to the test sample.
2) If starch is present, the solution changes from browny-orange to a dark, blue-black colour.
3) If there's no starch, it stays browny-orange.

## Use the Biuret Test to Test for Proteins

1) Put 2 $cm^3$ of your test sample in a test tube.
2) Add 2 $cm^3$ of biuret solution to the sample and mix the contents of the tube by gently shaking it.
3) If the food sample contains protein, the solution will change from blue to purple. If no protein is present, the solution will stay blue.

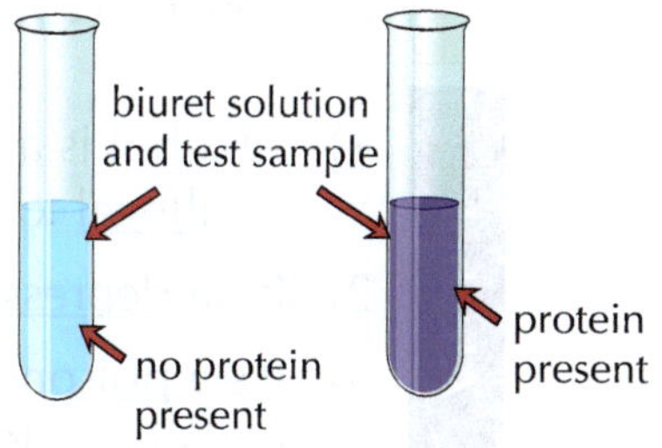


## Use the Emulsion Test for Lipids

1) Shake the test substance with ethanol for about a minute until it dissolves, then pour the solution into water.
2) If there are any lipids present, they will show up as a milky emulsion.
3) The more lipid there is, the more noticeable the milky colour will be.

An emulsion is when one liquid doesn't dissolve in another — it just forms little droplets.

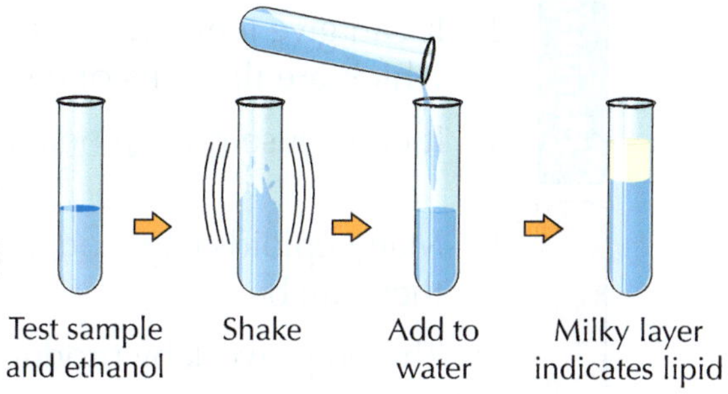


## Food testing isn't as tasty as it sounds...

Be careful when doing these food tests — e.g. wear safety goggles to protect your eyes from the chemicals.

# Drugs

Nearly all people take drugs in their life, without any negative effects on their health. But misusing drugs can cause all sorts of problems that can affect a person's health as well as their general behaviour.

## All Drugs Affect the Body

1) A drug is a substance that affects the way the body works. E.g. it may raise heart rate or affect vision.
2) Many drugs work by affecting the nervous system and the brain.
3) Your nervous system is responsible for sending messages around your body, so drugs can mean that messages aren't sent, or that your body doesn't respond properly to the messages.
4) By affecting your brain, drugs can also change the way you think and behave.

## Drugs can be Legal or Illegal, and Medical or Recreational

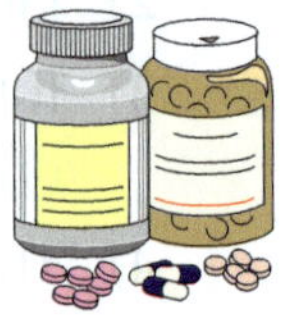

1) Many legal drugs have medical uses — they are used to improve health in some way, e.g. aspirin and antibiotics. Some legal drugs are not medical, e.g. caffeine and alcohol.
2) Cannabis, speed and ecstasy are examples of illegal drugs.
3) Recreational drugs are drugs used for enjoyment, rather than as medicine. They can be legal or illegal.
4) Many drugs are addictive — the effect that they have on the brain makes the person feel a really strong craving to keep having the drug. This can happen despite whether the person started taking the drug for medical or recreational reasons.

Taking drugs that harm your physical or mental health is known as substance misuse.

5) Here are some examples of common drugs that can be addictive:

**Tobacco**

1) Tobacco is a recreational drug smoked in cigarettes. It contains the drug nicotine. Nicotine is a legal drug, but it's illegal to buy it under the age of 18.
2) It gives feelings of pleasure, which can make the person want to keep smoking.
3) Tobacco smoke contains chemicals like tar, which damage the lungs (see page 24).

**Alcohol**

1) Alcohol is a recreational drug found in beers, wines and spirits. It's illegal to buy it under the age of 18.
2) It's a depressant, which means it decreases brain activity and slows down responses.
3) It's a poison which affects the brain and liver leading to various health problems, e.g. cirrhosis (liver disease). It also impairs judgement, which can lead to accidents.

**Marijuana**

1) Marijuana (also known as cannabis) is an illegal recreational drug that is usually smoked.
2) It can give feelings of well-being and relaxation. Sometimes it causes hallucinations, which are illusions of the mind.
3) It can cause mental health problems, including things like anxiety and paranoia.

**Opioids**

1) Many opioids (e.g. codeine, tramadol) are medical drugs — they can be prescribed by doctors as painkillers.
2) The drugs work by producing chemicals which stop pain, but the chemicals can also make a person feel more uplifted. People can get addicted to this feeling and continue taking the drugs (often in higher doses) even when they no longer need them for medical reasons.
3) Opioid addiction can cause problems with a person's breathing and can also lead to depression and anxiety.

# Preventing Disease

Micro-organisms might be tiny, but they're certainly mighty when it comes to disease. And because they're invisible to the naked eye, you just never know where they might be lurking...

## Micro-Organisms Cause all Sorts of Diseases

1) If micro-organisms get inside the body they can cause diseases, making you feel ill.
2) There are different types of micro-organism that can cause disease. E.g.:

### Viruses

1) Viruses invade living tissue and take over cells.
2) They kill or damage cells, making you feel ill.
3) Viral diseases include: colds, flu, chickenpox, German measles.

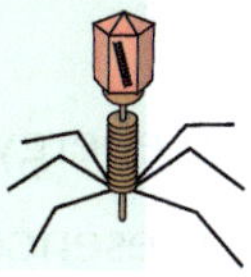

### Bacteria

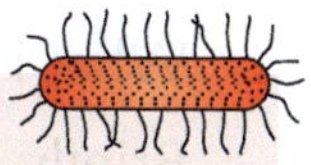

1) Bacteria are found in most places. Some are harmless but others cause disease.
2) They grow and reproduce very rapidly.
3) They attack body tissue or release poisons, making you ill.
4) Bacterial diseases include: tetanus, food poisoning, whooping cough.

## Being Clean Can Protect Us From Disease

The best way to defend against disease is to prevent the micro-organisms from entering our bodies in the first place. Keeping things clean is a really good way of doing this:

### Personal Cleanliness

1) People should wash their hands often (to wash off the micro-organisms that cling to our skin when we touch things). This is particularly important after going to the toilet as a person is likely to come in contact with many micro-organisms there. Hands should also be washed before eating, to help prevent micro-organisms entering the body through the mouth.
2) People should cover their mouth and nose with a tissue when sneezing or coughing, and then put the tissue in the bin. This helps to stop micro-organisms from being spread in the air or landing on nearby surfaces.

These measures are really important at home and also in public areas to stop micro-organisms being passed on to other people.

### Community Cleanliness

1) Places where food is made or prepared in the community need to be kept clean — this helps to prevent harmful micro-organisms getting into the food we eat.
2) Rubbish should be disposed of properly and collected regularly. If rubbish is left to build up, the harmful micro-organisms that grow on it can be passed on to humans by animals that feed on the rubbish (e.g. flies, rats).

REVISION TASK

### My computer has a virus — I must have sneezed on it...

Grab a friend, parent or pet, and see if you can explain to them two ways that personal cleanliness can prevent diseases, and two ways that community cleanliness can prevent diseases. Try not to sneeze on them and wash your hands when you've finished.

# Warm-Up & Practice Questions

Take a deep breath and ease yourself in gently with these Warm-Up Questions. Then attack the Practice Questions. All the answers are somewhere in this section, so there are no excuses.

## Warm-Up Questions

1) Name three structures that are found in both plant and animal cells. Describe what they all do.
2) What is the difference between a tissue and an organ?
3) Briefly describe how you would prepare a temporary microscope slide of a sample.
4) Give two nutrients that the body gets energy from.
5) Name one type of food that contains fibre.
6) Name one disease that is linked to a lack of calcium.
7) Give a health risk which is caused by taking in more energy than you use up.
8) Describe how you could test a food sample for the presence of lipids.
9) What does it mean if a drug is 'addictive'?
10) Explain why washing your hands can help prevent you from getting a disease.

## Practice Questions

1 The diagram below shows a plant cell.

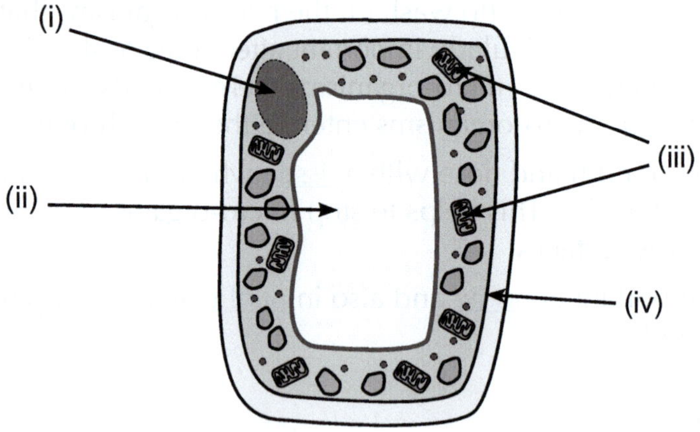


(a) Name the cell parts labelled (i)-(iv) on the diagram.

*(4 marks)*

(b) Name **two** structures that are found in plant cells, but not in animal cells.

*(2 marks)*

(c) Name the part of a cell that controls what the cell does.

*(1 mark)*

(d) Which life process are the mitochondria mainly needed for?

*(1 mark)*

# Practice Questions

2 (a) Use words from below to complete the following sentences.

**a tissue** **a cell** **an organ** **an organism**

......................... is the simplest building block of organisms.

Several of these can come together to make up ......................... ,

and several of these can work together to make ......................... .

*(3 marks)*

(b) What is an **organ system**?

*(1 mark)*

3 Alcohol is a recreational drug.

(a) Describe the difference between a recreational drug and a medical drug.

*(2 marks)*

(b) (i) Name **one** other type of recreational drug.

*(1 mark)*

(ii) Name **one** type of medical drug.

*(1 mark)*

(c) Give **one** way in which drinking alcohol affects the brain.

*(1 mark)*

PRACTICAL

4 Alana's class is investigating the cells in onion skin using light microscopes.
Alana collects a microscope from the teacher and positions it near a window.

(a) Light has to enter the microscope for it to work.

(i) Name the part of the microscope that can be adjusted to allow light in.

*(1 mark)*

(ii) Strong sunlight should not be allowed to enter the microscope.
Explain why.

*(1 mark)*

(b) Alana clips a slide with a piece of onion skin stuck to it onto the stage and focuses the microscope until she gets a clear image of the cells.

(i) Describe how Alana could make the image of the onion cells bigger.

*(2 marks)*

(ii) The cytoplasm of the onion cells is pink. Suggest why this is.

*(1 mark)*

(c) The eyepiece lens of the microscope Alana used had a magnification of × 10.
The objective lens she used had a magnification of × 10.
Calculate the total magnification Alana used to view the cells.

*(2 marks)*

# Summary Questions

Welcome to your very first set of Summary Questions. These questions have been written to help you find out what you know — and, more importantly, what you don't. Here's what to do...

- Try these questions and tick off each one when you get it right.
- When you've done all the questions for a topic and are completely happy with it, tick it off.

## Cells and The Light Microscope (p.11-p.14) ☐

1) What part of a cell holds the cell together and controls what goes in and out? ☐
2) What part of a cell is the place where most of the reactions for aerobic respiration happen? ☐
3) Describe the function of chloroplasts. ☐
4) List the seven life processes. ☐
5) Describe one example of a tissue being involved in one of the life processes. ☐
6) Give an example of a single-celled organism. ☐
7) What part of a microscope do you clip your slide onto? ☐
8) What do the focusing knobs on a microscope do? ☐
9) Describe three things you should do when drawing what you see under a microscope. ☐
10) How could you work out the total magnification of an object under a microscope, given the magnification of the eyepiece lens and objective lens? ☐

## Nutrition and Food Tests (p.15-p.17) ☐

11) Name all five nutrients in a balanced diet. Say what each is important for in the body. ☐
12) Apart from the five nutrients, give two things that are needed in a balanced diet. ☐
13) What health problem can be caused by a lack of vitamin C? ☐
14) Why is it not a good idea to have too much animal fat in your diet? ☐
15) Give five pieces of information that are usually highlighted on a food label. ☐
16) Describe how you could test for sugar in food. ☐
17) In a food sample, what is tested for using: a) iodine solution, b) biuret solution? ☐

## Drugs and Preventing Disease (p.18-p.19) ☐

18) What is a 'drug'? ☐
19) Give one negative effect that can be caused by: a) tobacco, b) marijuana. ☐
20) Name one medical drug that people can become addicted to. ☐
21) Name one disease caused by: a) viruses, b) bacteria. ☐
22) Other than washing their hands often, describe one other thing that people can do on a personal level to help stop micro-organisms from spreading. ☐
23) Explain two ways that community cleanliness can help to stop the spread of diseases. ☐

# Breathing

You breathe in and out about 20 000 times a day. That's a lot of breathing. Let's see how it happens...

## You Need to Breathe for Gas Exchange to Happen

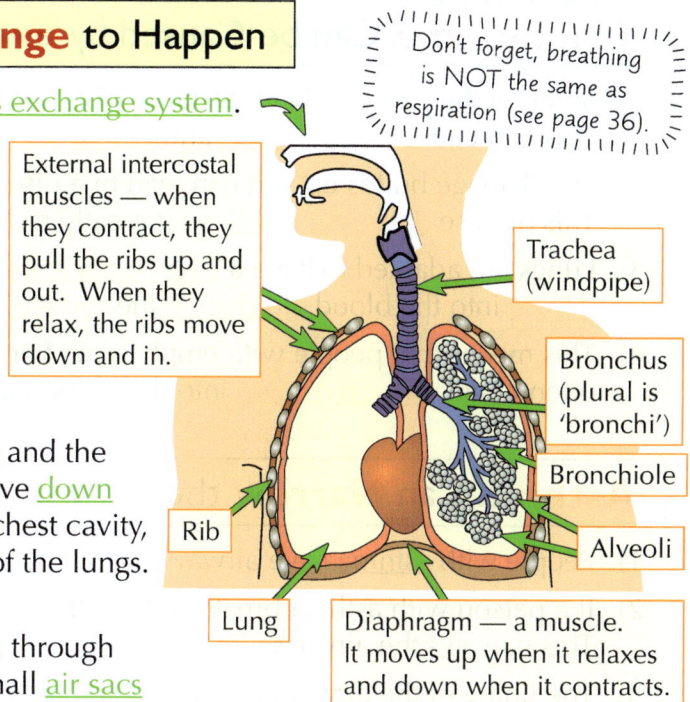

Don't forget, breathing is NOT the same as respiration (see page 36).

This diagram shows some of the structures in the gas exchange system. The process of getting air in and out of the lungs is called breathing. It happens like this:

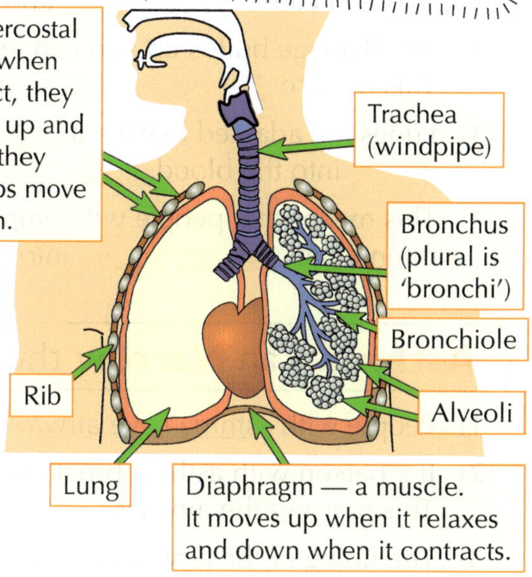


1) When you breathe in, the external intercostal muscles pull the ribs up and outwards and the diaphragm moves down. This increases the volume of the chest cavity, which decreases the pressure. So air rushes in to fill the lungs. This is called inspiration.
2) When you breathe out, the diaphragm moves up and the external intercostal muscles relax (so the ribs move down and inwards). This decreases the volume of the chest cavity, which increases the pressure. So air rushes out of the lungs. This is called expiration.
3) When you breathe in, air goes down the trachea, through the bronchi, through the bronchioles and into small air sacs in the lungs called alveoli.
4) These are where gas exchange takes place — oxygen diffuses from the air into the blood, and carbon dioxide diffuses out of the blood into the alveoli and is breathed out.

## The Mechanism of Breathing

The bell jar and parallelogram models show what's going on when you breathe:

**Bell Jar Model**

1) First you pull the rubber sheet down — like it's your diaphragm.
2) This increases the volume inside the bell jar, which decreases the pressure.
3) The drop in pressure causes air to rush into the balloons — this is like breathing in.
4) Let go of the rubber sheet — this is like relaxing your diaphragm.
5) The volume in the jar gets smaller. This increases the pressure, so air rushes out.

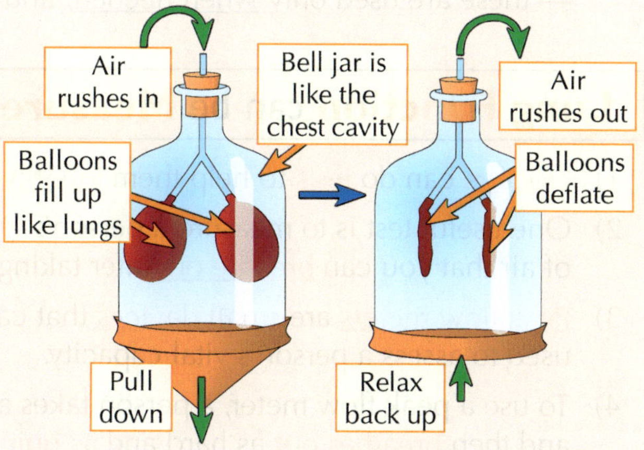


**Parallelogram Model**

1) The rubber band is like your intercostal muscles, the long rod is like your backbone and the horizontal rods are like your ribs.
2) Start by holding on to the long rod and pull the 'ribs' down so the rubber band stretches.
3) Then let go — the rubber band will contract and get shorter, which will pull the 'ribs' upwards. This is like the contraction of your intercostal muscles pulling your ribcage up when you breathe in.

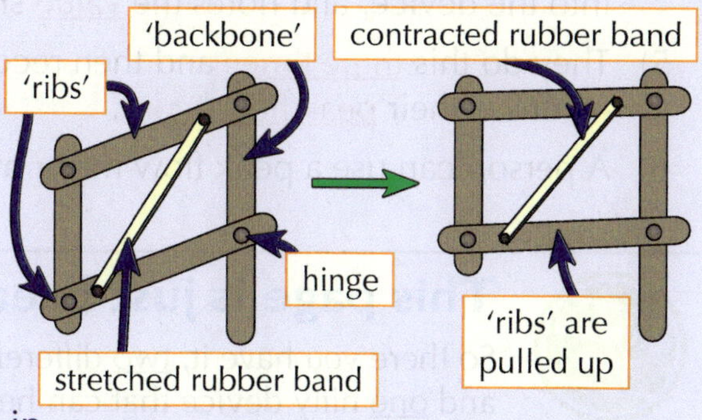

# More on Breathing

The gas exchange system is sensitive — here are a just a few things that can affect how well it works.

## Emphysema Can be Caused by Smoking

1) Some of the particles in cigarette smoke can irritate the lining of the airways. This can cause inflammation and damage to the lungs.
2) The damage builds up and can lead to a disease called emphysema. This disease destroys alveoli, so it greatly reduces the surface area of the lungs.
3) Lungs are adapted to have a large surface area to help as much oxygen as possible from the air diffuse into the blood. Reducing the surface area of the lungs makes gas exchange less efficient.
4) This means that people with emphysema find it difficult to breathe — they have to breathe more often to get enough oxygen into their blood and they often feel short of breath.

Emphysema can also be caused by other factors, such as drug use, air pollution, dust or fumes.

## Asthma Can Narrow the Airways

1) People with asthma have airways that are too sensitive to certain things (e.g. pet hair, pollen, smoke).
2) If a person with asthma breathes these things in, the muscles around their bronchioles contract. This narrows the airways.
3) The lining of the airways becomes inflamed and fluid builds up in the airways. This narrows the airways further and makes it hard to breathe (an asthma attack).
4) During an asthma attack, it's difficult for a person to get enough oxygen into their lungs and blood.
5) Inhalers contain drugs which help to open up the airways.
6) Some inhalers can be used to reduce the risk of having an asthma attack — they're designed to be used on a regular basis, but not all people with asthma need them.
7) Some inhalers can be used when a person is having an asthma attack — these are used only when needed, and all people with asthma should carry one.

## Lung Function can be Measured

1) Doctors can do tests to help them identify if someone has a medical condition that affects the lungs.
2) One useful test is to measure a person's vital capacity — this is the total amount of air that you can breathe out after taking your biggest breath in.
3) Peak flow meters are small devices that can be used to assess a person's vital capacity.
4) To use a peak flow meter, a person takes a deep breath and then breathes out as hard and as quickly as possible into the device, and notes the value shown on the scale.
5) They do this three times and then record the highest reading — this is their peak flow score.
6) A person can use a peak flow meter at home to monitor their condition.

REVISION TASK

### This page is just breathtaking...

So there you have it, two different conditions that have an impact on the gas exchange system, and one nifty device that can help to measure the impact. Make sure you get to grips with all of that — cover up the page and see how much you can write about each one.

# Human Reproductive Systems

In humans, males and females have different reproductive systems, made up of different organs (see page 12). These organs all work together to produce offspring (babies). No giggling now...

## The Male Reproductive System

1) Sperm are the male sex cells or 'gametes'.
2) Sperm are made in the testes after puberty.
3) Sperm mix with a liquid to make semen, which is ejaculated from the penis during sexual intercourse.

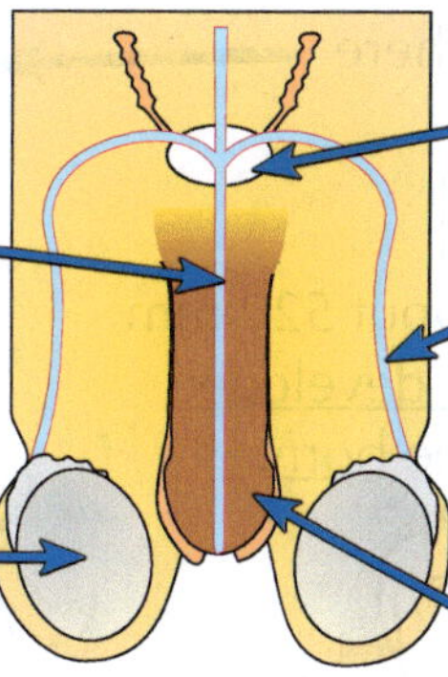

Urethra — a tube which carries sperm through the penis during ejaculation. Urine also passes through the urethra to exit the body.
Testis — where sperm are made.
Prostate gland — produces the liquid that's added to sperm to make semen.
Sperm duct — tube that carries sperm from a testis towards the urethra.
Penis — swells when filled with blood, for introducing sperm into the female.

## The Female Reproductive System

1) An egg (or 'ovum') is a female sex cell or 'gamete'.
2) One of the two ovaries releases an egg every 28 days.
3) It passes into the fallopian tube (or oviduct) where it may meet sperm, which have entered the vagina during sexual intercourse (sometimes known as copulation).
4) If it isn't fertilised by sperm (see below), the egg will die after about a day and pass out of the vagina.

*You say one ovum, but two (or more) ova.*

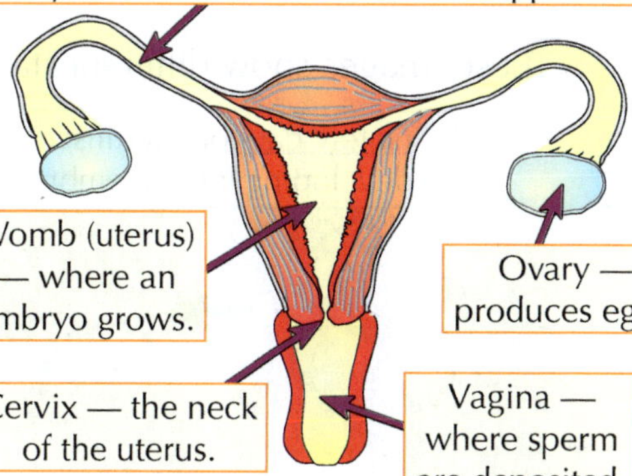

Fallopian tube — carries the egg from the ovary to the uterus. Fertilisation happens here.
Womb (uterus) — where an embryo grows.
Ovary — produces eggs.
Cervix — the neck of the uterus.
Vagina — where sperm are deposited.

## Fertilisation Needs to Happen to Make a Baby

*All mammals reproduce in a similar way to this.*

1) During sexual intercourse, millions of sperm are released from the penis into the vagina.
2) The sperm travel to the fallopian tubes where one may fertilise an egg.
3) An egg is fertilised when the nuclei of the sperm and egg cell fuse together. For this to happen the head of a sperm breaks through the membrane of the egg cell.
4) The fertilised egg is called a zygote.
5) The zygote divides — once it is a ball of cells it's called an embryo.
6) About one week after fertilisation, the embryo starts to implant (embed) in the wall of the uterus and the placenta (see page 26) begins to develop.

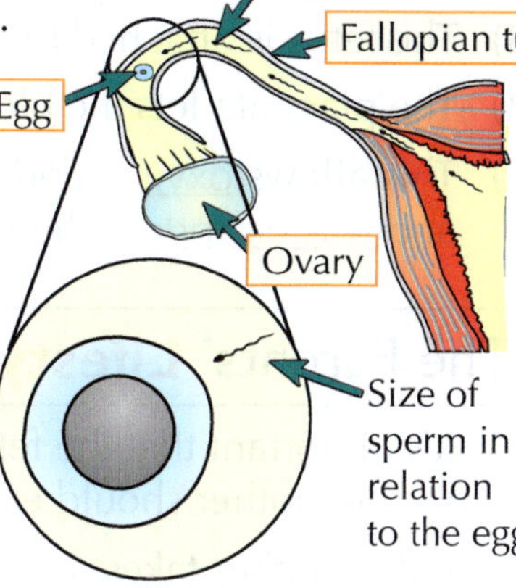

Sperm
Fallopian tube
Egg
Ovary
Size of sperm in relation to the egg

### Well, that's all a bit different to the stork story I got told...

I suspect you won't have too much difficulty remembering most of this stuff. Nevertheless, make sure you know the role of each organ in the reproductive systems and what fertilisation is all about before moving on.

# Having a Baby

Once an embryo has implanted in the wall of the uterus, the baby will develop until it's ready to be born.

## The Baby Develops in the Uterus

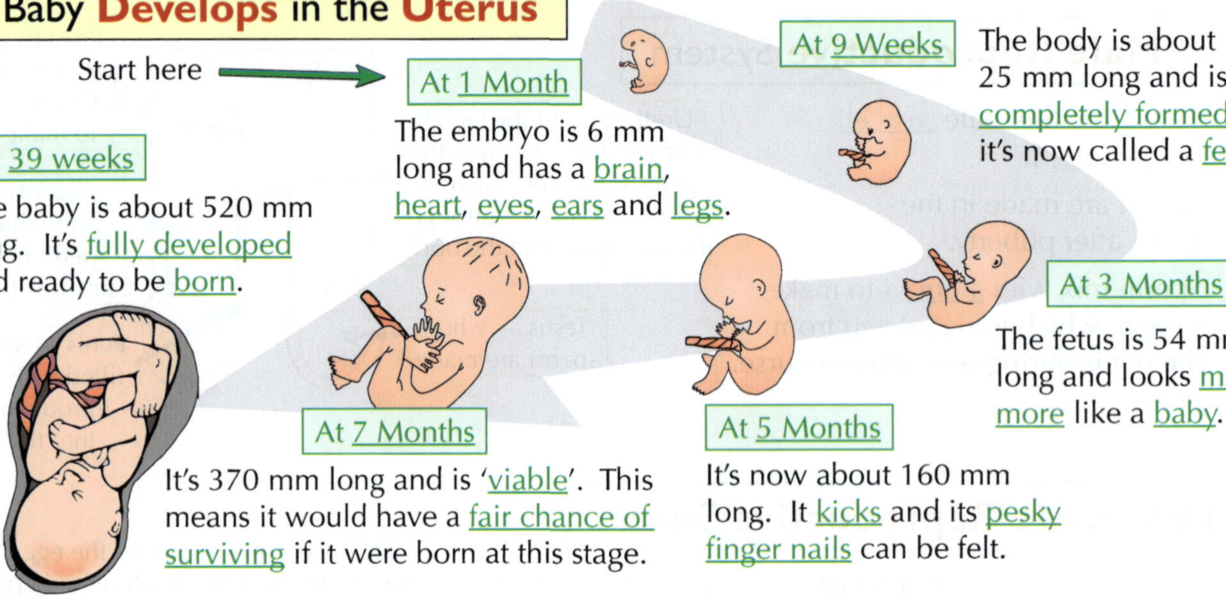


**At 1 Month**
The embryo is 6 mm long and has a brain, heart, eyes, ears and legs.

**At 9 Weeks**
The body is about 25 mm long and is completely formed — it's now called a fetus.

**At 3 Months**
The fetus is 54 mm long and looks much more like a baby.

**At 5 Months**
It's now about 160 mm long. It kicks and its pesky finger nails can be felt.

**At 7 Months**
It's 370 mm long and is 'viable'. This means it would have a fair chance of surviving if it were born at this stage.

**At 39 weeks**
The baby is about 520 mm long. It's fully developed and ready to be born.

These images show different stages of a baby's development:

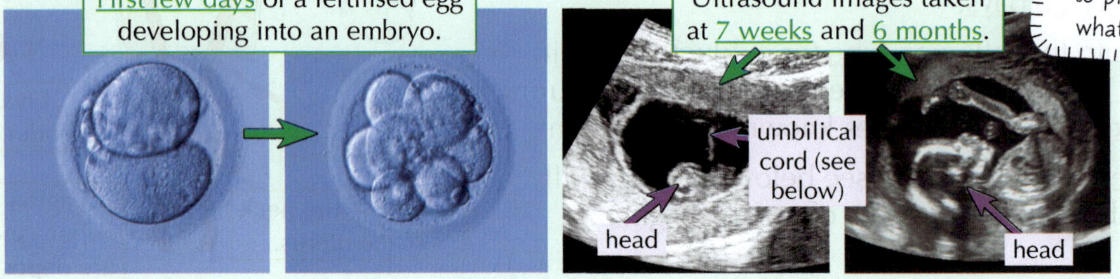


First few days of a fertilised egg developing into an embryo.

Ultrasound images taken at 7 weeks and 6 months.

Ultrasound images are created using sound waves to produce a picture of what's inside the body.

## The Placenta is Important for the Growing Fetus

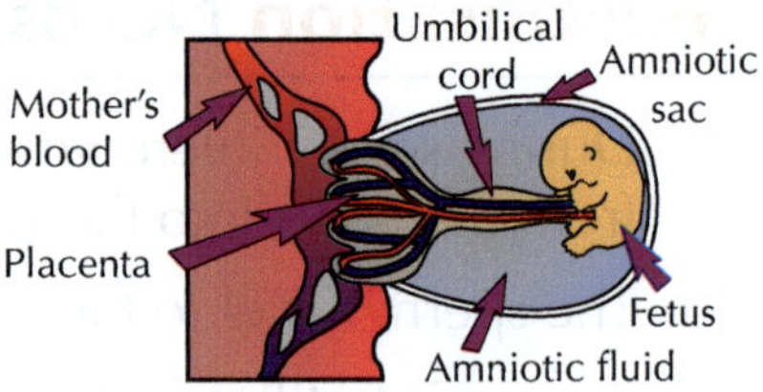


1) The placenta is an organ that's attached to the wall of the uterus.
2) The amniotic sac attaches to the placenta — this sac contains amniotic fluid, which protects the fetus against knocks and bumps.
3) The fetus is attached to the placenta by the umbilical cord.
4) The placenta lets the blood of the fetus and the blood of the mother get very close together.
5) This allows oxygen and nutrients to pass from the mother to the fetus and waste products like carbon dioxide to pass from the fetus to the mother.

## The Parents' Lifestyle can Affect the Fetus

1) It's important that the fetus receives all of the right nutrients as it grows, so the mother should eat a healthy, balanced diet.
2) If the mother takes drugs while she is pregnant, harmful molecules in her blood can cross the placenta and affect the fetus. For example, alcohol dependency and smoking can slow down the development of the fetus and cause a low birth weight.
3) The father's lifestyle may also be important — there's evidence that smoking and drugs (including alcohol) can affect sperm, which could then affect the fetus. And if anyone smokes around the mother while she's pregnant, she could breathe in the smoke, which might also affect the fetus.

# The Menstrual Cycle

The menstrual cycle — not the most exciting of things, but you wouldn't be here without it.

## The Menstrual Cycle Takes 28 Days

1) From puberty, females undergo a monthly sequence of events which are collectively known as the menstrual cycle.
2) This involves the body preparing the uterus (womb) in case it receives a fertilised egg.
3) If this doesn't happen, then the egg and uterus lining break down and are lost from the body through the vagina over a period of three to four days, usually.
4) The cycle has four main stages — they are summarised below:

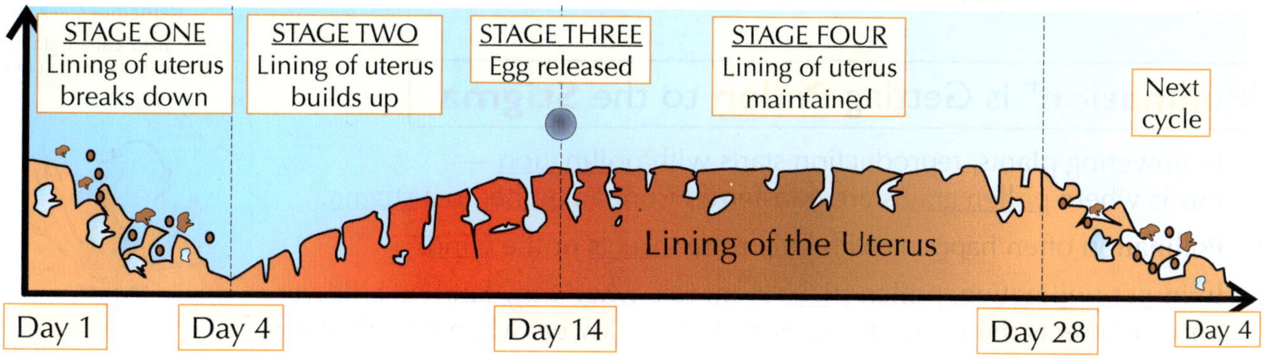


### Day 1

Bleeding starts as the lining of the uterus (womb) breaks down and passes out of the vagina — this is what's known as "having a period".

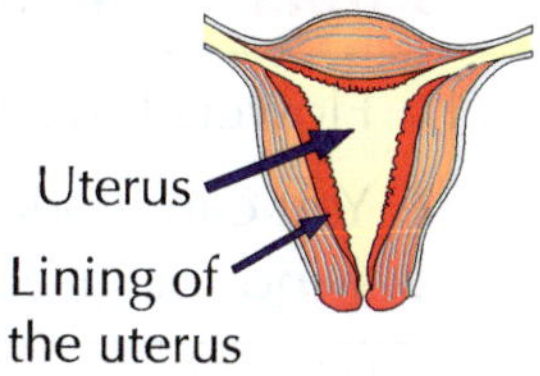


### Day 4

The lining of the uterus starts to build up again. It thickens into a spongy layer full of blood vessels ready for implantation (see 25).

### Day 14

An egg is released from the ovaries of the female, so this is the most likely time in which a female may become pregnant. (This day may vary from one woman to the next).

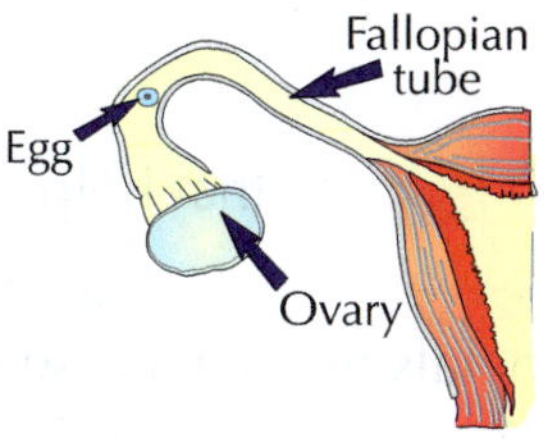


### Day 28

The wall remains thick awaiting the arrival of a fertilised egg. If this doesn't happen then this lining breaks down, passes out of the vagina, and the whole cycle starts again.

## A cycle that takes 28 days? That must hurt your legs...

Make sure you understand why the menstrual cycle is important — it's all about getting the uterus ready in case it receives a fertilised egg. If a fertilised egg does implant, the uterus lining stays thick so it can support the developing fetus and connect to the placenta. And if there's no fertilised egg, the cycle continues...

# Plant Reproduction

Plants, like all living things, need to reproduce. And that's where a plant's pretty flowers come in...

## The Flower Contains the Reproductive Organs

Stamens (the male part of the flower) consist of:

an anther — this contains pollen grains, which produce the male sex cells.

a filament — this supports the anther.

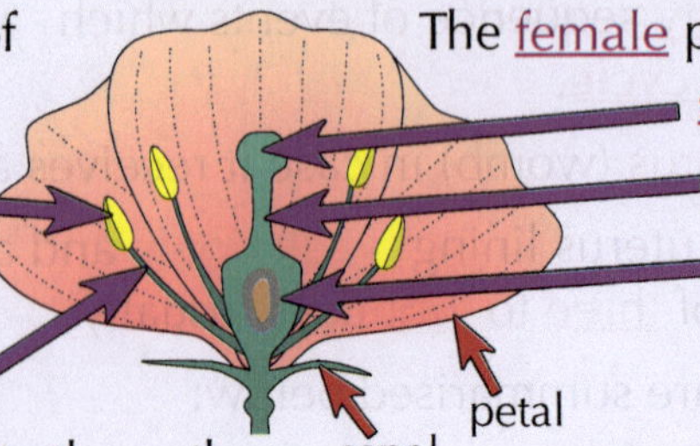


The female parts of the flower (carpels) consist of the:

stigma,

style and

ovary — the ovary contains the female sex cells inside ovules. Just like in humans, a female sex cell is called an egg cell or 'ovum'.

Remember, sex cells are also called 'gametes'.

## "Pollination" is Getting Pollen to the Stigma

1) In flowering plants, reproduction starts with pollination — this is where pollen grains are transferred from an anther to a stigma.
2) Pollination often happens with help from insects or the wind.
3) In insect-pollination, pollen sticks to insects when they land on a flower and the insects then carry the pollen to other flowers when they fly away.
4) In wind-pollination, pollen is blown off one plant and onto anther.

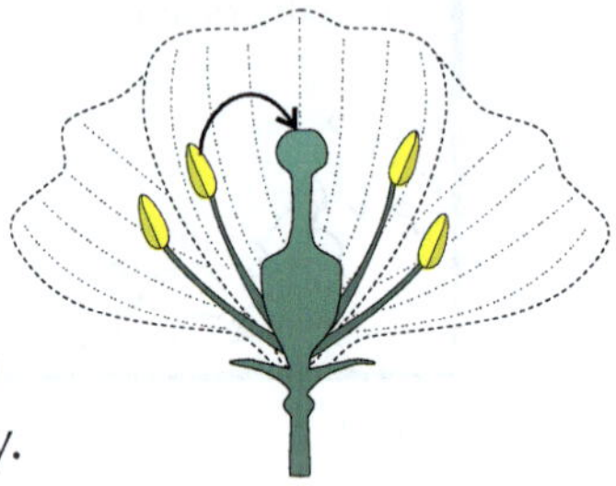

## Comparing Wind- and Insect-Pollinated Flowers

1) Flowers have different adaptations depending on how they are pollinated.
2) You can work out whether a plant is more likely to be wind- or insect-pollinated from the structure of the flower.

### Insect-pollinated Plants

Plant features that help insect pollination:

1) Scented flowers with bright coloured petals to attract insects.
2) Flowers containing nectar (a sugary liquid that insects feed on).
3) Sticky stigma to take the pollen off the insect as it goes from plant to plant to feed on the nectar.

### Wind-pollinated Plants

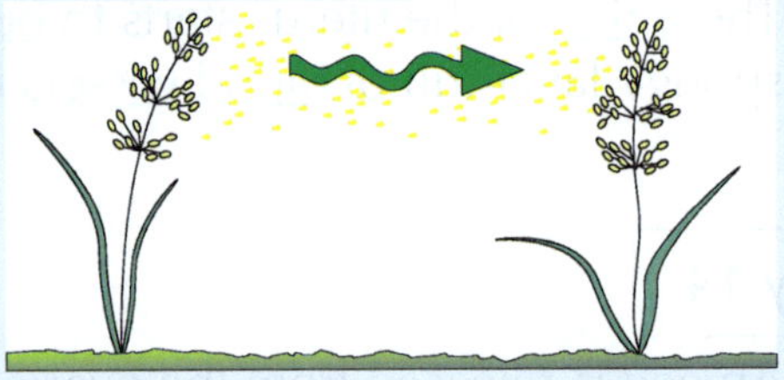

Features of plants that use wind pollination:

1) Usually have flowers with no scent and small dull petals.
2) No nectar in the flowers.
3) Long filaments hang the anthers outside the flower so a lot of pollen is blown away.
4) Stigmas are feathery to catch pollen as it's carried past in the wind.

REVISION TASK

**Now's your chance to spend the afternoon sniffing flowers...**

When you're ready for a break from 'proper' revision, look at a variety of flowering plants (by going outside or online). Use what you know to decide how each one is likely to be pollinated.

# Fertilisation and Seed Dispersal

After pollination, next up is fertilisation. Then the seeds produced get sent off into the great wide world.

## Fertilisation is the Joining of Sex Cells

Pollination brings pollen grains, producing the male gametes (sex cells) to a stigma. Then the plant's just got to get the male gametes to the female gamete (an egg cell). Here's how it works...

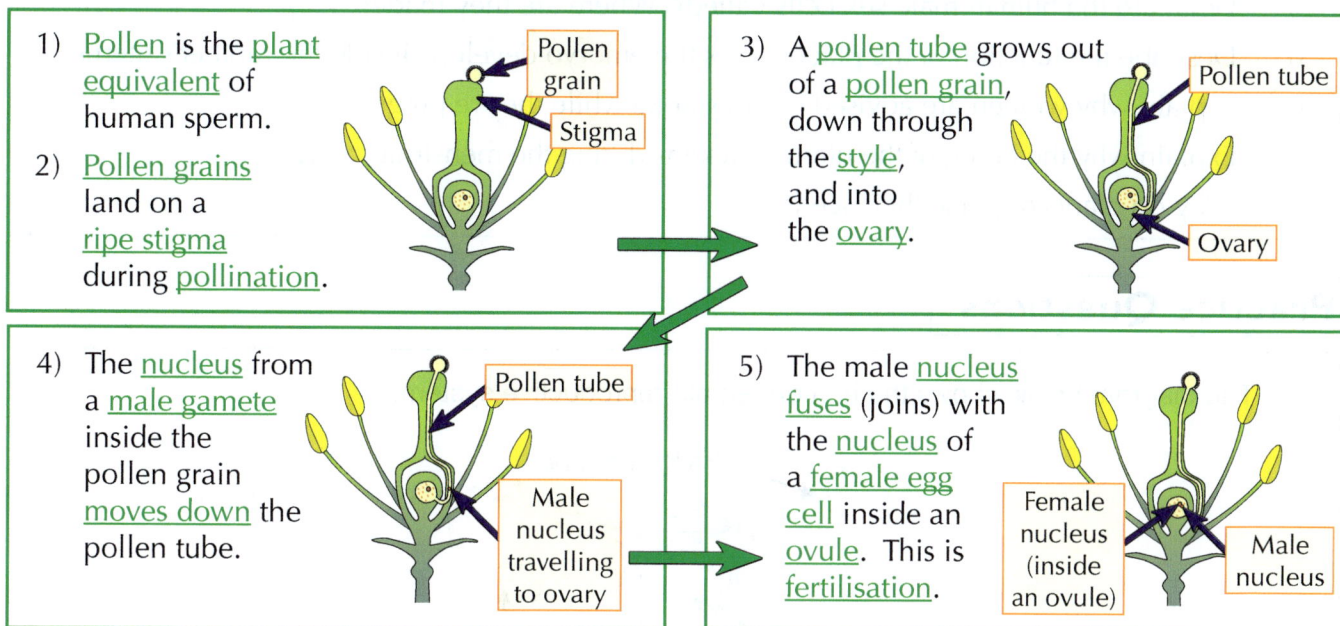

1) Pollen is the plant equivalent of human sperm.
2) Pollen grains land on a ripe stigma during pollination.

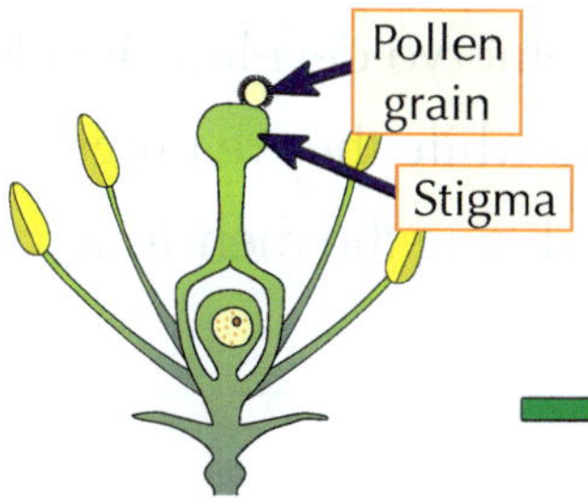


3) A pollen tube grows out of a pollen grain, down through the style, and into the ovary.

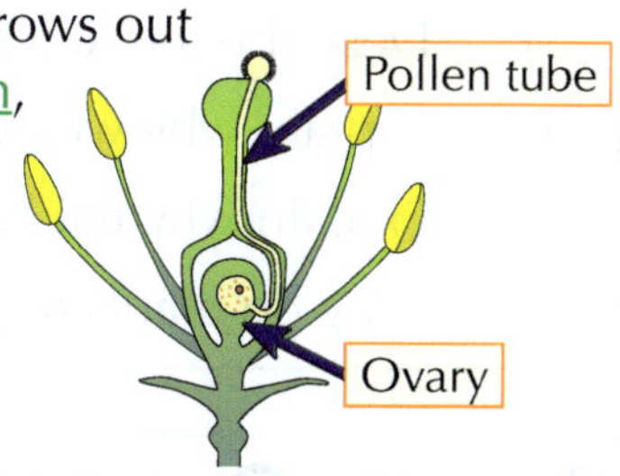


4) The nucleus from a male gamete inside the pollen grain moves down the pollen tube.

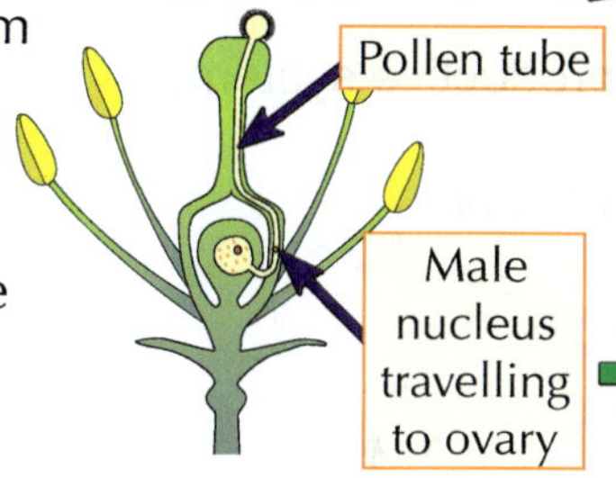


5) The male nucleus fuses (joins) with the nucleus of a female egg cell inside an ovule. This is fertilisation.

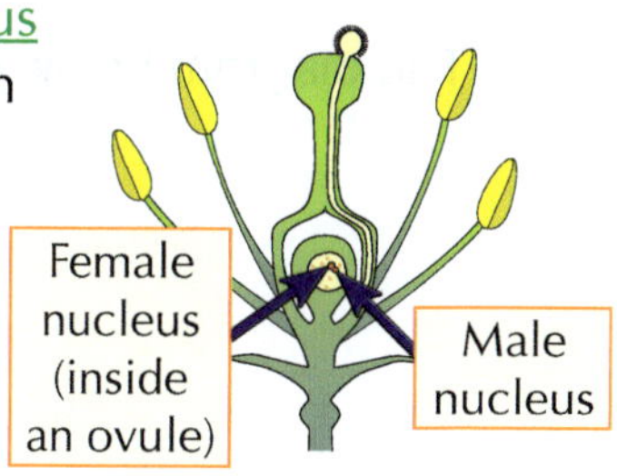


After fertilisation the ovule containing the fertilised egg develops into a seed, which can eventually grow into a new plant. In some plants the ovary develops into a fruit around the seed.

## Seed Dispersal is Scattering Seeds

Seeds need to be dispersed (spread out) so that they can grow without too much competition from the parent plant and from each other. Here are some ways in which seeds can be dispersed:

### 1) Wind dispersal

Wind-dispersed seeds are light. The shape of the fruit means they catch the wind, so the seeds are carried far away from the parent plant (e.g. dandelion seeds).

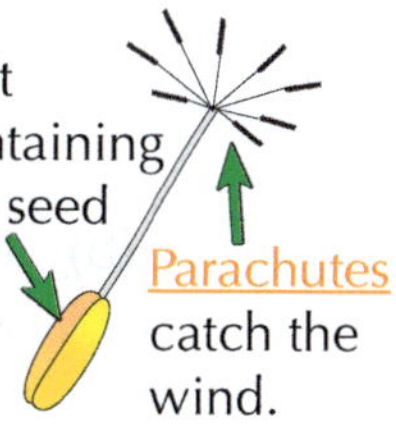


### 2) Animal dispersal

Some plants grow sugary fruit around the seeds, which attracts animals to eat it (e.g. berries). The seeds then come out in the animals' droppings, usually far away from the parent plant. Seeds can also be dispersed by the fruit sticking on to animals' coats.

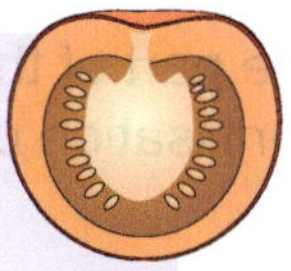

### 3) Explosions/ballistic

The fruit bursts open once it has ripened, scattering the seeds away from the parent plant. Seeds might then be carried further by animals.

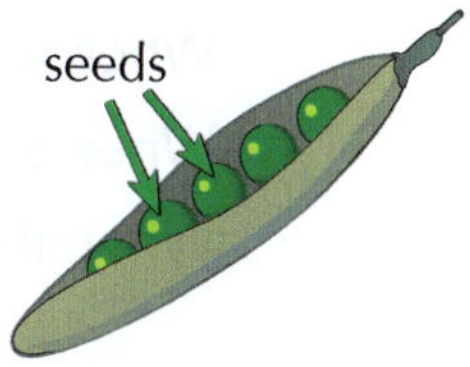


### 4) Drop and Roll

Fruit dispersed by drop and roll fall from the parent plant then roll away. Fruit that disperse by this method are often hard and heavy (e.g. coconuts). Drop and roll doesn't always take seeds very far, and some plants using it disperse their seeds in other ways too.

# Warm-Up & Practice Questions

Gosh, rather a lot happened in that section. Well, here are some questions to help it all sink in...

## Warm-Up Questions

1) Explain why a person finds it difficult to breathe during an asthma attack.
2) What are the human male sex cells called? Where are they made?
3) Describe the function of the placenta, as the embryo develops inside the mother's uterus.
4) Explain why women are advised not to smoke while they're pregnant.
5) Explain why the lining of the uterus thickens during the menstrual cycle.
6) Why do plants disperse their seeds?

## Practice Questions

1 The diagram below shows the human female reproductive system.

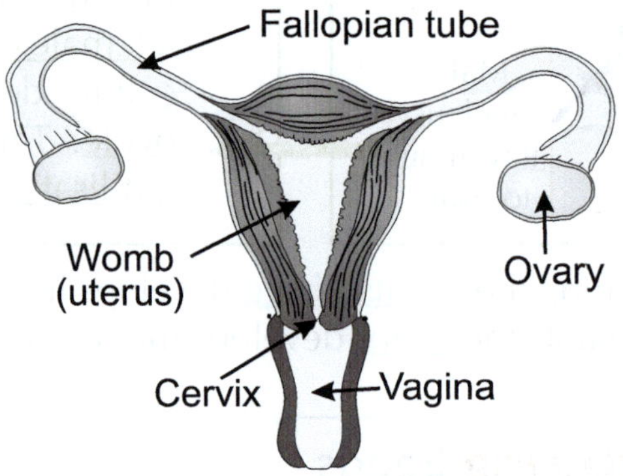


(a) During the menstrual cycle, the female reproductive system undergoes changes which prepare it for receiving a fertilised egg. State how many days a typical menstrual cycle takes.

*(1 mark)*

(b) Name the part of the female reproductive system where sperm are deposited during sexual intercourse.

*(1 mark)*

(c) (i) Name the part of the female reproductive system where fertilisation usually takes place.

*(1 mark)*

(ii) Underline the correct definition of **fertilisation** in the list below:

When an egg cell is released from the ovary

When the egg and sperm meet

When the nuclei of the egg and sperm join

When the egg and sperm attach to the uterus wall

*(1 mark)*

(d) After how many weeks of pregnancy is a human baby considered to be 'fully developed'?

*(1 mark)*

# Practice Questions

2 (a) Four parts of the human male reproductive system are named in the table below. Using the diagram, write the letter for each part next to its name.

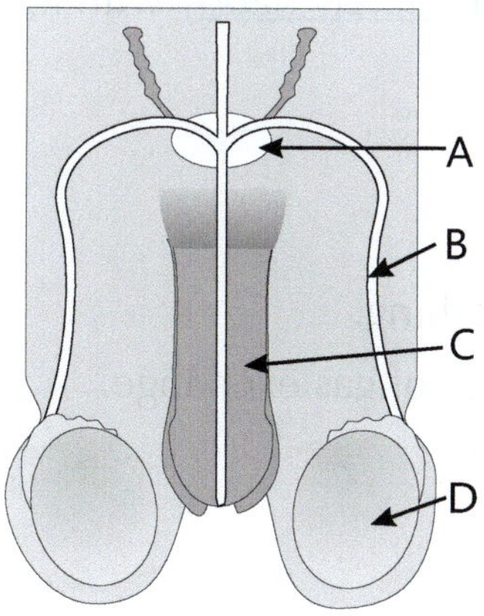


| name of organ | letter |
|---|---|
| sperm duct | |
| penis | |
| prostate gland | |
| testis | |

*(2 marks)*

(b) Name the tube that semen travels through before being ejaculated from the penis during sexual intercourse.

*(1 mark)*

3 (a) Apple trees are pollinated by bees. Explain **one** feature that you would expect apple blossoms to have, given that they are pollinated by bees.

*(2 marks)*

(b) After an apple blossom is pollinated, apples begin to grow. The apple fruit helps the seeds travel away from the original tree before growing into new apple trees. Suggest how each of the following characteristics helps the seed to move away from the original tree.

(i) The apple is round and heavy.

*(1 mark)*

(ii) The apple is a source of food for birds.

*(1 mark)*

4 The diagram below shows some of the structures in the gas exchange system.

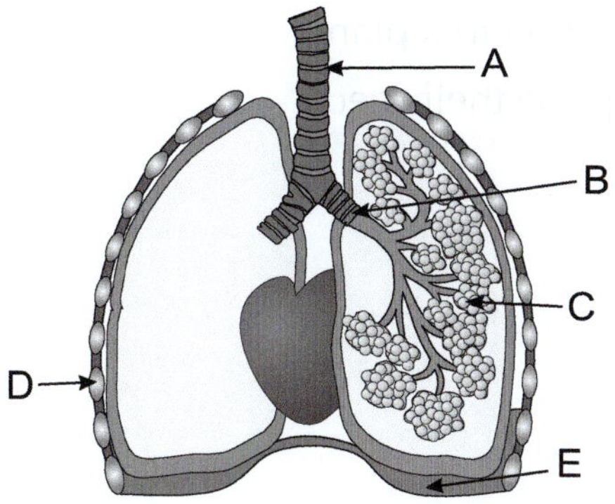


(a) Which letter (A-E) is the label for the diaphragm?

*(1 mark)*

(b) Explain what happens to the chest cavity as you breathe in.

*(4 marks)*

# Summary Questions

Well, there's certainly some interesting stuff in Section B2 — now let's see how much you remember...

- Try these questions and tick off each one when you get it right.
- When you've done all the questions for a topic and are completely happy with it, tick it off.

## Breathing (p.23-p.24) ☐

1) Explain how we breathe air out. ☐
2) Explain how the bell jar model demonstrates breathing. ☐
3) Describe what the parallelogram model shows about breathing. ☐
4) What is emphysema? Explain why it reduces the efficiency of gas exchange. ☐
5) How can an inhaler help a person with asthma? ☐
6) Why might a peak flow meter be used by someone with a medical condition that affects their lungs? ☐

## Human Reproduction (p.25-p.27) ☐

7) Name three organs in the male reproductive system. ☐
8) What are the human female sex cells called? Where are they released from? ☐
9) What happens between a sperm and an egg during fertilisation? ☐
10) Name the part of the female reproductive system in which a baby develops. ☐
11) Describe what a human fetus is like at: 9 weeks, 5 months, 7 months. ☐
12) Explain why the lifestyle of the parents is important for a fetus to develop healthily. ☐
13) Outline the four main stages of the menstrual cycle and say when they happen. ☐

## Plant Reproduction (p.28-p.29) ☐

14) What is the male part of a flower called? ☐
15) What is the female part of a flower called? ☐
16) What is 'pollination'? ☐
17) Describe how insects and the wind can help with pollination. ☐
18) Explain three differences between flowers pollinated by insects and flowers pollinated by wind. ☐
19) Describe the process of fertilisation in a plant. ☐
20) Give two ways that plants disperse their seeds. ☐

# Plant Nutrition

Nutrition is vital for plants, just like it is for all living organisms. But unlike most other living organisms, plants make their own grub. They just sit there in the sun and turn carbon dioxide and water into food.

## Photosynthesis: Making Food Using Sunlight

1) Photosynthesis is a chemical process which takes place in every green plant.
2) Photosynthesis basically produces food — in the form of glucose (a sugar).
3) Glucose is a carbohydrate. That means it's made up of the elements carbon, hydrogen and oxygen.
4) Plants can use glucose to increase their biomass — i.e. to grow. The faster the rate of photosynthesis, the more quickly sugar is formed and the faster the plant can grow.
5) Most plants convert the glucose into starch, which is easier to store.
6) Photosynthesis happens in the green bits of a plant, but mainly in the leaves.

See page 57 for more about elements.

You can test a plant's leaves for the presence of starch (see p.34).

## The Photosynthesis Word Equation

1) For photosynthesis to take place, plants need light, chlorophyll, water and carbon dioxide.
2) Chlorophyll absorbs sunlight and uses its energy to convert carbon dioxide and water into glucose. Oxygen is also produced.
3) This word equation summarises what happens during photosynthesis.

Chlorophyll is a green chemical found in chloroplasts (see p.11).

Carbon dioxide + Water —(Light / Chlorophyll)→ Glucose + Oxygen

These are the reactants. (Carbon dioxide + Water)

These are the products. (Glucose + Oxygen)

4) The rate of photosynthesis is affected by factors such as:
   - the amount of carbon dioxide there is available,
   - the amount of chlorophyll plant cells have,
   - the amount of light a plant is exposed to (see next page),
   - the temperature (generally warmer temperatures increase the rate of photosynthesis).

REVISION TIP

### Photosynthesis — a light snack...

Plants need to photosynthesise in order to create food. But they don't turn carbon dioxide and water into burgers or chips, they turn them into glucose. And then they use it to increase their biomass or store it as starch. Remember — plants STore glucose as STarch.

# PRACTICAL Photosynthesis Experiments

You can't tell photosynthesis is happening by looking at a plant — you need to do an experiment or two...

## You Can Investigate Photosynthesis by Collecting Gas

This is a simple experiment which shows that light intensity (the amount of light a plant gets) affects how fast photosynthesis happens:

1) Get a sample of an aquatic plant, such as *Elodea* or *Cabomba*.
2) Put it under a funnel in a beaker of sodium hydrogen carbonate solution — this provides carbon dioxide and water. Put a measuring cylinder over the top. Shine a bright lamp at the plant from 30 cm away.
3) The plant will produce bubbles of oxygen as it photosynthesises.
4) Use the measuring cylinder to measure the amount of oxygen produced in a given time — this will show how fast photosynthesis is happening.
5) Repeat the experiment twice more — once with the lamp positioned 20 cm away from the plant, and once with it positioned 10 cm away.
6) You should find that the closer the lamp is to the plant, the more oxygen is produced in a given time. This is because increasing the light intensity increases the rate of photosynthesis.

You can check that the gas you've collected is oxygen by seeing if it will relight a glowing splint (see p.76).

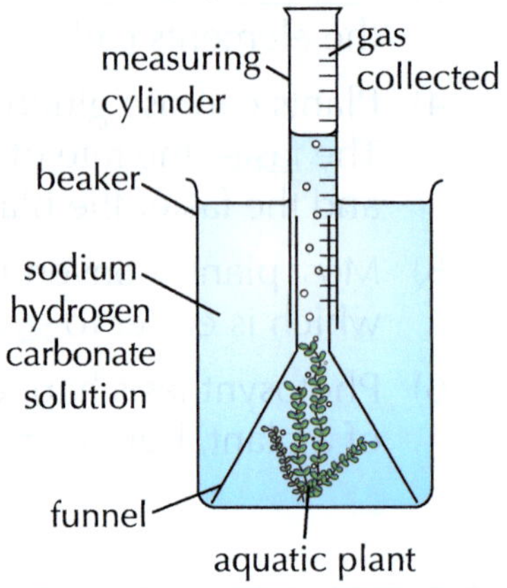


## The Almost Legendary Starch Test

1) In the starch test, iodine solution is used to test for the presence of starch. You just add a few drops of iodine solution to a sample and if it turns blue-black, then starch is present.
2) You can show that the green colour of leaves is linked to starch production with this experiment:

Choose a plant with variegated leaves (green and white bits) and leave it in the light for 24 hours.

Remove one leaf from the plant. Boil the leaf in water for a few minutes to soften it.

Once you've picked your leaf, sketch it to record which parts are green and white to start with.

Put the leaf in a boiling tube and cover it with ethanol. Put the boiling tube in hot water so the ethanol boils. This will remove the green colour (chlorophyll) from the leaf.

Dip the leaf in water to wash it.

Now do the iodine test for starch. Drip brown iodine solution all over the leaf. The iodine solution will turn blue-black where starch is present.

Make sure you're working safely (see p.5) — keep the ethanol away from the Bunsen burner.

**The results:**

1) Iodine solution goes blue-black in parts that have been photosynthesising (where there's starch).
2) If the iodine solution stays brown then there's no starch present — which means that those parts of the plant were not photosynthesising.
3) The bit of the leaf that was white didn't contain any chlorophyll, so didn't photosynthesise. So it didn't make any starch – which is why the iodine solution stayed brown.

# The Importance of Plants

Plants live a quiet life — they just sit there soaking up the sun and swaying in the breeze, not a care in the world... But simple as they are, they're super-important for life on Earth...

## Almost All Living Things Depend on Plants

Almost all life on Earth depends on plants. Without them, we just wouldn't be here. Here's why...

### Plants Capture the Sun's Energy

1) Almost all energy on Earth comes from the Sun.
2) Plants use some of the Sun's energy to make food (glucose) during photosynthesis (see page 33).
3) They then use this food to build "organic molecules" (things like carbohydrates and proteins), which become part of the plants' cells. These organic molecules store the Sun's energy.
4) The energy gets passed on from plants to animals when animals eat the plants. It gets passed on again when these animals are eaten by other animals.
5) This is why plants are called 'producers' (see page 42) — they 'produce' the molecules that other organisms in the food chain depend on for energy.

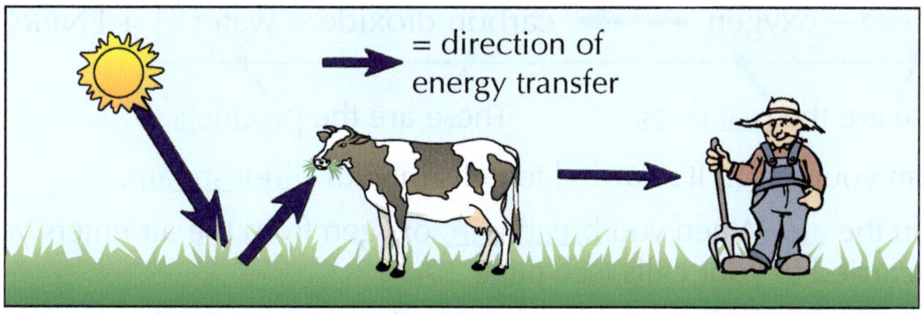


Without photosynthesis, we wouldn't have any food to eat. Everything we eat either comes from plants or things that have eaten plants.

6) Plants aren't the only photosynthetic organisms — algae (seaweeds) and some bacteria are also able to carry out photosynthesis, so they can be producers too.

### Plants Release Oxygen and Take in Carbon Dioxide

1) All living things respire (see page 36).
2) When plants and animals carry out aerobic respiration, they take in oxygen ($O_2$) from the atmosphere and release carbon dioxide ($CO_2$).
3) When plants photosynthesise, they do the opposite — they release oxygen and take in carbon dioxide.

4) So photosynthesis helps make sure there's always plenty of oxygen around for respiration. It also helps to stop the carbon dioxide level in the atmosphere from getting too high.

## Make sure this stuff is imPLANTed firmly into your brain...

If there's one thing you should get from this page it's this — plants are really, really important. Even if you live on a nothing-but-meat diet you still rely on plants for your food (without plants those tasty cows wouldn't even exist). And plants help to control the balance of gases in the atmosphere too.

# Aerobic Respiration

As life processes go, this is the big one — respiration. Without it, you'd be well and truly stuck.

## Respiration is a Chemical Reaction

Respiration is not the same as breathing — breathing is moving air in and out of the lungs (see p.23).

1) Respiration happens in every cell of every living organism.
2) Respiration is the process of releasing energy from food, such as glucose (a sugar).
3) The energy released by respiration is used for all the other chemical reactions that keep you alive. For example, the reactions involved in building proteins, muscle contraction and keeping warm.

## Aerobic Respiration Needs Plenty of Oxygen

Anaerobic respiration happens without oxygen. See the next page for more.

1) Aerobic respiration is respiration using oxygen. It takes place in the mitochondria (see page 11) of animal and plant cells.
2) In aerobic respiration, glucose and oxygen react to produce carbon dioxide and water. This reaction releases lots of energy.
3) Here's the word equation to show what happens in this reaction — learn it:

glucose + oxygen → carbon dioxide + water + ENERGY

These are the reactants. These are the products.

4) Glucose comes from your food. It's carried to cells in your bloodstream.
5) Oxygen comes from the air. When you breathe in, oxygen from the air enters your blood at the lungs and is carried to your cells (see page 23).
6) Blood also carries carbon dioxide away from your cells — it goes back to your lungs to be breathed out (exhaled).

## Testing Exhaled Air For Carbon Dioxide

PRACTICAL

You can show that exhaled air contains carbon dioxide by doing an experiment using limewater or hydrogen carbonate indicator.

1) Put some limewater or hydrogen carbonate indicator in a test tube. Pop a tube (a straw will do) into it.
2) Take a deep breath and breathe out into the tube. (You may need to do this a few times.)
3) The solution will change colour, showing that the air you are breathing out contains carbon dioxide.

### Using limewater

Limewater is a colourless solution — but it turns cloudy when you bubble carbon dioxide through it.

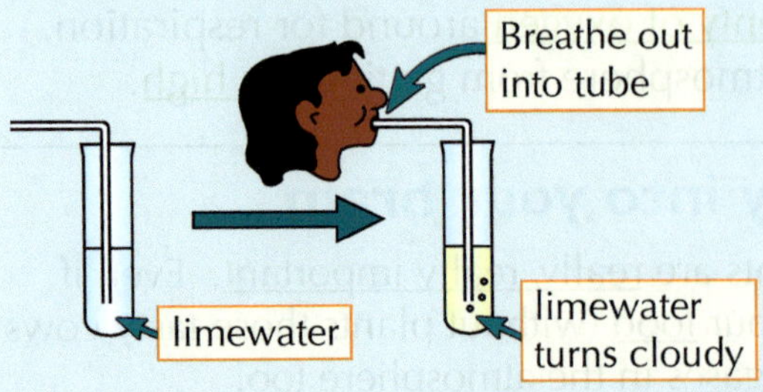


### Using hydrogen carbonate indicator

Hydrogen carbonate indicator is a red solution — but it turns orange or yellow when you bubble carbon dioxide through it.

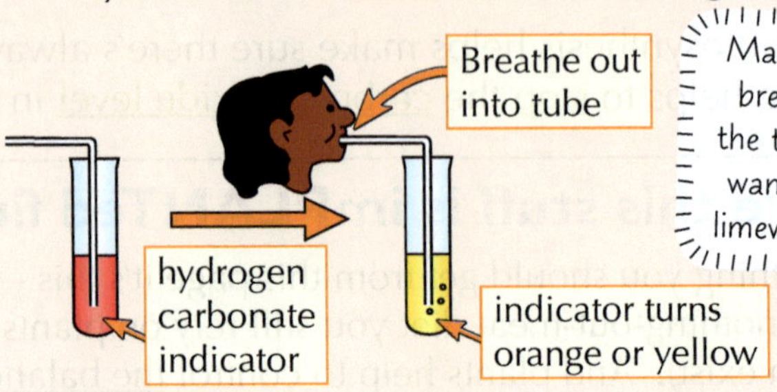


Make sure you don't breathe in through the tube, as you don't want to suck up the limewater or indicator.

# Anaerobic Respiration

As well as aerobic respiration, there's anaerobic respiration. You need to know all about this type too.

## Anaerobic Respiration Takes Place Without Oxygen

1) Anaerobic respiration is respiration without oxygen.
2) Anaerobic respiration is less efficient than aerobic respiration. This means that for every glucose molecule used, less energy is released.
3) Because of this, anaerobic respiration usually only happens when cells can't get enough oxygen.

**Example: Humans**

When you exercise, your body needs more energy — so your respiration rate increases. If you exercise hard, your body can't always get enough oxygen to your muscle cells. So your muscle cells start to respire anaerobically.

**Example: Plants**

If the soil a plant's growing in becomes waterlogged (full of water) there'll be no oxygen available for the roots — so the root cells will have to respire anaerobically.

## Anaerobic Respiration is Different in Different Organisms

1) In animals, anaerobic respiration produces a substance called lactic acid. Lactic acid can build up in your muscles during exercise and can be painful. This is the word equation for anaerobic respiration in animals:

$$\text{glucose} \rightarrow \text{lactic acid} \quad + \text{SOME ENERGY}$$

Yeast is a single-celled fungus.

2) In plants and yeast, anaerobic respiration produces carbon dioxide and alcohol. If alcohol builds up it can be toxic to plants and yeast. Here's the word equation:

$$\text{glucose} \rightarrow \text{carbon dioxide} + \text{alcohol} \quad + \text{SOME ENERGY}$$

The alcohol produced is called ethanol.

3) When anaerobic respiration produces alcohol, it's called fermentation. See the next page for more.

## You can Compare Aerobic and Anaerobic Respiration

| | Aerobic respiration | Anaerobic respiration |
|---|---|---|
| **Is oxygen needed?** | yes | no |
| **What products are made?** | $CO_2$ and water | lactic acid (muscles) / $CO_2$ and alcohol (plants & yeast) |
| **How much energy is transferred?** | A large amount. | A small amount. |

REVISION TASK

### Anaerobic respiration — all pain and not much (energy) gain...

You'll need to know the similarities and differences between aerobic and anaerobic respiration. A good place to start is memorising the word equations — cover the book and write them down.

# Fermentation

Yeast is a useful microorganism. It's used to make things like bread, wine and beer. So without yeast, human society would look a little different. And it's all down to what happens when the yeast respires...

## We Use Yeast for Making Bread...

1) A bread dough is made by mixing yeast with flour, water and a bit of sugar.
2) The yeast uses sugars in the dough for anaerobic respiration. This is known as fermentation, and produces carbon dioxide and alcohol (see previous page).
3) The carbon dioxide produced is trapped in bubbles in the dough, which makes the dough rise.
4) The dough is then baked in an oven, where the yeast continues to ferment until the temperature of the dough rises enough to kill the yeast.
5) Any alcohol made while the dough is rising evaporates away when it's baked.

## ...and for Making Beer and Wine

1) To make beer and wine, yeast is added to a source of glucose and other ingredients. In beer, the source of glucose is a type of grain (such as malted barley), and in wine it's crushed grapes.
2) The ingredients are left to ferment — the yeast respires anaerobically and uses the glucose to produce alcohol and carbon dioxide.
3) The carbon dioxide produced is often what makes beer fizzy.

## You Can Investigate Fermentation in Yeast

PRACTICAL

You can do experiments to investigate how fast yeast respires anaerobically under different conditions. For example, here's how to investigate the effect that temperature has on fermentation:

1) Mix together some sugar, yeast and water in a test tube.
2) To create anaerobic conditions, add a layer of oil to the top of the yeast mixture. This will prevent oxygen from the air getting into the mixture.
3) Attach a bung with a tube leading to a second test tube of water.
4) Place the test tube containing the yeast mixture in a beaker of water at 25 °C.
5) Leave the test tube to warm up and then count how many bubbles of carbon dioxide are produced in one minute.
6) Repeat the experiment with the test tube in beakers of water at different temperatures.
7) The more bubbles produced in one minute, the faster the fermentation is happening.

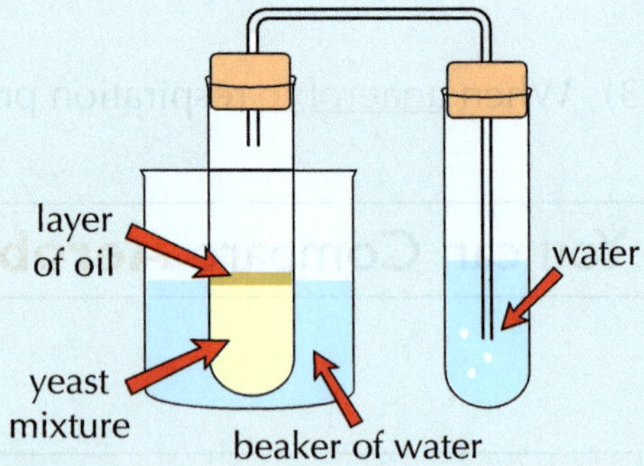


### At yeast there aren't any more formulae to learn...

...but you do need to know that fermentation has lots of important uses. Time for toast, anyone?

# Warm-Up & Practice Questions

Take a moment to appreciate how wonderful plants and yeast really are. Then try these questions...

## Warm-Up Questions

1) What four things are needed for photosynthesis?
2) Which part of a variegated leaf would test positive for starch — the green bit or the white bit? Explain why.
3) Explain how plants help to maintain the levels of oxygen and carbon dioxide in the atmosphere.
4) Explain why living organisms respire.
5) Which sort of respiration is the most efficient?
6) Give the word equation for anaerobic respiration in yeast.

## Practice Questions

1 Respiration is a very important life process for all organisms.
Sometimes respiration does not involve oxygen.

(a) (i) Name the sort of respiration that does not involve oxygen.

*(1 mark)*

(ii) Write the word equation for this process when it occurs in humans.

*(1 mark)*

(b) Other than whether the process involves oxygen, describe **one** difference between the two types of respiration.

*(1 mark)*

PRACTICAL

2 Farrah wants to make the aquatic plants in her fish tank grow faster.

(a) She decides to try to increase the rate of photosynthesis.

(i) Explain why increasing the rate of photosynthesis could make the plants grow faster.

*(2 marks)*

(ii) Farrah notices small bubbles coming from her plants.
Suggest what is likely to happen to the number of these bubbles released in a given time as the rate of photosynthesis increases. Explain your answer.

*(2 marks)*

(b) Farrah decides that the plants need more light to grow faster.

(i) Give **one** factor, other than light, that affects how fast the plants grow.

*(1 mark)*

(ii) Suggest how Farrah could test whether increasing the amount of light will increase the rate of photosynthesis.

*(2 marks)*

# Practice Questions

PRACTICAL

3 Azaria was investigating how the amount of sugar present affects the rate of fermentation in yeast. She set up the experiment shown below.

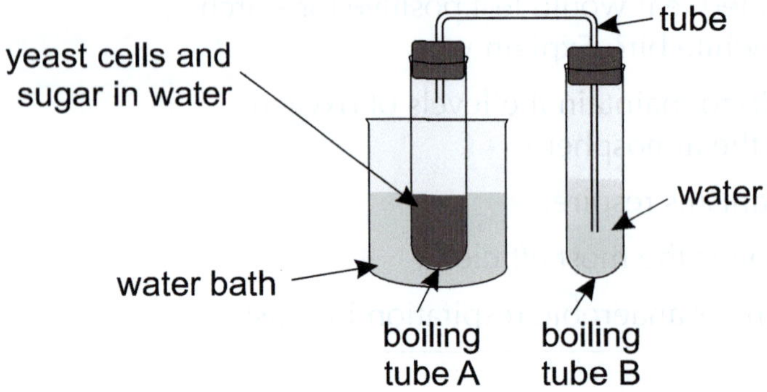


After a little while, bubbles of gas started to enter the water in boiling tube B. She counted how many gas bubbles were produced in one minute and recorded her results in a table. She repeated the experiment three times and found the mean of her results. She did the whole experiment twice more but changed the amount of sugar in boiling tube A each time.

(a) Choose the correct word(s) to complete the following sentence:

**hydrogen** **carbon dioxide** **oxygen**

During the experiment Azaria counted bubbles of ......................................... .

*(1 mark)*

(b) Other than the gas you wrote in part (a), give **one** substance that would be produced in the experiment if the yeast were respiring anaerobically.

*(1 mark)*

(c) Suggest what Azaria could have done when she was setting up the experiment to make sure that the yeast cells were respiring anaerobically from the start.

*(1 mark)*

(d) (i) State the independent variable in the experiment.

*(1 mark)*

(ii) Give **two** control variables in the experiment.

*(2 marks)*

(e) Suggest how the number of bubbles produced might have changed as the amount of sugar in boiling tube A increased. Explain your answer.

*(3 marks)*

(f) The fermentation of yeast is used to make some of the products we eat and drink. Name **one** of these products.

*(1 mark)*

# Summary Questions

I bet you're full of energy now. If not, grab yourself a plant-based snack and get stuck into this page.

- Try these questions and tick off each one when you get it right.
- When you've done all the questions for a topic and are completely happy with it, tick it off.

## Photosynthesis (p.33-p.35) ☐

1) What is the role of photosynthesis in plants? ☐
2) What do most plants store glucose as? ☐
3) Write out the word equation for photosynthesis. ☐
4) Give three factors that affect the rate of photosynthesis. ☐
5) Jamie does an experiment to test for the presence of starch in a leaf.
   a) During his experiment he soaks the leaf in boiling ethanol. Why does he do this? ☐
   b) What chemical should Jamie use to test for the presence of starch in the leaf? Describe what would happen if there was starch present. ☐
6) Explain why most living things rely on plants for energy. ☐
7) Name two photosynthetic organisms other than plants. ☐
8) Apart from providing us with energy, explain why it is important to other living things that plants carry out photosynthesis. ☐

## Respiration (p.36-p.38) ☐

9) Give one way that the energy released during respiration is used in animals. ☐
10) Where in a cell does aerobic respiration take place? ☐
11) Write down the word equation for aerobic respiration. ☐
12) Describe an experiment you could do to show that exhaled air contains carbon dioxide. ☐
13) Name the products of anaerobic respiration in yeast. ☐
14) What is fermentation? ☐
15) Give three differences between aerobic and anaerobic respiration. ☐
16) Give two products of fermentation that are important to society. ☐
17) Briefly describe how you could measure the rate of fermentation in yeast. ☐

# Interdependence and Food Webs

It probably won't surprise you to learn that organisms depend on other organisms for their survival.

## Organisms in an Ecosystem are Interdependent

1) The place where an organism lives is called its habitat, e.g. a freshwater pond or a hedgerow.
2) Many different organisms can live in the same habitat. E.g. look at this freshwater pond habitat:

3) An ecosystem is all the living organisms in one area, plus their habitats.
4) The organisms in an ecosystem are interdependent — they need each other to survive.

## Food Webs are Made of Lots of Food Chains

1) Food chains show what is eaten by what. For example:

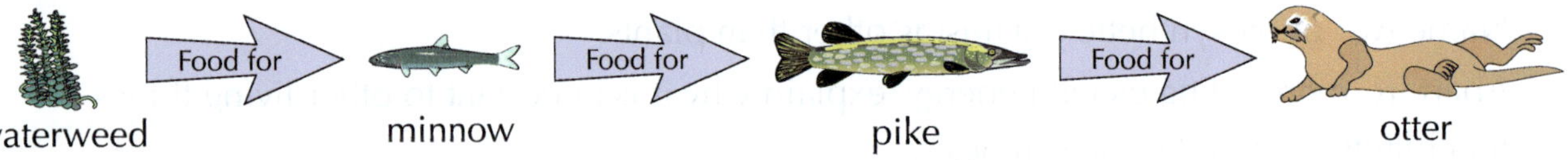


2) Food chains follow just one path of what eats what.
3) Food webs contain many interlinked food chains, like this:

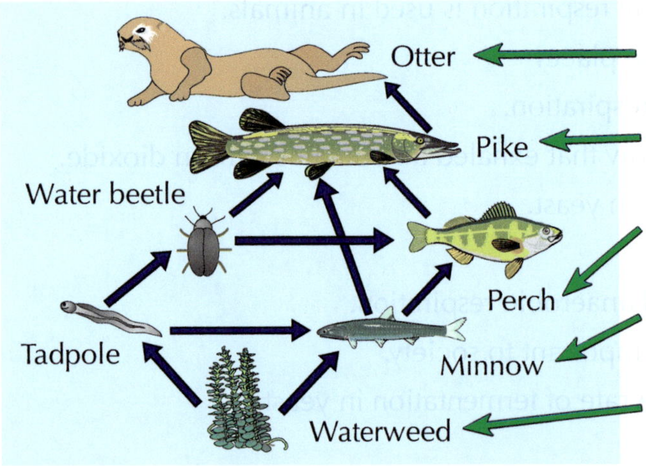


Top carnivore — an animal that is not eaten by anything else.

Tertiary consumer — an animal that eats secondary consumers.

Secondary consumer — an animal that eats primary consumers.

Primary consumer — an animal that eats producers (plants).

Producer — all plants are producers. They use the Sun's energy to make their own food.

4) Food chains can only have one producer, however food webs can have several producers.

The Sun is the original source of energy for many food chains.

5) The organisms in a food web are all interdependent, so a change in one organism can affect others.

**E.g. — What happens if the minnows all die?**

1) The tadpoles may be less likely to get eaten as there are no minnows there to eat them.
2) Water beetles may be more likely to get eaten (by perch who'll get hungry without minnows).
3) The waterweeds may be more likely to get eaten (since the numbers of tadpoles will increase).

REVISION TASK

### Learn about food webs — but don't get tangled up...

Once you've learnt everything on this page, have a go at this food web question:
"If the number of otters decreased, give one reason why the number of water beetles might a) decrease b) increase". You can find the answer to this question on page 144.

# Investigating Populations

PRACTICAL

A 'population' is how many of one particular type of organism there are in a particular place.

## Investigate Populations by Counting and Repeating

You might want to investigate the populations in a habitat, e.g. by finding out how the numbers and types of organisms found in one area of the habitat compare with those found in another area. To do this you need to do two things:

1) **Count the organisms in one area (a sample area).** Here are four sampling techniques you could use:

**Pitfall Traps**

1) PITFALL TRAPS are steep-sided containers that are sunk in a hole in the ground. The top is partly open.
2) To use a pitfall trap, leave it overnight in your sample area. Organisms (e.g. crawling insects, slugs, spiders) that come along fall into the container and can't get out again, so you can count them.

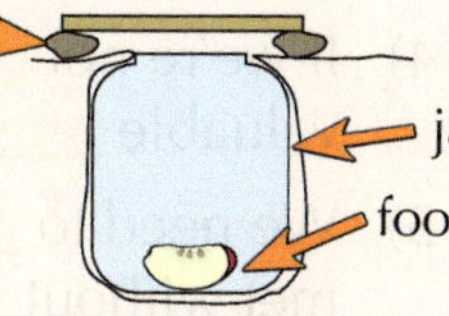

A pitfall trap.

**Sweep Nets**

1) A SWEEP NET is a net lined with strong cloth for collecting insects, spiders, etc. from long grass.
2) To use one, stand still in your sample area and sweep the net once from left to right through the grass. Then quickly sweep the net up and turn the organisms out into a container to count them.

**Pond Nets**

1) A POND NET is a net used for collecting insects, water snails, etc. from ponds and rivers.
2) To use one, stand in your sample area and sweep the net along the bottom of the pond or river. Turn the net out into a white tray with a bit of water in to count the organisms you've caught.

**Quadrats**

1) A QUADRAT is a square frame enclosing a known area, e.g. 1 m$^2$, that can be used to count small, slow-moving or still organisms (e.g. plants).
2) To use a quadrat, place it on the ground at a random point within your sample area. Then count how many of the organisms that you're studying are within the quadrat and record the result.

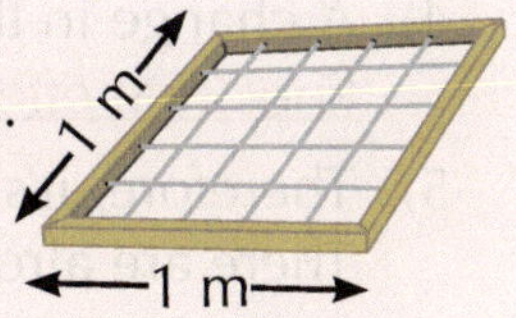

A quadrat.

Whichever technique you use, you need to repeat it at least three times at random locations in your sample area, and then work out the mean number of each organism found.

2) **Repeat in another sample area...** ...then compare your results.

To be able to make a fair comparison you need to control as many variables as you can, e.g. in each sample area use exactly the same sampling technique and equipment, and collect samples at the same time of day.

## Quadrats are Great for Estimating Population Size

To estimate the population size using a quadrat:

1) Count and repeat as many times as you can at random locations across the habitat.
2) Work out the mean number of organisms per quadrat.
3) Work out the mean number of organisms per m$^2$.
4) Finally, multiply the mean by the total area (in m$^2$) of the habitat.

If the quadrat has an area of 1 m$^2$, these are the same.

**Example**

Ty wants to estimate the number of daisies in a field with an area of 800 m$^2$. He counts the number of daisies in six 1 m$^2$ quadrats placed randomly in the field. These are his results: 18, 20, 22, 23, 23, 26.

$$\text{MEAN} = \frac{\text{TOTAL number of organisms}}{\text{NUMBER of quadrats}} = \frac{132}{6}$$

= 22 daisies per quadrat = 22 daisies per m$^2$

So the daisy population size is 22 × 800 = 17 600.

# Protecting Living Things

Humans depend on other organisms to survive — we need to protect them.

## Development Has to be Sustainable

1) Humans use resources from the Earth to survive. For example, we use many different animals and plants for things like food, drugs and clothes. Also, we use fossil fuels for energy (see p.77).
2) As the human population grows, we'll use more of these resources and produce more pollution.
3) Unfortunately, the resources of the Earth are limited and can run out.
4) If we're not careful, we could end up losing some of our valuable resources and damaging the environment.
5) We need to manage the way we use resources so that the needs of our growing population can be met without destroying things for future generations — this is called sustainable development.

## It's Important to Conserve Species and Habitats

1) Human activities can greatly affect the environment and the population size of a species.
2) Sometimes our actions cause the population size of a species to fall directly — e.g. by hunting.
3) Other times our activities affect habitats — e.g. chopping down trees to make way for buildings. This in turn can affect the population size of a species.
    - When an organism's habitat is destroyed or changed in some way, the organism may no longer be able to survive and reproduce successfully.
    - This could mean its population size falls dramatically.
4) A change in the population size of one species can have a huge knock-on effect for other species — e.g. by disrupting food webs.
5) Therefore, it's really important that we try to conserve (protect) species and habitats. There are already lots of conservation schemes set up to help us do this. For example:

### Captive Breeding Programs

1) Species that are low in numbers in the wild can be bred in captivity to help increase their numbers — e.g. pandas.
2) Animals bred in captivity can then be reintroduced to the wild.

### Fishing Quotas

1) Fish stocks are declining because we're overfishing — we're fishing too much.
2) This means there are fewer fish for us to eat, the oceans' food chains are affected and some species of fish may disappear altogether in some areas.
3) Fishing quotas are limits to the amounts of certain fish species that fishermen are allowed to catch.

### Protected Areas

1) Protected areas include places such as national parks and nature reserves.
2) They protect habitats by limiting the number of buildings that can be built, and limiting the amount of farming and other industry that can happen in the area.

## Net profits — the money that a fisherman makes...

Humans are always taking things from the planet, creating pollution and disrupting other organisms. We need to manage what we're doing now so that the Earth isn't too messed up for future generations.

# Warm-Up & Practice Questions

It's easy to think you've learnt everything in a section until you attempt the Warm-Up Questions and realise you can't answer them all. If that happens to you, don't worry, just go back over the pages and write out the bits you got wrong until you can answer them standing on your head. Then stand on your head and try to answer the Practice Question.

## Warm-Up Questions

1) All the organisms in an ecosystem are interdependent. What does this mean?
2) What is shown by the arrows in a food chain?
3) Give a definition for each of the following food web terminologies:
   a) top carnivore
   b) primary consumer
   c) producer
4) State two sampling techniques that can be used to investigate the population of different organisms.
5) Name a piece of equipment that is useful for estimating the number of still organisms (e.g. plants) in a habitat.
6) What is meant by sustainable development?

## Practice Question

1 Below is part of the food web of plants and animals in the Arctic.

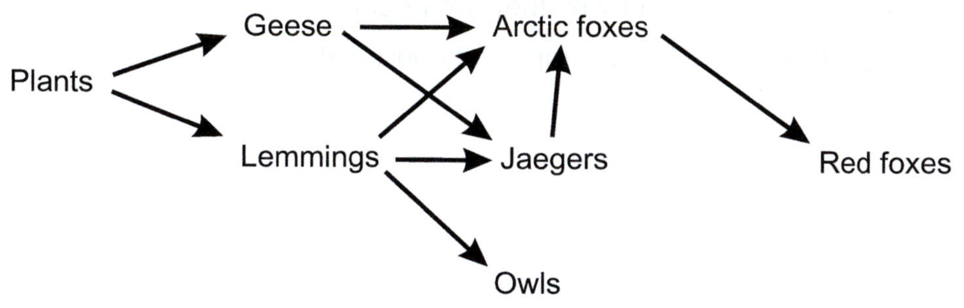


(a) Name **one** primary consumer in this food web.

*(1 mark)*

(b) The numbers of lemmings in the Arctic goes up and down a lot.

(i) Suggest **two** reasons why the number of lemmings may suddenly decrease.

*(2 marks)*

(ii) Suggest and explain what may happen to the number of Arctic foxes if the number of lemmings suddenly decreased.

*(2 marks)*

(c) One year, the number of geese drops significantly. Daya suggests that this is due to the fact that the number of owls has increased in recent years.
Explain whether Daya is likely to be correct.

*(2 marks)*

# Summary Questions

This section may have been short and sweet but you still need to make sure you know it all. Luckily for you, I've put together a set of questions that should test most of that key knowledge...

- Try these questions and tick off each one when you get it right.
- When you've done all the questions for a topic and are completely happy with it, tick it off.

## Interdependence and Food Webs (p.42) ☐

1) What is an organism's habitat? ☐
2) What is a food web? ☐
3) What is the difference between a tertiary consumer and a secondary consumer in a food web? ☐
4) True or false? Food chains only have one producer. ☐

## Investigating Populations (p.43) ☐

5) What does 'population' mean? ☐
6) Explain how a pitfall trap works. ☐
7) Describe a sampling technique that could be used to investigate the population of water snails in a pond. ☐
8) What is a quadrat? ☐
9) Describe how you could use a quadrat to estimate the number of daisies in a field. ☐

## Protecting Living Things (p.44) ☐

10) True or false? The resources of the Earth are limited. ☐
11) Explain why it is important to conserve habitats. ☐
12) Explain what fishing quotas are and why they are important. ☐
13) Other than fishing quotas, give two examples of conservation schemes. ☐

# Variation

All organisms are different. This difference is known as 'variation' — that's what this page is all about...

## Variation Can be Continuous or Discontinuous

Variation within a species can either be classed as continuous or discontinuous.

You also get variation between members of different species.

### Continuous Variation — A Variable That Can Take Any Value Within a Range

1) Examples of this are things like height, weight, skin colour, hand span, leaf area, etc. where the feature can have any value at all — within a certain range. If you did a survey of kids' heights you could plot the results on a chart like the one opposite (the heights would be collected into groups to give the bars).
2) The smooth distribution curve drawn on afterwards (the red line) better shows the continuous way that values for height actually vary.

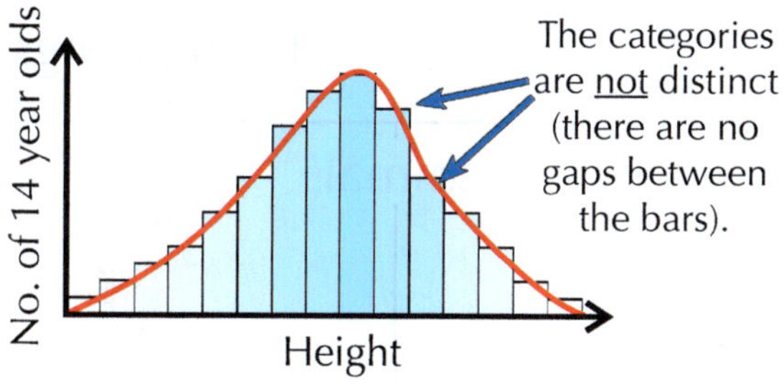


### Discontinuous Variation — A Variable That Can Only Take Certain Values

1) An example of this is a person's blood group, where there are just four distinct options, NOT a whole continuous range.
2) Hair colour and eye colour can also be classed as showing discontinuous variation, as there are only so many colours these characteristics could be described as (e.g. brown eyes, blue eyes, etc).

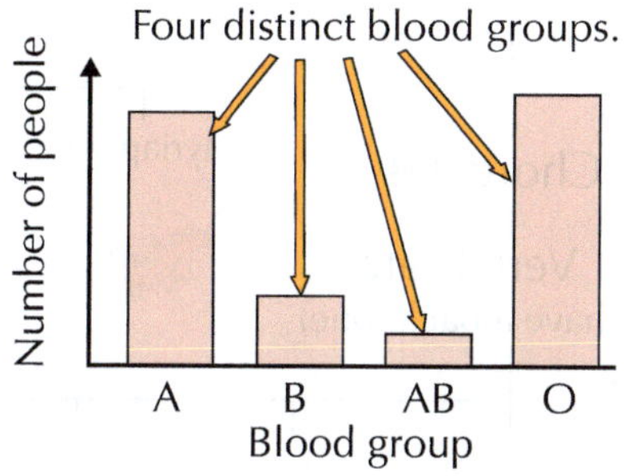


## You Can Measure Variation Between Organisms

PRACTICAL

You might also need to suggest possible causes for the variation.

**Example**

**A student plants a sunflower seed in each of five different gardens. After ten weeks he measures the height that each sunflower has grown to using a tape measure. His results are shown in the table and on the graph. Suggest possible causes for the variation between the heights of the sunflowers.**

| Sunflower | Height / cm |
|---|---|
| A | 185 |
| B | 196 |
| C | 152 |
| D | 201 |
| E | 198 |

1) The quality of the soil in each of the gardens could have been different.
2) Some gardens could get more sunlight than others.
3) Some flowers may have been watered more than others.
4) The temperature in each of the gardens could be different.

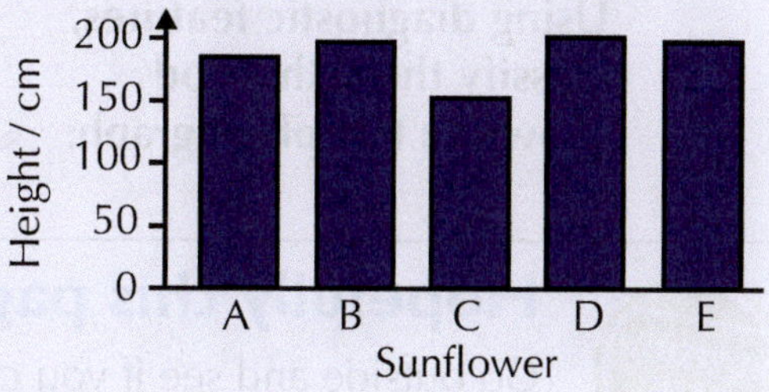


With questions like this, you just need to make sure you give sensible suggestions for why there could be variation.

# Classification

It seems to be a basic human urge to want to classify things — that's the case in biology anyway...

## All Living Things Can Be Classified Into Groups

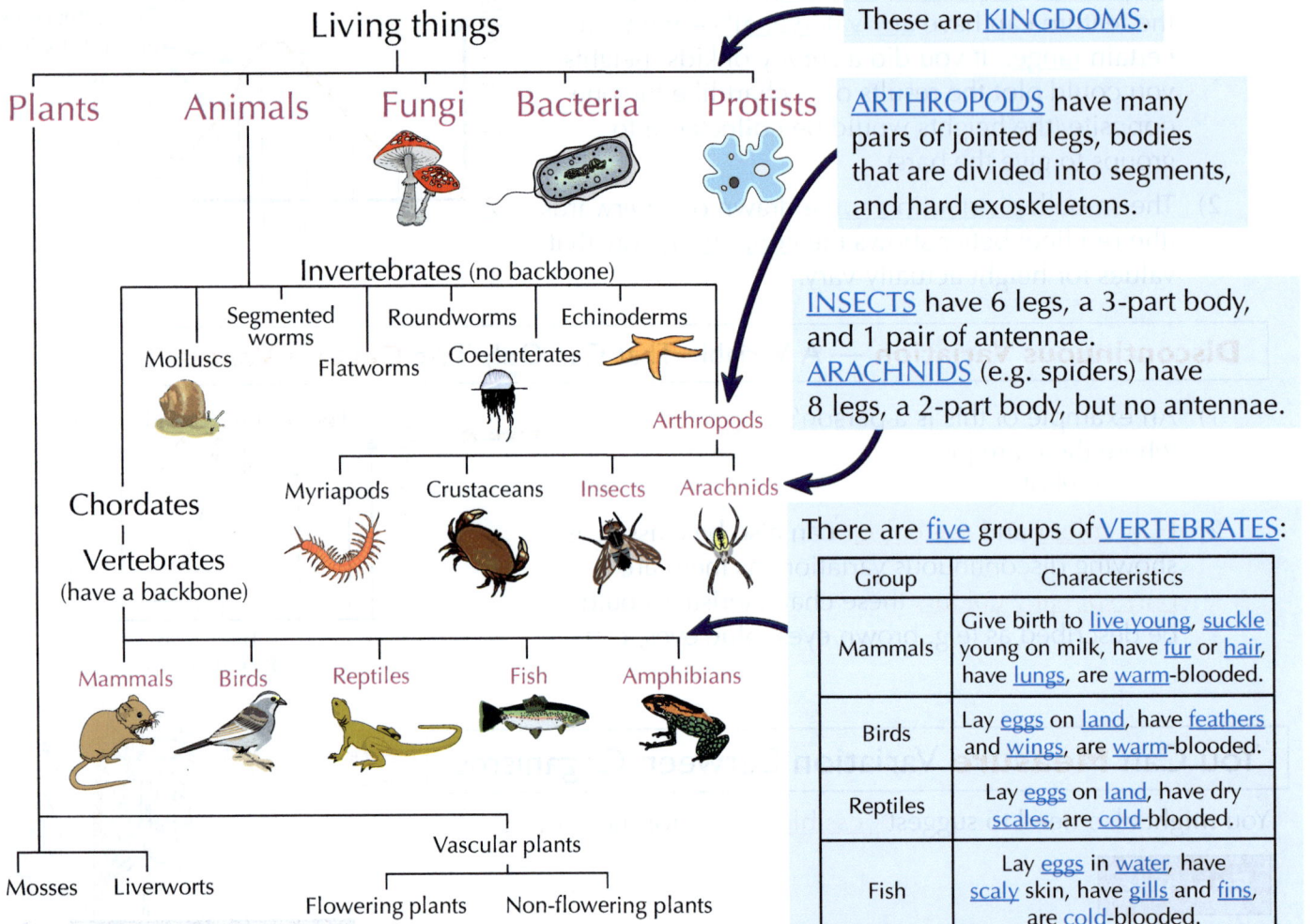

1) The similarities and differences between organisms allow us to classify them into taxonomic groups.
2) Living things are first divided into five kingdoms: plants, animals, fungi, bacteria and protists.

There's more about the different kingdoms on the next page.

3) The kingdoms are then subdivided into smaller and smaller groups as the diagram below shows...

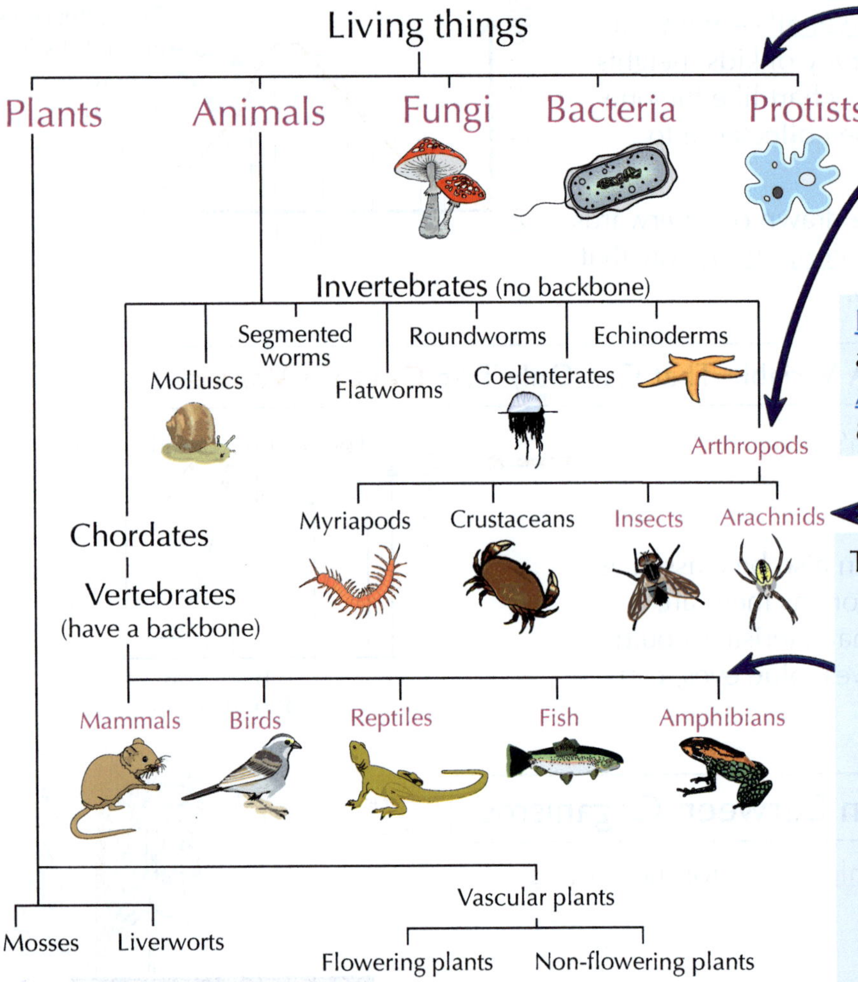


These are KINGDOMS.

ARTHROPODS have many pairs of jointed legs, bodies that are divided into segments, and hard exoskeletons.

INSECTS have 6 legs, a 3-part body, and 1 pair of antennae. ARACHNIDS (e.g. spiders) have 8 legs, a 2-part body, but no antennae.

There are five groups of VERTEBRATES:

| Group | Characteristics |
|---|---|
| Mammals | Give birth to live young, suckle young on milk, have fur or hair, have lungs, are warm-blooded. |
| Birds | Lay eggs on land, have feathers and wings, are warm-blooded. |
| Reptiles | Lay eggs on land, have dry scales, are cold-blooded. |
| Fish | Lay eggs in water, have scaly skin, have gills and fins, are cold-blooded. |
| Amphibians | Lay eggs in water, have smooth moist skin, are cold-blooded. |

Amphibians live near water to keep their skin moist.

4) The information given in the blue boxes for each group are known as diagnostic features (or characteristic features). They help to classify different species.

**Example**

**Using diagnostic features, classify the arthropod shown in this photograph:**

The arthropod has 6 legs, 1 pair of antennae and a 3-part body, so it is likely to be an insect.

### Hopefully this page hasn't been too taxing...

REVISION TASK

Go outside and see if you can find five arthropods or vertebrates. Then try to classify each one into one of the groups above. Revision whilst being outside — winner. Unless it's raining.

# Structures of Different Organisms

There's a great variety of organisms on Earth, and they all have different attributes that help them survive.

## Different Kingdoms have Different Structures and Life Processes

As you saw on the previous page, all living organisms are split into one of five different kingdoms. There are similarities and differences between the organisms in each kingdom:

| Kingdom | Single-celled? | Cells have a nucleus? | Cells have a cell wall? | Able to move around? | Able to make own food? |
|---|---|---|---|---|---|
| Plants | ✗ | ✓ | ✓ | ✗ | ✓ |
| Animals | ✗ | ✓ | ✗ | ✓ | ✗ |
| Fungi | Can be | ✓ | ✓ | ✗ | ✗ |
| Bacteria | ✓ | ✗ | Most do | ✓ | Some can |
| Protists | Most are | ✓ | Can have | ✓ | Some can |

## The Structures of an Organism are Related to Their Function

Different organisms have different structures that help them to survive and reproduce. The structures of an organism are related to their function. Here are some examples:

### GULL

Beak with curved tip — this helps the bird to catch prey (e.g. fish) and helps to prevent the prey from escaping.

Webbed feet — these increase the surface area of the feet, which help the bird to swim, or walk on soft ground.

Large feathers on wings — these are strong but lightweight. They push against the air when the bird flaps its wings, which enables the bird to fly. They are also smooth, which helps the bird to glide through the air.

### TROUT

Scales — these grow from the fish's skin and are made from a bone-like substance. They help to protect the fish, e.g. from predators.

Gills (under flaps on the side of the head) — as water flows across the gills, oxygen is absorbed from the water into the fish's blood.

Fins — these help the fish to swim by stabilising it in the water and allowing it to change direction easily.

### CONIFER TREE

Cones — when the 'scales' on the pine cone are closed, the seeds inside are protected from animals and harsh weather conditions. When the 'scales' open, the seeds are released, which allows the tree to reproduce.

Needles (instead of broad leaves) — these are narrow, meaning snow is less likely to build up on them and cause damage. There are lots of them on each branch, which means the tree can carry out lots of photosynthesis.

# Warm-Up & Practice Questions

If you don't take time to ease into things you risk serious brain-strain. So try these Warm-Up Questions first to get in the zone, then launch yourself into the Practice Questions...

## Warm-Up Questions

1) What are the two different classes of variation? How are they different?
2) True or false? Mammals, fish and birds are different types of kingdom.
3) What is a 'diagnostic feature'?
4) Which two kingdoms could an organism belong to if it was single-celled and had a nucleus?
5) Name two kingdoms that contain organisms that are not able to move around.

## Practice Questions

1 Kate wants to get a pet rabbit. She looks at several rabbits in the pet shop and notices that some have straight ears and some have floppy ears, even though they all belong to the same species.

(a) Explain why the rabbits can have different types of ear even though they belong to the same species.

*(1 mark)*

(b) Explain whether this variation in ear type is continuous or discontinuous.

*(2 marks)*

2 The photographs below show two reptiles, a turtle and a tortoise.

Turtle

Tortoise

(a) Give **two** diagnostic features that the turtle and tortoise will have in common, which cannot be seen on the photographs.

*(2 marks)*

(b) Both organisms have a shell on their back. Suggest **one** function of the shell.

*(1 mark)*

(c) The turtle lives in water, whereas the tortoise lives on land.

(i) Use the photographs to identify **one** way that the structure of the turtle differs from that of the tortoise.

*(1 mark)*

(ii) Suggest how the structure you identified in part (i) helps the turtle to survive in water.

*(1 mark)*

# Summary Questions

Just one more page of questions standing between you and the first Chemistry section. Exciting, eh...

- Try these questions and tick off each one when you get it right.
- When you've done all the questions for a topic and are completely happy with it, tick it off.

## Variation (p.47)

1) What does variation mean?
2) What is continuous variation? Give three examples.
3) What is discontinuous variation? Give two examples.
4) Describe how a graph showing continuous variation would differ from one showing discontinuous variation.

## Classification (p.48)

5) All living things can be classified into one of five groups. What do we call these groups? List them.
6) Give three features of an arthropod.
7) How do insects differ from arachnids? Give two ways.
8) What is the difference between a vertebrate animal and an invertebrate animal?
9) List the five groups of vertebrates, and give three characteristics for each group.

## Structures of Different Organisms (p.49)

10) Give two similarities between animals and plants.
11) Name three kingdoms in which organisms have cells with cell walls.
12) Give two ways in which fungi are different to plants.
13) Give one way in which bacteria are different to protists.
14) For each of the following organisms, state two structures that it has and describe how each of those structures is related to its function: a) a seagull, b) a trout, c) a conifer tree.

# The Particle Model

The particle model — sounds pretty fancy. But actually it's pretty straightforward.

## The Three States of Matter — Solid, Liquid and Gas

1) A material can be a solid, a liquid or a gas — these are called the three states of matter.
2) All materials are made up of tiny particles.
3) The particles in a substance stay the same whether it's a solid, a liquid or a gas.
4) What changes is the arrangement of the particles and their energy.

Water is commonly found in different states.

## Solids — Particles are Held Very Tightly Together

Particles in a Solid

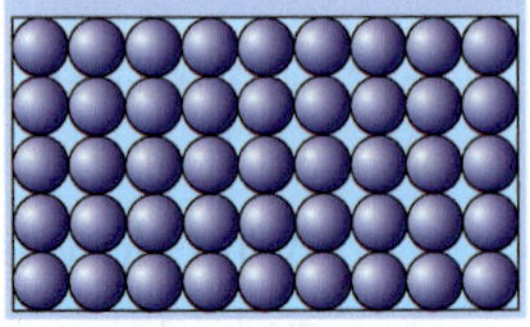

1) There are strong forces of attraction between particles.
2) The particles are held closely in fixed positions in a very regular arrangement. But they do vibrate to and fro.
3) The particles don't move from their positions, so all solids keep a definite shape and volume — they can't flow like liquids.
4) Solids can't be compressed because the particles are very closely packed.
5) Solids are usually very dense, as they have lots of particles in a small volume.

See page 113 for more about density.

## Liquids — Particles are Close Together But They Can Move

Particles in a Liquid

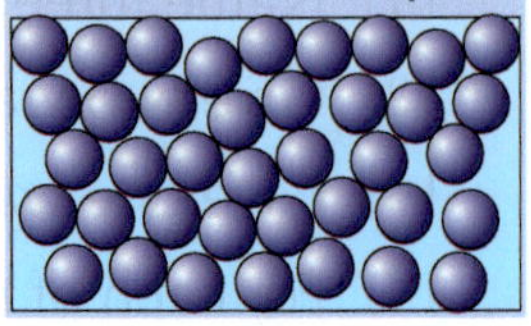

1) There are some forces of attraction between the particles.
2) The particles are close, but free to move past each other — and they do stick together. The particles are constantly moving in all directions.
3) Liquids don't keep a definite shape and can form puddles. They flow and fill the bottom of a container. But they do keep the same volume.
4) Liquids don't compress easily as the particles are packed closely together.
5) Liquids are quite dense, as they have quite a lot of particles in a small volume.

## Gases — Particles are Far Apart and Whizz About a Lot

Particles in a Gas

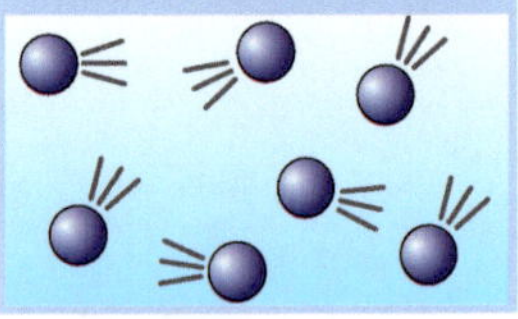

1) There are very weak forces of attraction between the particles.
2) The particles are far apart and free to move quickly in all directions.
3) The particles move fast, and so collide with each other and the container.
4) Gases don't keep a definite shape or volume and will always expand to fill any container. Gases can be compressed easily because there's a lot of free space between the particles.
5) Gases have very low densities, because there are not many particles in a large volume.

REVISION TASK

### Solid, liquid, gas — they all matter...

It's pretty clever the way you can explain all the differences between solids, liquids and gases with a page full of snooker balls. Anyway, that's the easy bit. The not-so-easy bit is making sure you understand it. Try explaining each state to someone who doesn't understand, your little brother, or your dog for instance. Just having to say it out loud will help you to work out which bits you've got sussed, and which you might need to spend a little more time on...

# Changes of State

Changes of state are physical changes. They don't change a substance's particles or its mass — they just change the particles' arrangement and energy.

## Most Things Expand on Heating and Contract on Cooling

1) When you heat a solid, liquid or gas, the particles move more and move further apart. So the substance expands and becomes less dense.
2) When you cool a substance, the particles move less and get closer together. So the substance contracts and becomes more dense.
3) This is what makes a thermometer work — when it is heated, the liquid inside it (e.g. mercury or ethanol) expands and moves up the tube (and vice versa).

Ice is an unusual case though — when it melts, the particles move closer together and the density increases (see p.69).

## Changes of State — i.e. changing from one state of matter to another.

1. When a solid is heated, its particles gain more energy.
2. This makes the particles move more which weakens the forces that hold the solid together.
3. At a certain temperature, the particles have enough energy to break free from their positions. This is called melting — the solid turns into a liquid.
4. When a liquid is heated, the particles gain even more energy.
5. This energy makes the particles move faster, which weakens the forces holding the liquid together.
6. At a certain temperature, the particles have enough energy to break the forces. This is called boiling and the liquid turns into a gas.

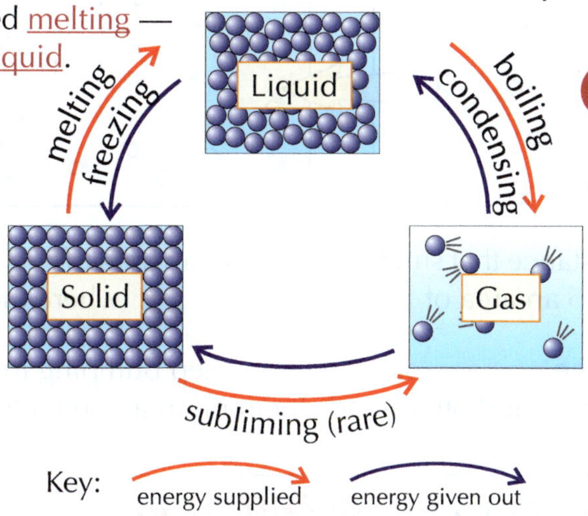


Evaporation and boiling both describe a change from a liquid to a gas, but they're not the same. Evaporation can happen slowly at any temperature, but boiling occurs rapidly at a specific temperature (known as the boiling point). Different liquids have different boiling points, e.g. pure water boils at 100 °C, but olive oil boils at a relatively higher temperature.

## You can Watch Iodine Subliming

**PRACTICAL**

1) Put a tripod and gauze over a Bunsen burner.
2) Put a beaker on the tripod and gauze, and add some iodine crystals.
3) Place an evaporating dish on top of the beaker and add some ice cubes to the dish.
4) Use the Bunsen burner to gently heat the beaker.
5) As the iodine heats up, it will sublime and turn into a purple gas.
6) When the gas touches the cold evaporating dish, it will turn back into a solid (you'll see iodine crystals form on the bottom of the dish).

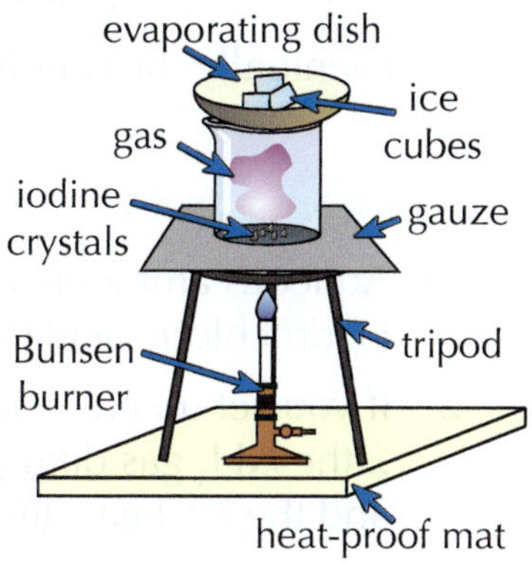


There are lots of other ways you could see changes of state taking place in the lab. E.g. stand a beaker of water on a tripod over a Bunsen burner — drop in some ice cubes and watch them melt, then let the water heat up until you see it boil. Turn off the Bunsen, then hold a test tube close to the steam coming from the beaker and watch the water condense on the glass.

# Gas Pressure and Diffusion

The particle model can be used to explain all sorts of exciting things, like gas pressure and diffusion.

## Gas Pressure is Due to Particles Hitting a Surface

1) When a gas is in a container, the gas particles bounce off the walls as they whizz about at high speeds.
2) These collisions create a pushing force on the walls of the container. This force is called gas pressure.

## Diffusion is Just Particles Spreading Out

1) Particles suspended in a liquid or gas move about randomly, in all directions.
2) Due to this movement, they end up spreading out. This process is called diffusion.
3) An example of diffusion in a gas is when a smell spreads slowly through a room:

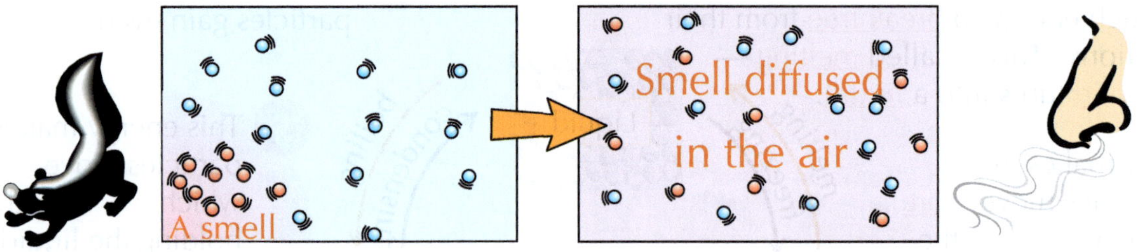


The particles of the substance that smells move from an area of higher concentration (i.e. where there are lots of them) to an area of lower concentration (where there's only a few of them).

4) Diffusion is slow because the particles of smelly gas keep bumping into air particles, which stops them making forward progress and often sends them off in a completely different direction.

## You Can do Experiments to Show Diffusion

PRACTICAL

### Potassium Manganate(VII)

1) Put some potassium manganate(VII) (which is purple) in a beaker of water.
2) The particles of potassium manganate(VII) will diffuse among the particles of water.
3) Eventually the purple colour will be evenly spread out throughout the water.

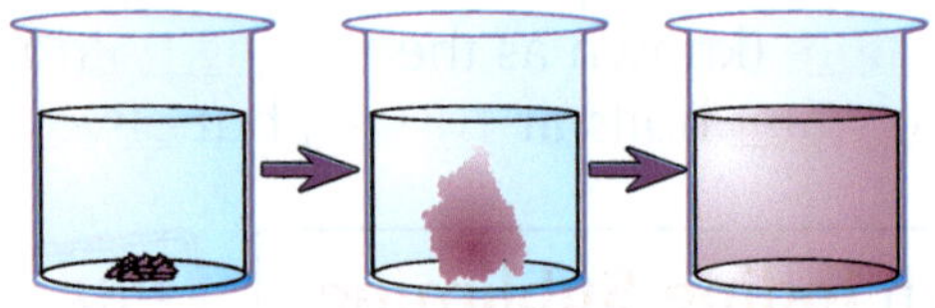

Potassium manganate(VII) can also be called potassium permanganate.

### Ammonia and Hydrogen Chloride

1) Aqueous ammonia ($NH_3$) gives off ammonia gas. Hydrochloric acid (HCl) gives off hydrogen chloride gas.
2) If you set up an experiment like this... ...the $NH_3$ gas diffuses from one end of the tube and the HCl gas diffuses from the other.
3) When they meet they react to form a ring of ammonium chloride.

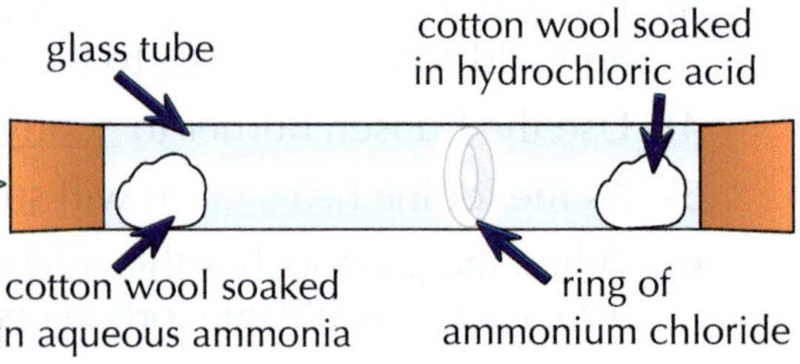


The ring forms nearest the end where the HCl was. This is because particles of HCl gas are larger and heavier than particles of $NH_3$ gas, so they diffuse more slowly and don't travel as far along the tube in the same amount of time.

# Warm-Up & Practice Questions

There's a bit too much gas in this section in my opinion.
Tackle the Warm-Up Questions first, then move on to the trickier Practice Question.

## Warm-Up Questions

1) In which state of matter are the particles fixed in a regular pattern?
2) Name the only state of matter that can be easily compressed.
3) True or false? When particles are heated they move around less.
4) What is sublimation?
5) Explain how particles diffuse from where there is a higher concentration of them to where there is a lower concentration of them.

## Practice Question

1 Jenny boils 2 litres of water in a large pan in her kitchen. After half an hour Jenny cools the water and measures it in a jug. There is 1 litre left.

(a) The pan is a solid.
Copy and complete the following sentence about solids using words from below:

**high** **easy** **low** **difficult**

Solids usually have a ........................ density and are ........................ to compress.

*(2 marks)*

(b) The water in the jug is a liquid.
Draw a diagram to show the arrangement of particles in a liquid.
Use a circle to represent each particle.

*(1 mark)*

(c) State what has happened to the water that is not in the jug.

*(1 mark)*

(d) Jenny notices that there are droplets of water on her kitchen window.
Name the process that has taken place to form the droplets.

*(1 mark)*

(e) Jenny freezes the water in the jug to make some ice cubes.
Explain whether the particles change when the water freezes.

*(1 mark)*

# Summary Questions

So, that's another section done — it may be short but it's full of important stuff that you need to know.

- Try these questions and tick off each one when you get it right.
- When you've done all the questions for a topic and are completely happy with it, tick it off.

## The Particle Model (p.52)

1) What are the three states of matter?
2) Describe the main properties of a liquid.
3) True or false? Liquids don't compress easily because the particles are packed closely together.
4) Which state of matter has very weak forces of attraction between the particles?
5) Draw how the particles are arranged in a gas.

## Changes of State (p.53)

6) Why do solids, liquids and gases (usually) expand when they are heated?
7) Explain why the liquid inside a thermometer moves down the tube when it is cooled.
8) Give the names of five changes of state. For each change, give the initial and final state.
9) A substance changes from a liquid to a solid. During this change of state, will the substance need energy supplied to it, or will it give out energy?
10) A substance changes from a solid to a gas. During this change of state, will the substance need energy supplied to it, or will it give out energy?
11) Describe the difference between evaporation and boiling.
12) Describe an experiment you could do to watch sublimation occurring.

## Gas Pressure and Diffusion (p.54)

13) Explain what gas pressure is in terms of the gas particles.
14) Explain what diffusion is.
15) If you put some potassium manganate(VII) in a beaker of water, what will happen to the water? Why will this happen?
16) Describe how you could show diffusion with some aqueous ammonia, some hydrochloric acid, two cotton wool balls, two bungs and a glass tube.

# Atoms and Elements

If you've ever wondered what everything is made of, then the simple answer is atoms.

## You Need to Know About **Atoms**...

1) Atoms are a type of tiny, tiny, particle.
2) Dalton's atomic model says that all matter is made up of atoms.
3) There are different types of atom, and each element (see below) contains a different type.

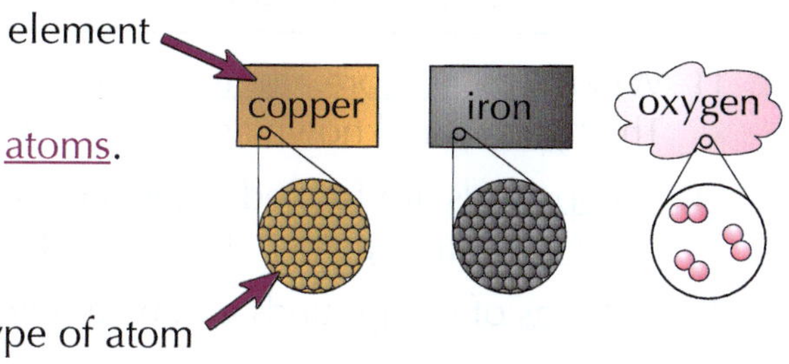


## ...and **Elements**

1) An element is a substance that contains only one type of atom.
2) Samples of the same element will always contain the same type of atom.
3) Different elements can have very different properties.

## All Elements Have a **Name** and a **Symbol**

1) Each element has a symbol — usually of one or two letters.
2) This symbol can also be used to mean just one atom of that specific element.
3) You need to know the symbols for these elements.

| Name | Symbol |
|---|---|
| hydrogen | H |
| helium | He |
| carbon | C |
| nitrogen | N |
| oxygen | O |
| sodium | Na |
| magnesium | Mg |
| sulfur | S |
| chlorine | Cl |
| calcium | Ca |
| iron | Fe |
| copper | Cu |

## The **Periodic Table** Lists **All** the **Elements**

1) The periodic table shows all of the elements we have discovered — there are about 100.
2) Elements with similar properties are arranged into vertical columns in the table.
3) The vertical columns are called groups, and the horizontal rows are called periods.

| Periods | Group 1 | Group 2 | | | | | | | | | | | Group 3 | Group 4 | Group 5 | Group 6 | Group 7 | Group 0 |
|---|---|---|---|---|---|---|---|---|---|---|---|---|---|---|---|---|---|---|
| 1 | | | | | | | | 1 H Hydrogen 1 | | | | | | | | | | 4 He Helium 2 |
| 2 | 7 Li Lithium 3 | 9 Be Beryllium 4 | | | | | | | | | | | 11 B Boron 5 | 12 C Carbon 6 | 14 N Nitrogen 7 | 16 O Oxygen 8 | 19 F Fluorine 9 | 20 Ne Neon 10 |
| 3 | 23 Na Sodium 11 | 24 Mg Magnesium 12 | | | | | | | | | | | 27 Al Aluminium 13 | 28 Si Silicon 14 | 31 P Phosphorus 15 | 32 S Sulfur 16 | 35.5 Cl Chlorine 17 | 40 Ar Argon 18 |
| 4 | 39 K Potassium 19 | 40 Ca Calcium 20 | 45 Sc Scandium 21 | 48 Ti Titanium 22 | 51 V Vanadium 23 | 52 Cr Chromium 24 | 55 Mn Manganese 25 | 56 Fe Iron 26 | 59 Co Cobalt 27 | 59 Ni Nickel 28 | 63.5 Cu Copper 29 | 65 Zn Zinc 30 | 70 Ga Gallium 31 | 73 Ge Germanium 32 | 75 As Arsenic 33 | 79 Se Selenium 34 | 80 Br Bromine 35 | 84 Kr Krypton 36 |
| 5 | 86 Rb Rubidium 37 | 88 Sr Strontium 38 | 89 Y Yttrium 39 | 91 Zr Zirconium 40 | 93 Nb Niobium 41 | 96 Mo Molybdenum 42 | 99 Tc Technetium 43 | 101 Ru Ruthenium 44 | 103 Rh Rhodium 45 | 106 Pd Palladium 46 | 108 Ag Silver 47 | 112 Cd Cadmium 48 | 115 In Indium 49 | 119 Sn Tin 50 | 122 Sb Antimony 51 | 128 Te Tellurium 52 | 127 I Iodine 53 | 131 Xe Xenon 54 |
| 6 | 133 Cs Caesium 55 | 137 Ba Barium 56 | 57-71 Lanthanides | 179 Hf Hafnium 72 | 181 Ta Tantalum 73 | 184 W Tungsten 74 | 186 Re Rhenium 75 | 190 Os Osmium 76 | 192 Ir Iridium 77 | 195 Pt Platinum 78 | 197 Au Gold 79 | 201 Hg Mercury 80 | 204 Tl Thallium 81 | 207 Pb Lead 82 | 209 Bi Bismuth 83 | 210 Po Polonium 84 | 210 At Astatine 85 | 222 Rn Radon 86 |
| 7 | 223 Fr Francium 87 | 226 Ra Radium 88 | 89-103 Actinides | | | | | | | | | | | | | | | |

Don't worry — you won't be tested on the details in this table.

metals | non-metals | separates metals from non-metals

### Anyone know any good jokes about sodium? Na...

Some of the symbols are a bit weird (like Fe for iron) — it's 'cause they're often based on Latin words. Thankfully most of the ones in that list you need to know are pretty straightforward, like O for oxygen.

# Compounds

Throw a few elements together and you end up with some compounds or a mixture. It's getting exciting...

## Compounds Contain Two or More Elements Joined Up

1) When <u>two or more atoms</u> join together, a <u>molecule</u> is made. The "<u>joins</u>" are known as <u>chemical bonds</u>.
2) <u>Compounds</u> are formed when atoms of <u>different elements</u> join together. Like in <u>carbon dioxide</u>, $CO_2$:

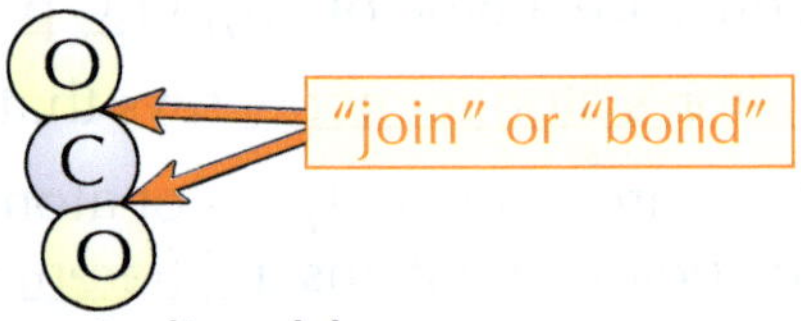


3) <u>Millions</u> of compounds can be made from the elements in the periodic table.

An <u>ELEMENT</u> made up of <u>atoms</u>

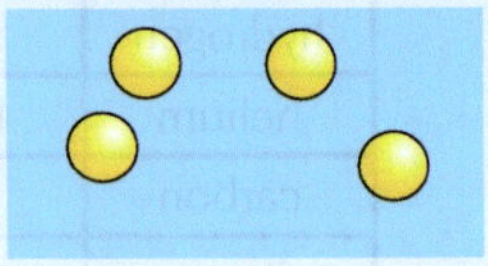

The atoms are all the same and not joined up — it must be an <u>element</u>.

An <u>ELEMENT</u> made up of <u>molecules</u>

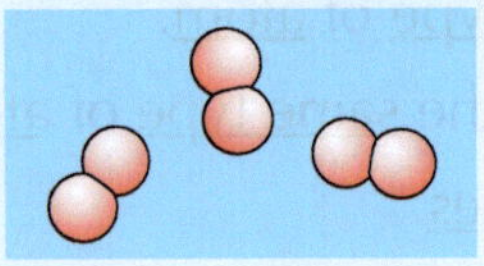

The atoms are joined, but there's only one type, so it's still an <u>element</u>, e.g. $O_2$.

A <u>COMPOUND</u> made up of <u>molecules</u>

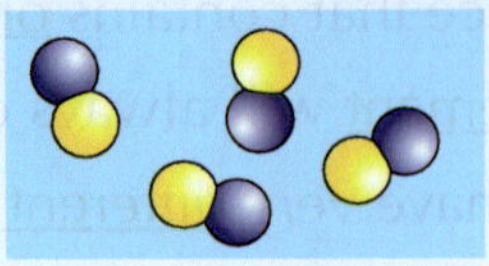

Here we have different atoms joined together — that's a <u>compound</u> alright.

A <u>MIXTURE</u> of different <u>elements</u>

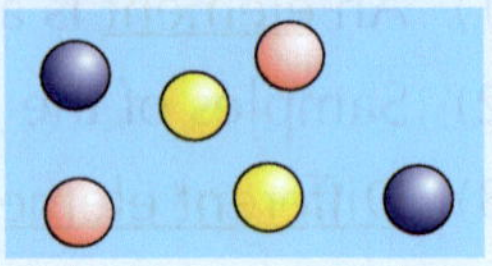

This is <u>not</u> a compound because the elements aren't joined up — it's a <u>mixture</u>.

Mixtures can also contain compounds, e.g. a sugar solution is a mixture containing sugar (a compound) and water (another compound).

## Compounds have Different Properties to their Elements

1) In a <u>chemical reaction</u>, chemicals <u>combine together</u> or <u>split apart</u> to form <u>new substances</u>. The chemicals you <u>start with</u> are called <u>reactants</u>. The chemicals you <u>end up with</u> are called <u>products</u>.
2) When a <u>new</u> compound is <u>synthesised</u> (made), elements <u>combine</u>.
3) The <u>new compounds</u> produced by chemical reactions have <u>different properties</u> from the <u>original elements</u> (or reactants). A <u>classic example</u> of this is <u>iron</u> reacting with <u>sulfur</u>...

### Iron is Magnetic but Iron Sulfide is Not

PRACTICAL

1) Take a test tube that contains a <u>mixture</u> of <u>iron powder</u> and <u>sulfur</u>.
2) Hold a <u>magnet</u> to the side of the test tube. The mixture will <u>separate</u> — the iron powder will move <u>towards</u> the magnet, but the sulfur <u>will not</u>. This is because iron is <u>magnetic</u>, but sulfur <u>is not</u>.

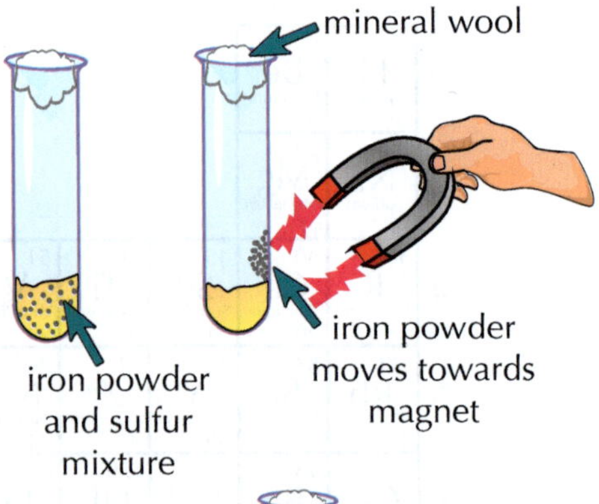


3) Next, the iron powder and sulfur need to be <u>heated</u> to create the <u>compound iron sulfide</u>. (Your teacher may do the heating with you in class, or you may be given a pre-made sample of iron sulfide in a test tube).
4) Hold a <u>magnet</u> to the side of the test tube, just like you did before. Iron sulfide is <u>not magnetic</u>, so it should <u>not</u> move towards the magnet. The iron and sulfur are <u>chemically bonded</u> — the magnet <u>can't</u> separate the iron from the sulfur.

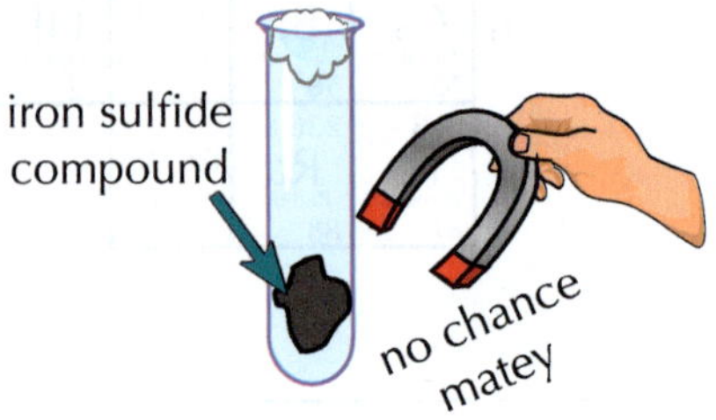


You might notice that the iron sulfide has a weak attraction to the magnet — this could be because some of the iron powder hasn't reacted and is trapped inside the iron sulfide.

# Chemical Formulae

When elements combine to make a compound, their names change slightly. Intrigued? Then read on...

## All Compounds Have a Chemical Formula

1) All compounds have a chemical formula. It contains the symbols for the elements it's made from.
2) Small (subscript) numbers in a formula tell you if there's more than one atom present in a molecule of a particular element. → $CaCO_3$ ← a subscript number

E.g. the formula for water is $H_2O$. A molecule contains 2 hydrogen (H) atoms and 1 oxygen (O) atom.

3) Elements made up of molecules have chemical formulae too, e.g. the formula for oxygen is $O_2$.

## Naming Compounds — Two Simple Rules

RULE 1: When two different elements combine the ending is usually "something -ide".

The metal keeps the same name. The non-metal gets the "-ide" on the end.

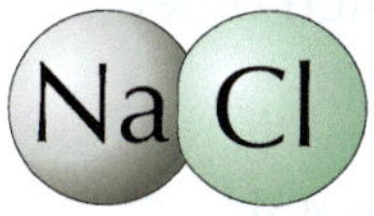


NaCl ← Formula

Sodium and Chlorine ← Elements present

give: sodium chloride ← Name of Compound

Similarly: Sulfur → Sulfide
Iodine → Iodide
Bromine → Bromide
Fluorine → Fluoride

RULE 2: When three or more different elements combine and one of them is oxygen, the ending is "something -ate".

The metal keeps the same name. The non-metal that isn't oxygen gets the "-ate" on the end. (The oxygen doesn't get a bit.)

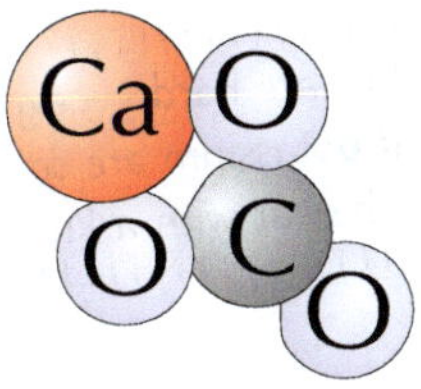


$CaCO_3$ ← Formula

1 Calcium
1 Carbon
3 Oxygens ← Elements present

calcium carbonate ← Name of Compound

And in just the same way:
Copper + Sulfur + 4 Oxygens makes:
copper sulfate ($CuSO_4$)

## ...But There are Exceptions to These Rules

1) Unfortunately, not every compound follows these rules.
2) The table on the right gives a few other names of compounds that you need to be familiar with.

| Compound | Formula |
|---|---|
| carbon dioxide | $CO_2$ |
| hydrochloric acid | $HCl$ |
| sulfuric acid | $H_2SO_4$ |
| methane (natural gas) | $CH_4$ |
| sodium hydroxide | $NaOH$ |

$CO_2$: There are two oxygen atoms, so you put 'di-' in front of the 'oxide' bit.

$HCl$: Technically it's called hydrogen chloride if it's a gas, but you'll only really find it as an acid.

$NaOH$: This one's just a bit odd and doesn't follow Rule 2.

### -ides and -ates — it's the game of the name, pal...

REVISION TASK

There are 10 chemical formulae on this page that you need to know: $H_2O$, $O_2$, $NaCl$, $CaCO_3$, $CuSO_4$, $CO_2$, $HCl$, $H_2SO_4$, $CH_4$ and $NaOH$. Jot down the numbers 1-10 on a blank piece of paper, then write the name of one of the compounds and its formula beside each number.

# Properties of Metals

Metals are jolly useful. We use them all the time in bendy wires, bridges, musical instruments and more.

## 1) Metals Can be Found in the Periodic Table

Most of the elements in the periodic table are metals. They are shown here in purple, to the left of the zigzag.

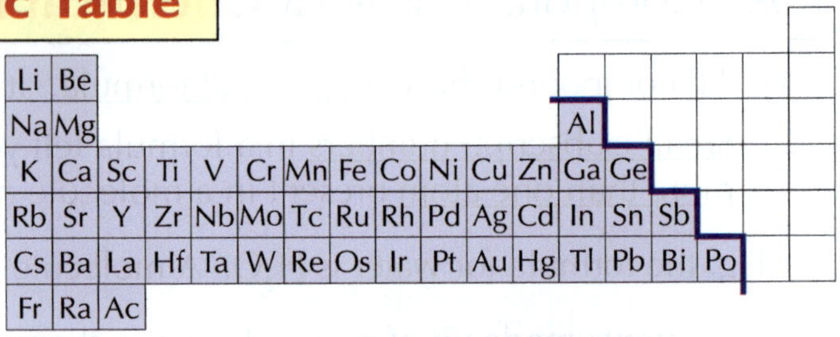

Li Be
Na Mg
Al
K Ca Sc Ti V Cr Mn Fe Co Ni Cu Zn Ga Ge
Rb Sr Y Zr Nb Mo Tc Ru Rh Pd Ag Cd In Sn Sb
Cs Ba La Hf Ta W Re Os Ir Pt Au Hg Tl Pb Bi Po
Fr Ra Ac


## 2) Metals are Shiny

Polished or freshly cut metals give strong reflection of light from their smooth surface. This makes them look shiny.

## 3) Metals are Malleable and Ductile

1) Metals are easily shaped (malleable) because the atoms in metals can slide over each other.
2) This means metals can be hammered into thin sheets or bent — all without shattering.

If an iron nail or a length of copper wire is put on a bench and hammered, the metal will bend or start to go flat. If the same thing is done with a material made from a non-metal element (e.g. the graphite from the middle of a pencil) it will shatter.

Graphite is made from carbon (a non-metal element).

3) Metals are also ductile, which means they can be drawn into wires.

## 4) Metals can be Hard

1) If a material is hard it means it is difficult to cut into, dent or scratch.
2) Metals are hard because they have strong forces between their atoms.
3) Tungsten, titanium and chromium are particularly hard metals.

Not all metals are hard — e.g. sodium and potassium are so soft they can be cut with a knife.

## 5) Metals Conduct Electricity

1) Electric current is the flow of electrical charge around a circuit.
2) Metals are electrical conductors, which means they allow electrical charge to pass through them easily.
3) The moving charges are negatively charged particles called electrons.
4) Metals contain some electrons that are free to move between the metal atoms. These free electrons can carry an electrical charge from one end of the metal to the other.

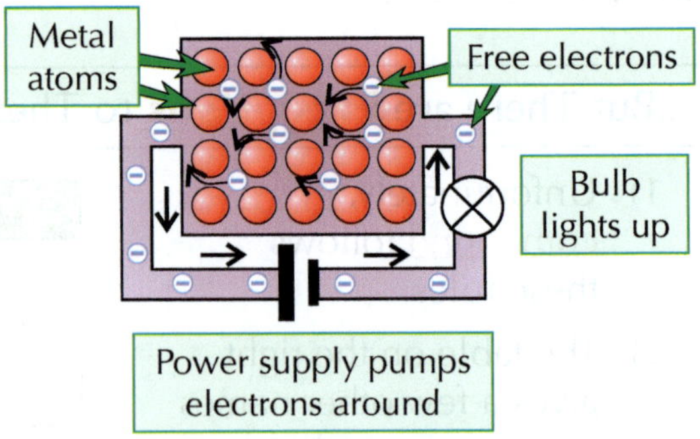


You can set up a circuit like the one above to check the theory...

PRACTICAL

1) Set up a simple circuit like this... ...and notice that the bulb lights up.
2) Replace the copper strip with different metal objects, e.g. aluminium foil or an iron nail.
3) Each time the bulb will light up because the electrical charge is able to pass through the metal object.

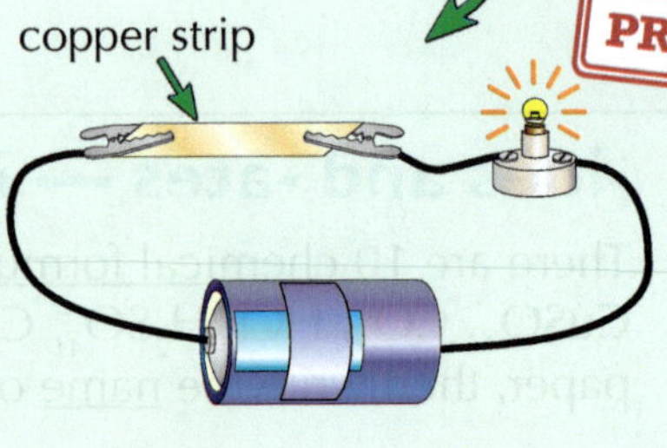

# Properties of Metals

## 6) Metals Conduct Heat

1) Metals are thermal conductors. This means metals let heat pass through.
2) If you heat one end of a piece of metal, the "hot" particles will vibrate strongly.
3) Because the particles are very close together, the vibrations are easily passed on through the metal.
4) Free electrons in the metal also help to transfer heat from the hot parts of the metal to the cooler parts as they move around.

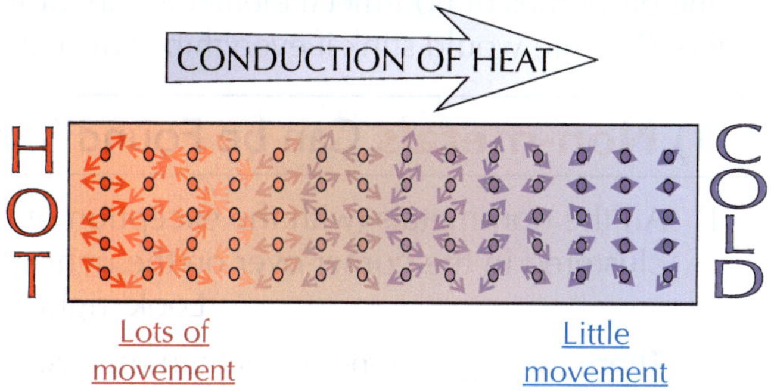


Some metals are better thermal conductors than others, e.g. copper and aluminium are much better thermal conductors than iron.

### Testing Conduction of Heat

PRACTICAL

1) Take a metal rod and drop beads of melted wax onto one end of it. The beads of melted wax will then set.
2) Put the metal rod in a clamp stand and use a Bunsen burner to heat the end where there's no wax.
3) Gradually, heat will be conducted along the rod, so the beads will melt and fall off, starting with the one closest to the Bunsen burner.

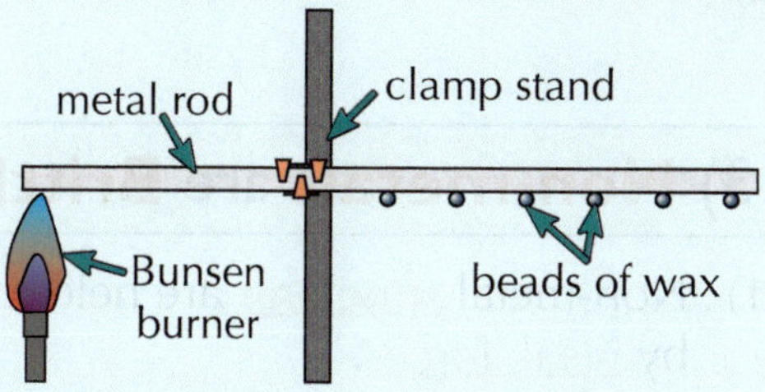


4) You could time how long it takes for all of the beads to fall off, then repeat the experiment with rods made from different metals to see which one is the best thermal conductor, i.e. which one loses its beads the fastest.

## 7) Metals have High Melting and Boiling Points

1) A lot of energy is needed to melt metals and even more to boil them.
2) This is because their atoms are joined by strong forces.
3) The table gives the melting and boiling points of some metals.
4) Most metals are solids at room temperature. Mercury is the only exception. It's a liquid at room temperature.

| Metal | Melting Point (°C) | Boiling Point (°C) |
|---|---|---|
| Aluminium | 660 | 2520 |
| Copper | 1085 | 2562 |
| Magnesium | 650 | 1090 |
| Iron | 1538 | 2861 |
| Zinc | 420 | 907 |

## 8) Some Metals are Magnetic

1) Only certain metals are magnetic.
2) Most metals aren't magnetic. Iron, nickel and cobalt are.
3) Alloys made with these three metals will also be magnetic — e.g. steel is made mostly from iron, so it is also magnetic.

Iron or nickel or cobalt (or a combination of different metals containing one of them)

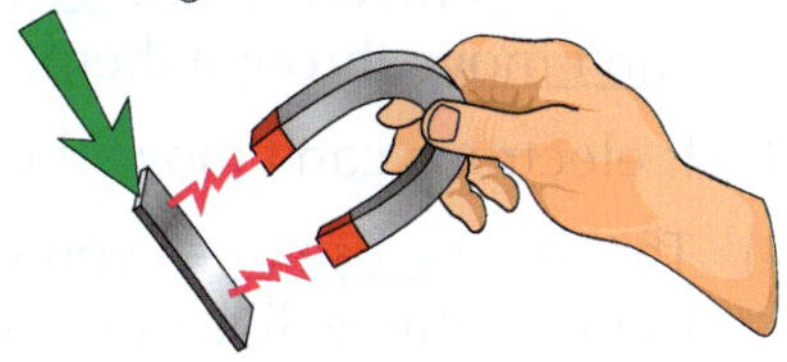

### My friends call me FeNiCo — I have a magnetic personality...

Two pages of facts about metals just waiting to be soaked up into that giant sponge lurking between your ears. You need to know all these properties well enough so that you can spot a metal from a mile away.

# Properties of Non-Metals

The properties of non-metal elements vary quite a lot.
Good — life would stink if everything was like sulfur...

## 1) Non-metals Can be Found in the Periodic Table

1) All the non-metals (with the exception of hydrogen) are clustered in the corner over on the right of the zigzag. Look, right over there.
2) There are fewer non-metals than metals.

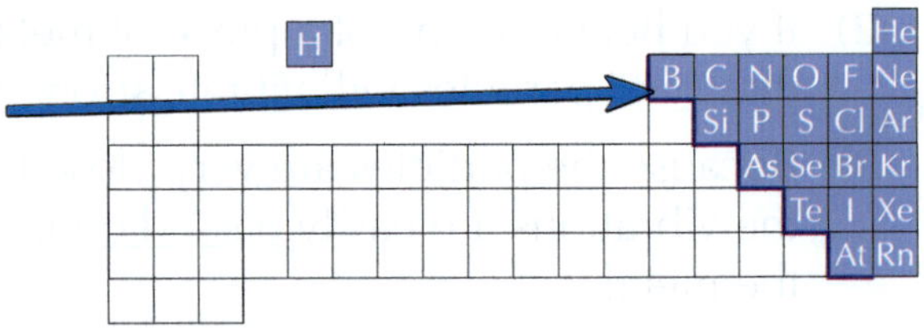


## 2) Non-metals are Dull

1) Most non-metals don't reflect light very well at all. Their surfaces are not usually as smooth as metals.
2) This makes them look dull.

## 3) Non-metals are Brittle

1) Non-metal structures are held together by weak forces.
2) This means they're not very malleable as they shatter all too easily.

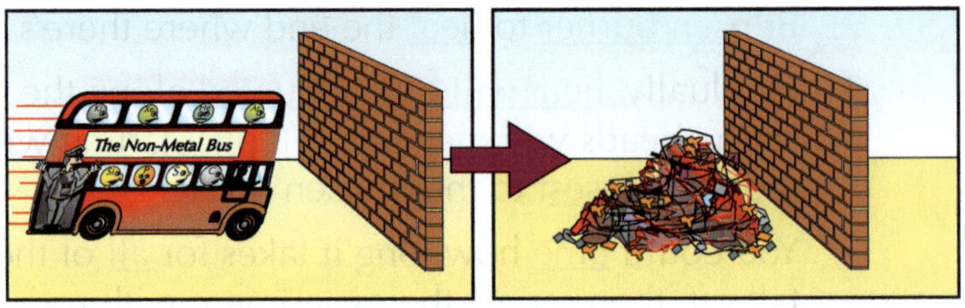


## 4) Non-metals are not Strong or Hard-Wearing

1) The forces between the particles in most non-metals are weak — this means they break easily.
2) It's also easy to scrub atoms or molecules off them — so they wear away quickly.

## 5) Non-metals are Poor Conductors of Electricity

1) Most non-metals are electrical insulators, which means that they don't conduct electricity.
2) The way that atoms in non-metals are arranged means that electrons (negative charges) can't move through them.
3) If electrons can't move then no electric current flows.
4) This is very useful — you can use non-metal compounds to make things like plugs and electric cable coverings.

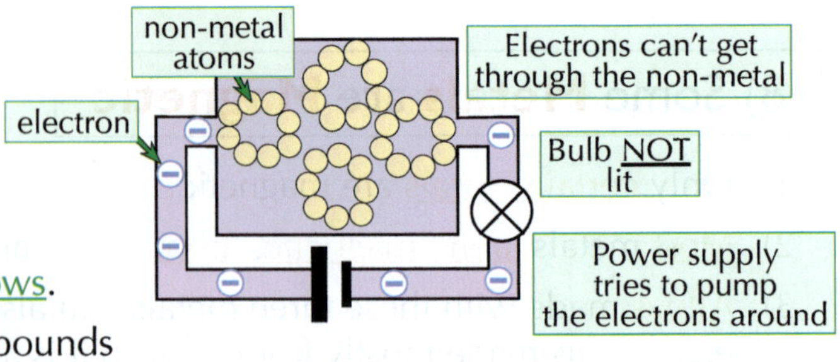


One exception to this rule is graphite — a non-metal made purely from carbon atoms. Its atoms are arranged in layers, which allow electrons to move along them, so graphite can conduct electricity.

You can test whether non-metal objects conduct electricity by putting them in a circuit (see p.60)

# Properties of Non-Metals

## 6) Non-metals are Poor Conductors of Heat

1) Heat does not travel very well at all through non-metals.
2) If you heat one end of a non-metal, the "hot" particles don't pass on their vibrations very well.
3) This makes non-metals really good thermal insulators (insulators of heat).
4) That's why non-metal compounds are used to make things like saucepan handles.

## 7) Most Non-metals Have Low Melting and Boiling Points

1) The forces which hold the particles in non-metals together are usually very weak. This means they melt and boil very easily.
2) The table gives the melting and boiling points of some non-metal elements.
3) At room temperature, most non-metal elements are gases or solids. Only one (bromine) is a liquid.

| Non-Metal | Melting Point (°C) | Boiling Point (°C) |
|---|---|---|
| Sulfur | 113 | 445 |
| Oxygen | -218 | -183 |
| Chlorine | -101 | -35 |
| Helium | -272 | -269 |
| Neon | -249 | -246 |
| Bromine | -7 | 59 |

## 8) Non-metals are Not Magnetic

All non-metals are most definitely non-magnetic.

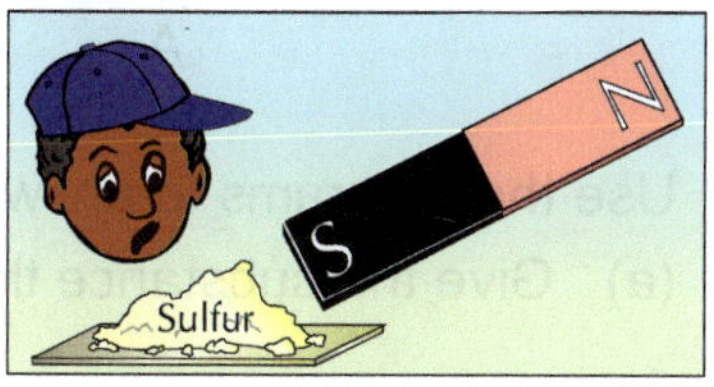


## You Can Use the Properties of an Element to Classify it

1) You could be asked to decided whether an element is a metal or a non-metal.
2) All you need to do is look at the properties of the element.

**Example**

**A sample of an element is shiny, can be bent and allows a current to flow when it is part of a circuit. Is the element a metal or a non-metal?**

It must be a metal because metals have a shiny appearance, are malleable and are good conductors of electricity.

REVISION TASK

### Non-Metals — they really are dull aren't they...

There are 8 fascinating facts about non-metals to learn on these pages. Why not make a poster with all 8 on, and hang it up where you can see it to help you learn all of them? As a matter of fact, make two posters — one for metals as well. You can never have too many posters...

# Warm-Up & Practice Questions

Here are five simple questions to get you going, then some more challenging Practice Questions to make sure you really understand atoms, elements, molecules, compounds and the periodic table.

## Warm-Up Questions

1) What is an element?
2) What is the difference between a compound and a mixture?
3) Name three magnetic metals.
4) Out of metals and non-metals, which are the:
   a) shiniest, b) most brittle, c) best insulators?
5) What physical state (or states) are most non-metal elements at room temperature?

## Practice Questions

1 The diagrams below represent the arrangement of atoms and molecules in four different substances, A, B, C and D.

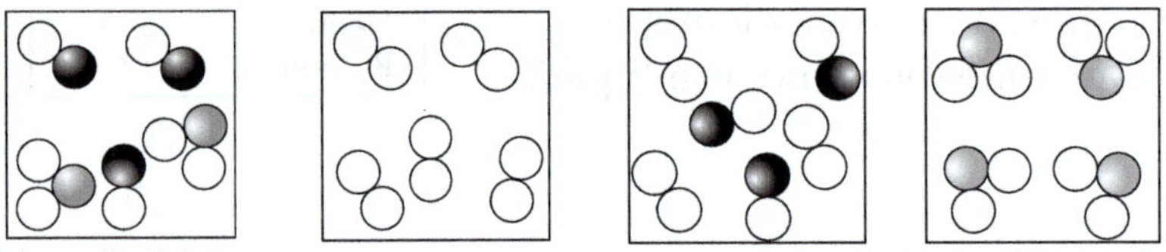

A B C D

Use the diagrams to answer the following questions.

(a) Give the substance that is a mixture of compounds.

*(1 mark)*

(b) Give the substance that you would expect to find in the periodic table.

*(1 mark)*

(c) Give the substance that is most likely to be water, $H_2O$.

*(1 mark)*

2 Sulfur is a non-metal.

Copy and complete the following sentences using words from the box:

| | | | |
|---|---|---|---|
| **shiny** | **left** | **brittle** | **poor** |
| **dull** | **right** | **flexible** | **good** |

Sulfur can be found on the ................-hand side of the periodic table.

It has a ................ consistency and a ................ yellow surface.

It is a ................ conductor of heat.

*(4 marks)*

# Practice Questions

3 Elements can be metals or non-metals.
All known elements are arranged in the periodic table.

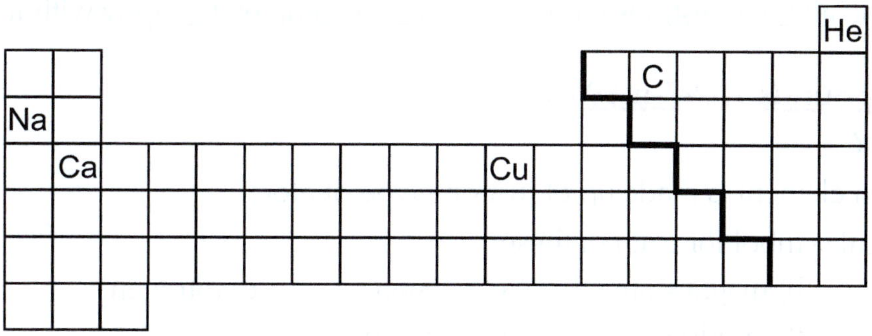


(a) From the table above, give the symbol of one element which

(i) is a metal.

*(1 mark)*

(ii) is a non-metal.

*(1 mark)*

(iii) is a gas at room temperature.

*(1 mark)*

(b) Name the element that is represented by each of the following symbols:

(i) He

*(1 mark)*

(ii) Cu

*(1 mark)*

**PRACTICAL**

4 A scientist mixed iron powder and sulfur together then put the mixture in a test tube. She heated the contents of the test tube until iron sulfide was formed. Before and after heating, she held a magnet close to the test tube and recorded what happened. Her results are shown below.

| | |
|---|---|
| Before heating | A substance moved towards the magnet |
| After heating | No movement towards the magnet |

(a) (i) Give the chemical symbol for iron.

*(1 mark)*

(ii) Give the chemical symbol for sulfur.

*(1 mark)*

(b) Name the substance in the test tube that moved towards the magnet before the chemicals had been heated. Explain how you know.

*(2 marks)*

(c) Heating the contents of the test tube caused a chemical reaction to take place. Explain why nothing moved towards the magnet after the chemical reaction.

*(3 marks)*

# Summary Questions

If you know your metals from your non-metals go straight ahead. If not, a U-turn will be needed here.

- Try these questions and tick off each one when you get it right.
- When you've done all the questions for a topic and are completely happy with it, tick it off.

## Atoms and Compounds (p.57-p.59)

1) What is an atom?
2) True or false? An element is made up of just one type of atom.
3) Give the chemical symbol for each of these:
   a) sodium b) magnesium c) oxygen d) nitrogen
   e) carbon f) chlorine g) calcium
4) What does the periodic table show?
5) What is a molecule?
6) When you're doing a chemical reaction, what are the chemicals that you start with called?
7) True or false? Compounds always have the same properties as the elements they are made from.
8) Give the names of each of the following compounds:
   a) $CH_4$ b) $CO_2$ c) HCl d) $CaCO_3$ e) NaOH
9) Give the chemical formulae of each of the following:
   a) water b) oxygen c) sodium chloride d) copper sulfate e) sulfuric acid

## Properties of Metals and Non-Metals (p.60-p.63)

10) What does malleable mean? Describe how you could show that a metal is malleable.
11) What does it mean if a metal is 'hard'? Name two very hard metals.
12) Describe how you could use a simple circuit to test whether a metal conducts electricity.
13) What is the physical state of most metals at room temperature?
14) Describe how the appearance of most solid non-metals differs from the appearance of metals.
15) True or false? Most non-metals are good thermal insulators.
16) How do the melting points of most non-metal elements compare to the melting points of most metal elements?

# Purity and Mixtures

A mixture in chemistry is a bit like a big salad — all the components are mixed up in a bowl, but you can pick out the olives if you really want to. Well, it's slightly more technical than that...

## Pure Substances Have Fixed Melting and Boiling Points

1) A pure substance is made up of only one type of particle (these particles could be elements or compounds). It can't be separated into anything simpler without a chemical reaction.

E.g. pure water is made up of $H_2O$ molecules only. These molecules can't be separated into H and O atoms without a chemical reaction.

2) Every pure substance has a fixed melting and boiling point (e.g. pure water melts at 0 °C and boils at 100 °C). This helps us to identify substances...

There's more about pure water coming up on page 69.

**Example**

PRACTICAL

1) Stearic acid is a pure substance with a melting point of 69 °C.
2) Candle wax is an impure substance — it's made of stearic acid and a mixture of hydrocarbons (see p.76). There is no set temperature at which it melts — it will melt over a range of temperatures depending on the substances it's made from.
3) If you had a sample of stearic acid and a sample of candle wax and wanted to identify which was which, you would just need to find their melting points.
4) Add one of the samples to a test tube and heat it in a beaker of water over a Bunsen burner. Use a thermometer to measure the temperature when it melts — if it's 69 °C you'll know it's pure stearic acid.

## Mixtures are Substances That are NOT Chemically Joined Up

1) A mixture contains two or more different substances which aren't chemically joined up — so you can separate them using physical methods (i.e. without a chemical reaction — see p.69-71).
2) The properties of a mixture are a mixture of the properties of its components (the parts it's made from). E.g. in a mixture of iron and sulfur, the iron is magnetic and the sulfur is non-magnetic (see p.58).

## You Can Dissolve a Solid to Make a Mixture

1) Dissolving is one way of making a mixture.
2) When you add a solid (the solute) to a liquid (the solvent) the forces between the solute particles sometimes break.
3) The solute particles can then mix with the molecules in the liquid forming a solution.
4) The particles in the solution are arranged randomly.

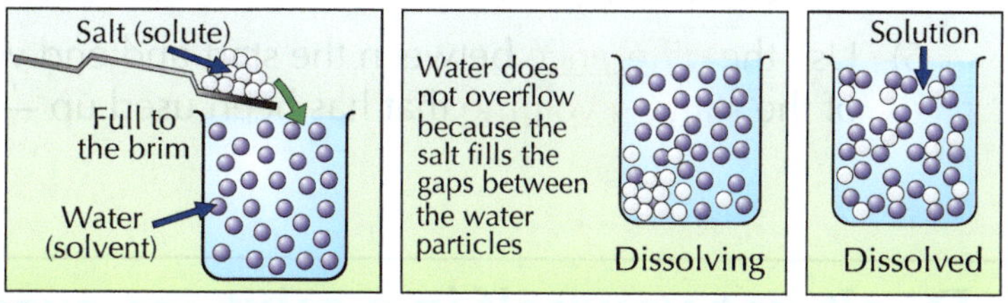


A solution is a mixture, so can be separated using physical methods like evaporation. See page 69 for more about using evaporation to separate solutions.

# Air

Air is a good example of a mixture. Deep breath, now let's begin...

## Air is a Mixture of Gases

1) Air contains around:

   78% nitrogen ($N_2$)     21% oxygen ($O_2$)

> Even though it makes up most of air, there's not a lot to say about nitrogen — it's very unreactive.

2) It also contains small amounts of other gases, like argon, water vapour and carbon dioxide.
3) The carbon dioxide and oxygen in air are both involved in life processes:
   - Photosynthesis uses carbon dioxide and produces oxygen (see p.33).
   - Aerobic respiration uses oxygen and produces carbon dioxide (see p.36).

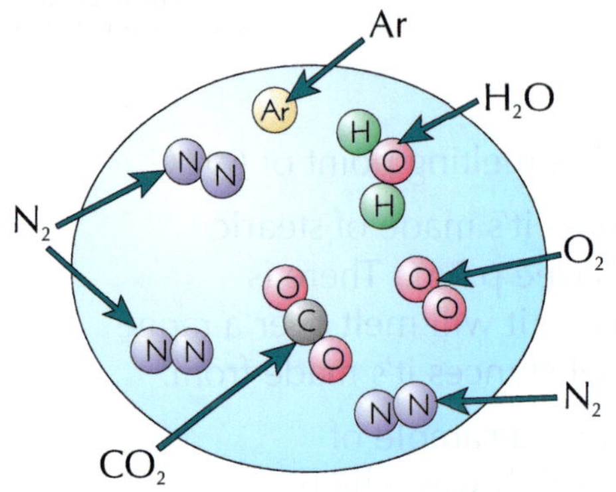

## You Can Show that Around 20% of Air is Oxygen

PRACTICAL

Iron reacts with oxygen and water (or water vapour) to form iron oxide — rust (see p.82). When iron forms rust, it removes oxygen from air. This means you can use rusting experiments to show that air is around 20% oxygen. Here's how:

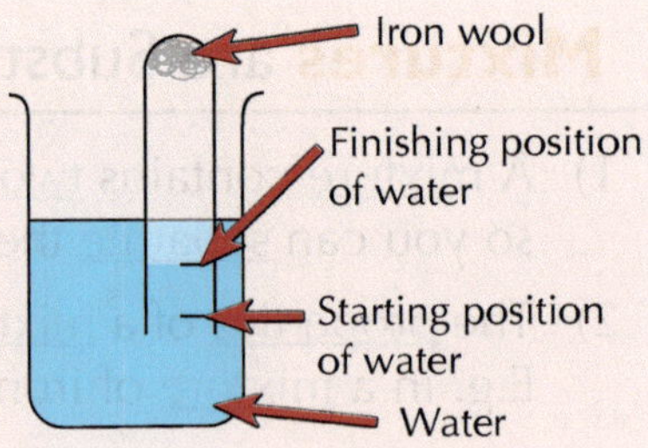


1) First soak some iron wool in water.
2) Then push the wool into a test tube, put your thumb over the end and put the tube upside down in a beaker of water. Remove your thumb and mark the starting position of the water on the test tube.
3) Over time, the level of the water in the test tube will rise. This is because the iron reacts with the oxygen in the air to make iron oxide (rust). The water rises to fill the space the oxygen took up.
4) About a week later, once the reaction has stopped, mark the finishing position of the water.
5) Remove the test tube from the beaker. Fill the tube with water up to each mark and pour the contents into a measuring cylinder to find out the volume of air in the tube at the start and the end.
6) Use the difference between the start and end volumes to work out the percentage of the starting volume that has been used up — it should be about 20%.

### Don't get yourself in a mixture over this page...

Instead of grumbling when your bike spokes next start to rust away, just be grateful that air's still got oxygen in it — I reckon that's a win in the grand scheme of things... Before you move on, make sure you've got that rust experiment sussed — it's a bit confusing the first time you read it, so take your time with it.

# Properties of Water

Water is really important — and for more reasons than just being able to get a nice hot bath...

## Water is an Important Solvent

PRACTICAL

Water is a very useful solvent, because it dissolves lots of solutes really easily. Because it's such a good solvent, you rarely find it in its pure form — it normally has solutes dissolved in it.

- Seawater is far from pure. It contains sodium chloride and other salts.
- Tap water contains some dissolved salts — some soluble impurities in the water can't be filtered out in water treatment plants. To make pure water you need to remove all the salts.
- Distilled water is totally pure water with nothing dissolved in it. It's produced by distillation — boiling water to make steam and condensing the steam (see next page).

## You Can Separate Solutes From a Solution By Evaporation

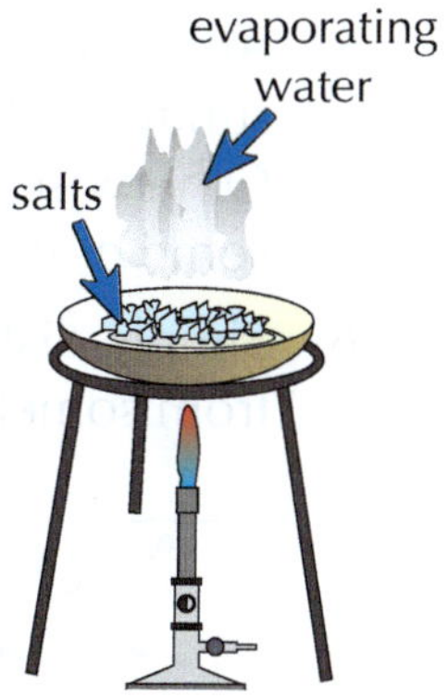


1) You can find out if different types of water contain dissolved salts:
   1) Put a small amount of sea, tap or distilled water in an evaporating basin.
   2) Heat the water gently with a Bunsen burner. The water will evaporate off, leaving any dissolved salts behind.
   3) Seawater will leave lots of salts behind, tap water will leave some salts but distilled water should leave no salts at all.
2) Forming salt crystals like this is called crystallisation. To get big salt crystals, boil off half the water and then leave the dish in a warm place for the rest to evaporate slowly.

Don't confuse boiling and evaporation. Boiling occurs rapidly at a specific temperature. Evaporation is slower and can happen at any temperature (see p.53).

## You Can Test the Purity of Water

1) You saw on page 67 that pure water melts at 0 °C and boils at 100 °C. Impurities change melting and boiling points, e.g. impurities in water cause it to boil above 100 °C.
2) This means you can test to see if a sample of water is pure by measuring its melting point and boiling point. If it doesn't melt at 0 °C or boil at 100 °C, then it isn't pure.
3) Here's how you'd measure the boiling point of water:
   1) Gently heat a small sample of water in a boiling tube.
   2) Use a thermometer to measure the temperature of the gas produced when the liquid is boiling.

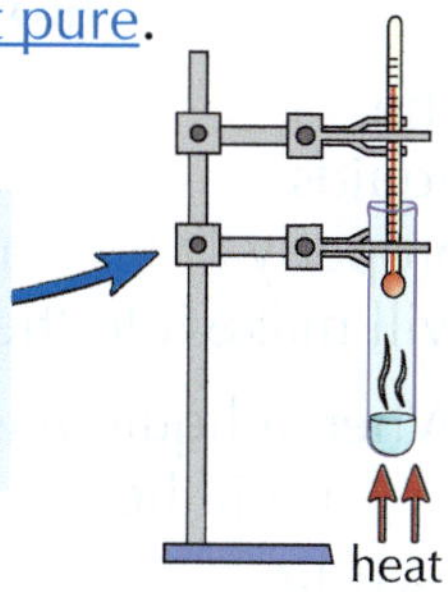


## Water Has Some Unusual Properties

1) When a substance freezes (turns from liquid to solid), the particles usually get closer together (see p.53). This means the substance is more dense.
2) But when water freezes, the particles get further apart.
3) This makes solid water (ice) less dense than liquid water. This difference in density means that ice floats on liquid water.
4) Because the particles get further apart, they take up more volume too. This is why a plastic bottle that's full of water might split if you freeze it. The water inside it expands, causing the bottle to bulge and crack.

# Distillation

As you saw on the previous page, you can use evaporation to separate the solutes from a solution. Distillation makes use of evaporation too, but it lets you keep hold of the solvent...

## Simple Distillation Separates a Solvent from a Solution

PRACTICAL

1) Simple distillation is used to separate out mixtures of liquids and solids.
2) The liquid is heated and evaporates off as a gas, leaving the solid behind.
3) The gas is then passed into a Liebig condenser — a glass tube surrounded by a 'jacket' of cold water, which makes the inside of the tube nice and cool.
4) When the hot gas from the flask touches the cold tube of the Liebig condenser, it condenses into a liquid. The liquid flows down the tube and is collected in a beaker.
5) After collecting the liquid, make sure the delivery tube is above the surface of the liquid in the beaker. Do this before you turn off the heat. Otherwise, as the air inside the flask cools and contracts, some of the liquid can get sucked back into the flask.
6) Simple distillation is great for getting pure water from something like seawater or ink.

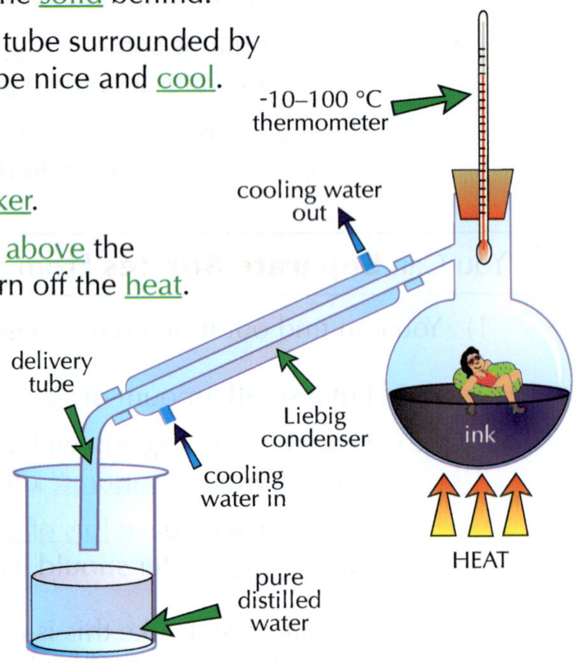

## Distillation Can Also be Used to Separate Mixed Liquids

1) A method known as fractional distillation is used for separating a mixture of liquids like crude oil.
2) Different liquids in a mixture will boil off at different temperatures, around their own boiling point.
3) The fractionating column ensures that the "wrong" liquids condense back down, and only the liquid properly boiling at the temperature on the thermometer will make it to the top.
4) When a liquid has boiled off, the temperature reading rises until the next fraction starts to boil off.
5) Real-life examples include:
   - distilling whisky,
   - separating crude oil into petrol, diesel and other fuels.

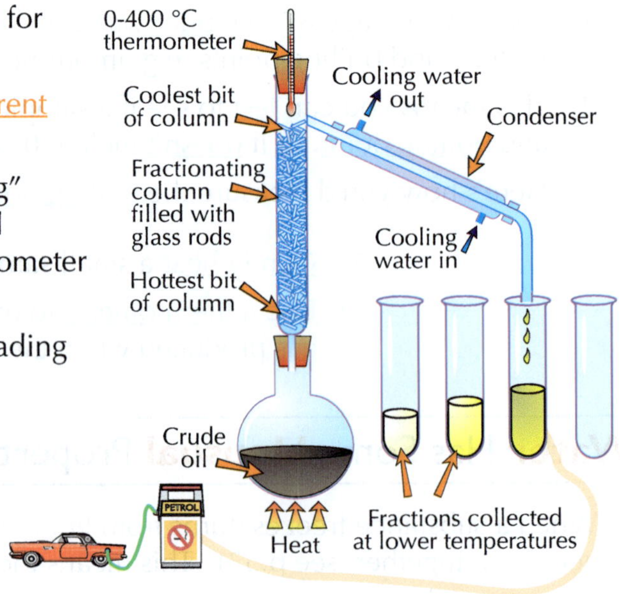


### Separate what you know from what you don't...

REVISION TASK

Pick a pal and explain to them how distillation can be used to separate mixtures of liquids and solids and mixtures of liquids. Tell them how you'd do it, and explain how it works. Having to explain something to someone else is a great way to check if you actually understand it yourself.

# Chromatography

Chromatography can be used to ~~make pretty patterns~~ separate dyes.

## Chromatography is Ideal for Separating Dyes

PRACTICAL

1) Inks and food colourings are made up of mixtures of different dyes.
2) Chromatography uses a solvent soaking through filter paper to separate the dyes.
3) Different dyes are carried by the solvent through the paper at different speeds. Some stick to the paper more and move quite slowly, while others move more quickly and go further up the paper.
4) Two things that affect how fast (and therefore how far) each dye travels are:
   - How soluble the dye is in the solvent — more soluble dyes travel faster.
   - How attracted the particles are to the paper — those that are less attracted travel faster.
5) By looking at the results (called a chromatogram) you can compare the dyes in different substances.

The solvent is often water, and the dyes are solutes. Filter paper is used because it's really absorbent — it soaks up the solvent.

### Method

1) Draw a line near the bottom of a sheet of filter paper — this is the baseline. (Use a pencil to do this — pencil marks won't dissolve in the solvent.)
2) Add spots of different inks along the line (e.g. different coloured felt tip pens). (Alternatively, you could investigate the food colouring in the coating of a sweet. Put the sweet in a couple of drops of water for a few minutes. Then transfer some of the liquid around the sweet onto the filter paper and let it dry. Do this a few times to produce a concentrated spot.)
3) Put the paper in a beaker with a little solvent at the bottom. Make sure the level of solvent is below the baseline — you don't want the inks to dissolve into the solvent yet.
4) Place a lid on top of the container to stop the solvent evaporating.
5) The solvent seeps up the paper, carrying the ink dyes with it.
6) Each dye will form a spot in a different place.

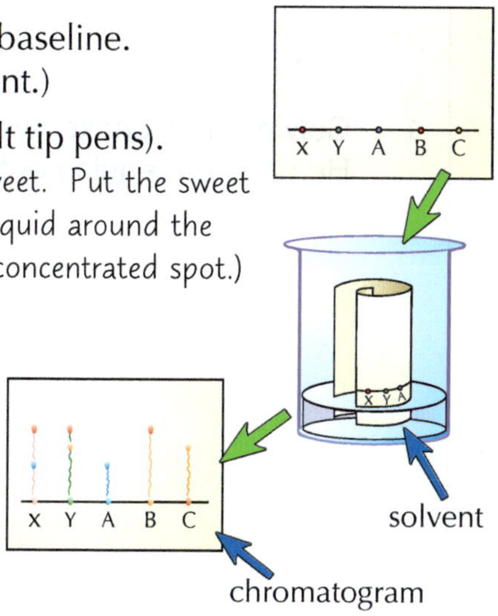


6) You can use a chromatogram to identify an unknown substance by comparing it to the chromatogram created by a known substance. For example:
   1) A particular ink will always leave a characteristic pattern of spots on a chromatogram. So, if you wanted to find out who forged a signature, you could compare the ink from the forgery with the ink from some suspects' pens.
   2) The culprit's ink will have exactly the same pattern of spots as the ink from the forgery. So here suspect C is most likely to be guilty. Case closed.

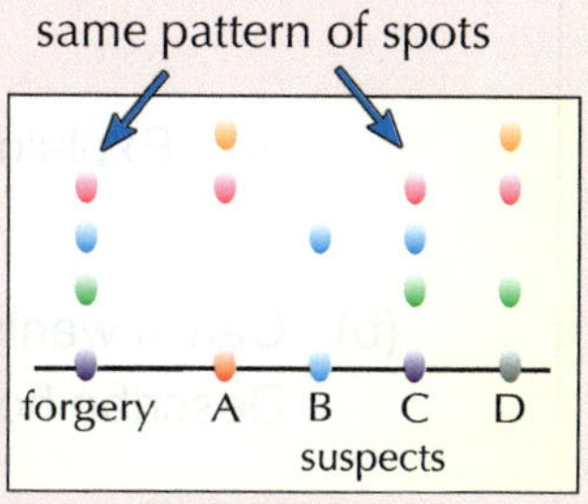


## Solubility Varies Between Solvents

1) Different solutes are more soluble in some solvents than others. E.g. nail varnish is insoluble in water but soluble in propanone (nail varnish remover).
2) This means dyes travel different distances up the paper depending on the solvent you use.
3) When you're choosing a solvent, make sure it's suitable for the substance you're trying to dissolve. Water is a good solvent, but if the dyes you are trying to separate by chromatography are insoluble in water, you'll have to use another solvent. Propanone is a useful alternative for chromatography.

Propanone is also called acetone.

# Warm-Up & Practice Questions

Five pages later, it's time for some more questions to check you're learning as well as reading. If you don't know the answer to any of the questions, go back and read the pages again.

## Warm-Up Questions

1) Why are mixtures (usually) easier to separate than compounds?
2) What gas makes up most of the air?
3) Describe what would be left over if each of these substances was gently heated in an evaporating basin: a) seawater, b) tap water, c) distilled water.
4) Describe what happens to the particles in water when it freezes. How does this affect its volume and its density?

## Practice Questions

PRACTICAL

1 Calvin has a beaker with some ink in it.
He uses the equipment shown below to separate the water from the ink.

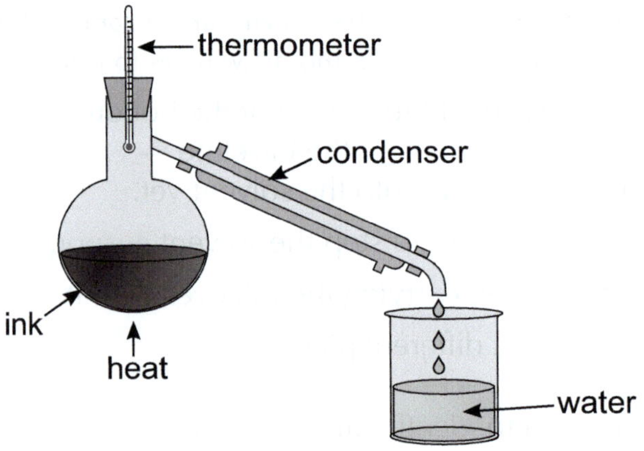


(a) (i) Name the separation method that Calvin used.

*(1 mark)*

(ii) Explain how this separation method works in Calvin's experiment.

*(3 marks)*

(b) Calvin wants to know if the water he has collected in the beaker is pure.
Describe how Calvin could test whether the water is pure.

*(2 marks)*

PRACTICAL

2 Al is investigating the dyes used in the food colourings of some brightly coloured sweets.
He puts concentrated spots of each colouring on a line at the bottom of some filter paper.

(a) Describe what he should do next, in order to separate the dyes.

*(1 mark)*

(b) The separated dyes form spots on the filter paper at different distances above the original spots of food colouring. Explain why this happens and give **two** factors that affect how far the dyes travel.

*(4 marks)*

# Summary Questions

Section C3 — small but perfectly formed. And as if by magic, it's another page of summary questions for you to get stuck into...

- Try these questions and tick off each one when you get it right.
- When you've done all the questions for a topic and are completely happy with it, tick it off.

## Purity, Mixtures and Air (p.67-p.68)

1) What is a pure substance?
2) Explain how the boiling point of a substance can be used to check its purity.
3) What is a mixture?
4) What determines the properties of a mixture?
5) Describe what happens when a substance dissolves.
6) What percentage of air is oxygen?
7) Which gas in air is an important reactant in photosynthesis?
8) Describe an experiment you could do to show the proportion of oxygen in air.

## Properties of Water (p.69)

9) What property of water means that you rarely find it in its pure form?
10) Describe how you could find out if a sample of water contains dissolved salts.
11) True or false? Evaporation can happen at any temperature.
12) Explain why ice floats on liquid water.

## Distillation and Chromatography (p.70-p.71)

13) Describe how a Liebig condenser is used to condense a gas during simple distillation.
14) Give one use of simple distillation.
15) Explain how mixed liquids can be separated using distillation.
16) What sort of paper is used in chromatography?
17) True or false? In chromatography, a dye that is more soluble in the solvent will travel further up the paper than a dye that is less soluble.
18) What is the name given to the results that you get at the end of a chromatography experiment?
19) Suggest an alternative solvent to water for use in chromatography.

# Chemical Reactions

In a chemical reaction, the reactants might give off heat, make a loud bang, or do a little dance. All that's really going on though is the rearrangement of atoms...

## Chemical Reactions are Really Important

1) Pretty much all the materials around us have been made by some sort of chemical reaction. E.g:
   - the rust on a garden spade
   - water in your cells
   - carbon dioxide in the air
2) Chemical reactions are always going on around us too. Examples you might see at home include: frying an egg, superglue setting, a banana ripening, candles burning, etc.
3) Heating a substance often causes a chemical reaction to occur. For example, heating copper in oxygen forms a new compound — copper oxide.
4) Chemical reactions involve a change in energy, i.e. reactions always give out or take in energy. This is usually causes the temperature in a reaction to go up or down.
5) Visible changes can occur in the reaction mixture. These show that a reaction has taken place, and a new substance has been formed. E.g. gas is given off, a solid is made, or the colour changes.

## Word Equations Show What Happens in a Chemical Reaction

1) In a word equation, the reactants are shown on the left, with an arrow pointing to the products on the right. For example, the reaction between magnesium and oxygen can be written as:

magnesium + oxygen ⟶ magnesium oxide

The reactants combine... ...to make a product.

2) Products can be split up back into their original reactants but it won't just happen by itself — you have to supply a lot of energy to make the reaction go in reverse.

## Atoms Rearrange Themselves in a Chemical Reaction

1) In a chemical reaction atoms are not created or destroyed.
2) The atoms at the start of a reaction are still there at the end.
3) Bonds get broken and made in the reaction, as atoms rearrange themselves in going from the reactants to the products. But the atoms themselves are not altered. E.g:

zinc + copper sulfate ⟶ zinc sulfate + copper

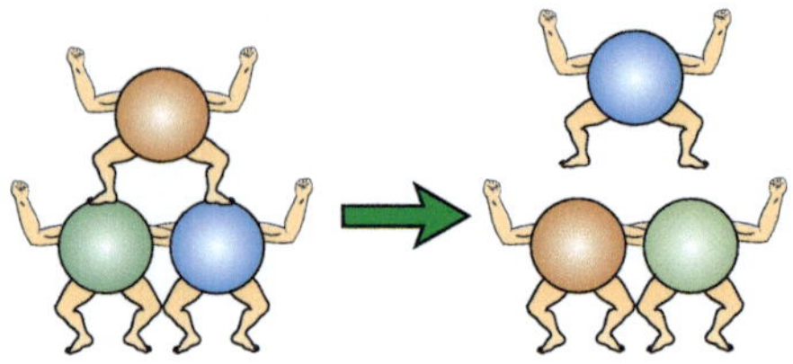

### Chemical reactions — just a case of atomic acrobatics...

Regardless of what a chemical reaction involves (colour changes, stinky fumes, explosions...), remember that there's one thing that will always stay the same — the number of atoms, before and after the reaction.

# More on Reactions and Using Bunsen Burners

Lab coats on, Bunsen burners at the ready... First though, a little more on chemical reactions...

## The Mass is Conserved in a Chemical Reaction

1) In a chemical reaction no mass is lost or gained when the reactants turn into the products.
2) This is because the total number of each type of atom is the same before and after the reaction — the atoms are just rearranged (see previous page).

### If the Mass Seems to Change, There's Usually a Gas Involved

1) In some reactions, you might observe an increase in mass.
2) This is probably because one of the reactants is a gas (e.g. oxygen).
3) Before the reaction, the gas is floating around in the air. It's there, but it's not contained within anything so you can't account for its mass.
4) When the gas reacts to form part of the product, it becomes contained inside whatever you're carrying out the reaction in (e.g. a crucible, boiling tube, etc.) — so the total mass increases. E.g:

If the mass decreases, it's probably because a gas is given off.

A crucible is a small cup that can withstand very high temperatures.

1) If you heat a crucible containing magnesium, the mass of the crucible's contents increases.
2) This is because the magnesium reacts with oxygen in the air to form magnesium oxide.
3) The mass of the magnesium oxide produced equals the total mass of the magnesium and the oxygen that reacted from the air.

## Bunsen Burners are Used for Heating in the Lab

1) Many chemical reactions need heat to get them going — you can often use a Bunsen burner to provide the heat.
2) Bunsen burners burn methane gas and provide a consistent and adjustable heat source.
3) They have an air hole that can be opened or closed by different amounts to vary the amount of oxygen that enters the burner. This affects the colour and temperature of the flame.
4) A Bunsen burner can produce three different types of flame:

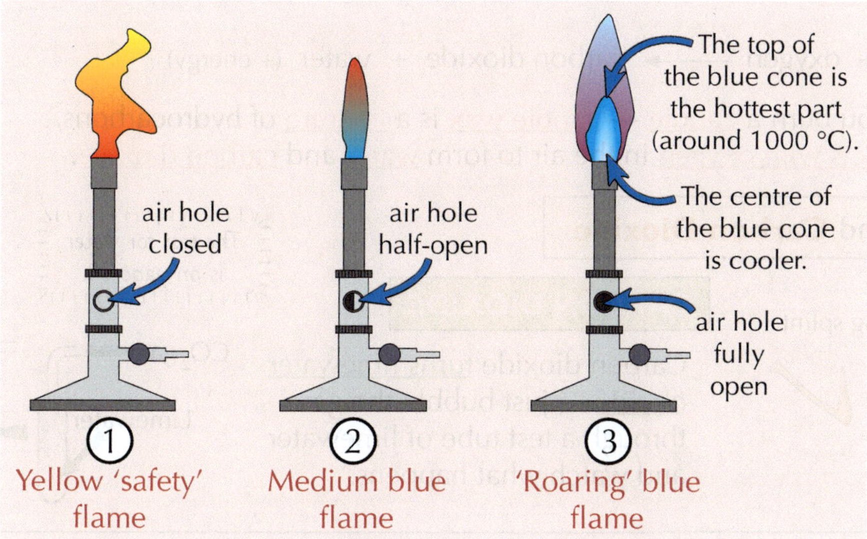


1) Yellow 'safety' flame
This is what you set the burner to when you're not using it. This isn't used for heating as it makes too much soot.

2) Medium blue flame
This is what you use for gentle heating. It's hotter than the safety flame but not as hot as the roaring blue flame.

3) 'Roaring' blue flame
This is used for vigorous heating. It's the hottest flame. This is because fully opening the air hole increases the oxygen supply for combustion (see next page).

Always be careful when working with Bunsen burners. Aside from being a fire hazard, the equipment you use with them will get very hot.

# Combustion

A pretty common chemical reaction for you now — combustion (otherwise known as burning stuff)...

## Combustion is Burning in Oxygen

1) Combustion is burning — it's when a substance reacts with oxygen to release energy. This energy is transferred away by heating and light.
2) Combustion is the process behind candles, wood fires, car engines, etc.
3) Three things are needed for combustion — fuel, heat and oxygen.
4) Here are a few combustion reactions you need to know about:

EXAMPLE: Carbon reacts with oxygen when heated to form carbon dioxide.

carbon + oxygen ⟶ carbon dioxide

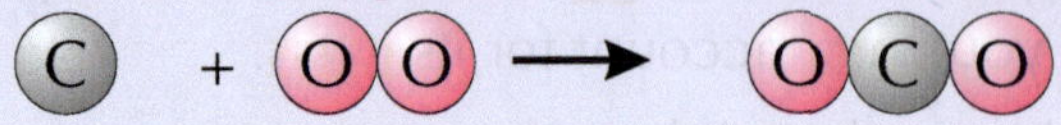


EXAMPLE: Magnesium reacts violently when heated in oxygen, burning with a bright flame. Magnesium oxide is produced.

magnesium + oxygen ⟶ magnesium oxide

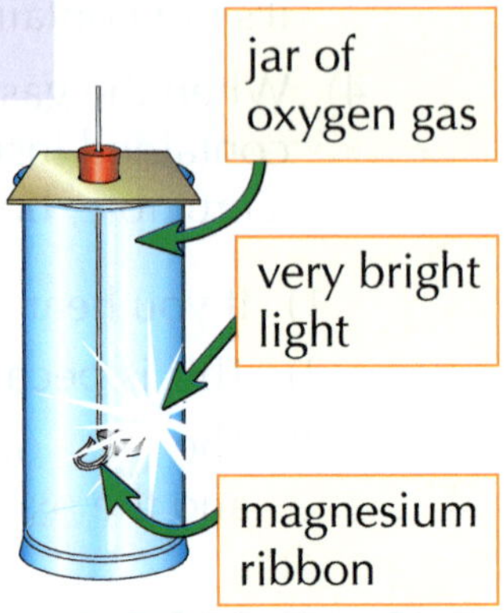


EXAMPLE: Sulfur produces a dark blue flame when heated in oxygen. Sulfur dioxide is produced.

sulfur + oxygen ⟶ sulfur dioxide

Try burning a substance in air first with a Bunsen burner — then place the burning substance in a jar of oxygen. It will burn more brightly in pure oxygen than in air, since air is only about 20% oxygen.

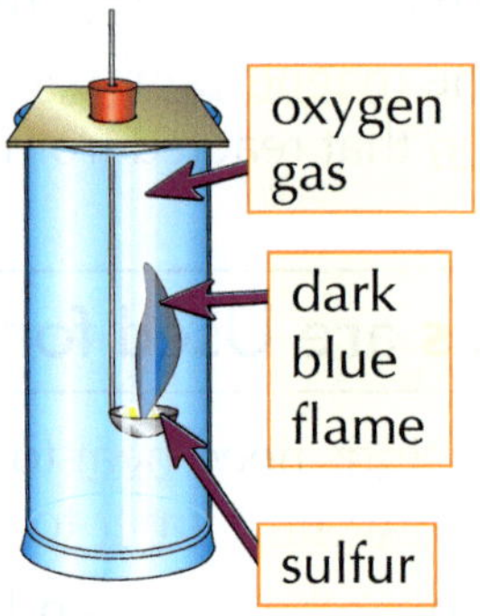


Both magnesium and sulfur produce a really bright light when they burn. Don't look directly at it — it could damage your eyes.

## Hydrocarbons are Fuels Containing Only Hydrogen and Carbon

1) When there's enough heat and oxygen, hydrocarbons combust (burn) to give water and carbon dioxide.

hydrocarbon + oxygen ⟶ carbon dioxide + water (+ energy)

2) This is what happens when you burn a candle — candle wax is a mixture of hydrocarbons, so when it burns, the wax reacts with oxygen in the air to form water and carbon dioxide.

## You can Test for Oxygen and Carbon Dioxide

The test for water is on page 78.

**OXYGEN**

Oxygen relights a glowing splint.

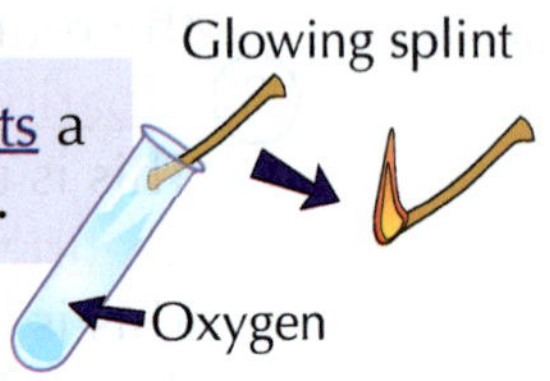


**CARBON DIOXIDE**

Carbon dioxide turns limewater cloudy — just bubble the gas through a test tube of limewater and watch what happens.

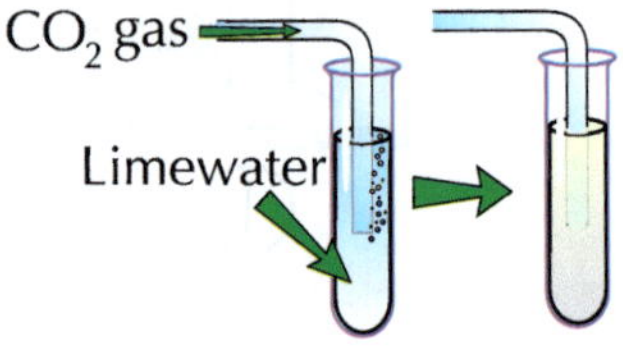


### All this revision is burning me out...

Oxygen — we need it for burning fuels, driving cars, and lighting your favourite bathtime candle.

# The Effects of Fossil Fuels

We burn a lot of fossil fuels these days — unfortunately this makes a bit of a mess of the environment...

## Burning Fossil Fuels Releases Gases and Particles

1) We burn huge amounts of fossil fuels (oil, coal and natural gas) to make electricity — see p.95. Cars also burn lots of fossil fuel (petrol and diesel are made from oil).
2) Fossil fuels are hydrocarbons — they contain carbon and hydrogen.
3) As you saw on the previous page, this means that during their combustion, carbon dioxide and water vapour are released into the atmosphere. Energy is also produced.
4) If there's not enough oxygen, some of the fuel doesn't burn (incomplete combustion), and solid particles (called particulates) of soot (carbon) and unburnt fuel are released. Carbon monoxide (a poisonous, polluting gas) is also released.
5) The easiest way of reducing the amount of soot released is to burn fewer fossil fuels. You can also try to trap the soot, e.g. by putting particulate filters on vehicles burning diesel.

This is why you get the sooty yellow flame when you close the air hole on a Bunsen burner. The oxygen supply is limited, so some of the fuel doesn't burn.

## Sulfur Dioxide Causes Acid Rain

1) If a fuel contains sulfur impurities, the sulfur will be released as sulfur dioxide (another polluting gas) when the fuel is burnt.
2) When the sulfur dioxide mixes with clouds it forms dilute sulfuric acid. This then falls as acid rain.
3) Acid rain can cause plants and animals to die and can also damage buildings (see page 87).

### You can Reduce Acid Rain by Reducing Sulfur Emissions

1) Sulfur can be removed from fuels before they're burnt, or afterwards from the waste gases.
2) For example, sulfur is removed from petrol and diesel before it is used in vehicles, and gas scrubbers are used in power stations to remove sulfur from the waste gases after combustion.
3) The other way of reducing acid rain is simply to reduce our usage of fossil fuels.

## Increasing Carbon Dioxide Causes Climate Change

1) Carbon dioxide is what's known as a greenhouse gas. This means it traps heat from the Sun in the Earth's atmosphere. This stops some heat from being lost into space and helps to keep the Earth warm.
2) But burning fossil fuels increases the level of carbon dioxide in the atmosphere — and so the Earth is gradually getting hotter.
3) This increase in the Earth's temperature is called global warming.
4) Global warming is a type of climate change. It seems to be having some serious effects — e.g. rising sea levels due to the polar ice caps melting (which could cause coastal areas to flood), changing rainfall patterns which make it harder for farmers to grow crops.

### We Need to Reduce Carbon Dioxide Levels

1) The most obvious thing we can do is to reduce the amount of fossil fuels we burn.
2) We can also reduce deforestation and plant more trees. Trees use carbon dioxide for photosynthesis (see page 33), so more trees means more carbon dioxide is removed from the atmosphere.

# Thermal Decomposition Reactions

Keep your chemical reaction hat on — another type of reaction is coming right up. 'Thermal' means heat and 'decomposition' means breaking down, so you might be able to guess what this page is about.

## Thermal Decomposition is Breaking Down With Heat

1) Thermal decomposition is when a substance breaks down into two or more new substances when heated.
2) Some metal carbonates break down on heating. Carbonates are substances with $CO_3$ in them, like copper(II) carbonate ($CuCO_3$) and calcium carbonate ($CaCO_3$).
3) They break down into a metal oxide (e.g. copper(II) oxide, $CuO$) and carbon dioxide. This sometimes results in a colour change.

EXAMPLE: The thermal decomposition of copper(II) carbonate.

copper(II) carbonate $\xrightarrow{\text{heat}}$ copper(II) oxide + carbon dioxide

This is green...  ...and this is black. 

Remember, you can tell if the gas produced is carbon dioxide by seeing if it turns limewater cloudy — see p.76.

EXAMPLE: The thermal decomposition of calcium carbonate.

calcium carbonate $\xrightarrow{\text{heat}}$ calcium oxide + carbon dioxide

This is white...  ...and so is this... 

4) Hydrated metal compounds can also be broken down on heating.
5) They break down into anhydrous metal compounds and water. You will usually see a colour change as the reaction happens.

Hydrated means that the substance contains some water. Anhydrous substances don't contain any water.

EXAMPLE: The thermal decomposition of hydrated copper(II) sulfate.

hydrated copper(II) sulfate $\xrightarrow{\text{heat}}$ anhydrous copper(II) sulfate + water

This is blue...  ...and this is white. 

**Testing for Water**

This colour change can be used to test for water.

Water will turn white anhydrous copper(II) sulfate blue.

6) Some substances don't break down when they're heated though — for example, if you heat copper oxide, it doesn't do anything.

### This page is easy — let me break it down for you....

REVISION TASK

Grab yourself a piece of paper and make a quick poster showing these examples of thermal decomposition. Jazz it up with some felt tip pens to include the colour changes that happen. Not only will it brighten up your room, it should help you learn them too. Win win.

# Warm-Up & Practice Questions

You need to learn all the stuff in this section. Might as well make a start on it now...

## Warm-Up Questions

1) 92 g of sodium reacts with 142 g of chlorine to make sodium chloride. Calculate the total mass of the sodium chloride produced from this reaction.
2) What type of flame do you get if you half close the air hole on a Bunsen burner?
3) What is produced when magnesium is heated in oxygen?
4) How can you test to see if a gas is oxygen?
5) Name the polluting gas formed if fossil fuels are burnt without enough oxygen present.
6) Why might global warming cause sea levels to rise?
7) What colour is hydrated copper(II) sulphate?

## Practice Questions

1 Channing heated some calcium carbonate, to produce solid calcium oxide and a gas.

(a) What type of reaction is this?

*(1 mark)*

(b) Channing heated the calcium carbonate on the hottest flame of a Bunsen burner. Describe the position of the air hole on the Bunsen burner when it produces this type of flame.

*(1 mark)*

(c) Channing bubbled the gas produced through limewater. Describe and explain what will have happened to the limewater.

*(2 marks)*

(d) Channing then decided to heat copper(II) carbonate using the same method. Write the word equation for this reaction.

*(1 mark)*

2 The combustion of hydrocarbons, such as coal, provides energy.

(a) (i) State the **three** things needed for combustion to take place.

*(1 mark)*

(ii) Other than energy, state the products of complete combustion of a hydrocarbon.

*(1 mark)*

(b) Combustion of hydrocarbons can result in acid rain. Name the polluting gas released if hydrocarbons containing sulfur impurities are burnt and explain how the production of this gas can result in acid rain.

*(2 marks)*

(c) Explain how the combustion of hydrocarbons can lead to global warming.

*(2 marks)*

# Summary Questions

Hooray, that's the end of another section. Now you get to find out if any of it has sunk in.

- Try these questions and tick off each one when you get it right.
- When you've done all the questions for a topic and are completely happy with it, tick it off.

## Chemical Reactions (p.74-p.75)

1) Give two examples of chemical reactions that might happen in your home.
2) What happens to atoms in a chemical reaction?
3) Explain whether the mass changes during a chemical reaction.
4) What are the three types of flame that a Bunsen burner can produce?

## Combustion and Fossil Fuels (p.76-p.77)

5) What is combustion?
6) What does the combustion of carbon produce?
7) Do magnesium and sulfur burn brighter in air or in pure oxygen?
8) Name a gas that relights a glowing splint.
9) Name two products that are released if there's not enough oxygen available when burning fossil fuels.
10) Describe how burning fossil fuels is affecting the level of carbon dioxide in the atmosphere.
11) Describe two effects of global warming.
12) Give two ways that carbon dioxide levels can be reduced.

## Thermal Decomposition (p.78)

13) What is thermal decomposition?
14) What two products are formed when a metal carbonate breaks down by thermal decomposition?
15) Describe the colour change that occurs during the thermal decomposition of copper(II) carbonate.
16) Give the word equation for the thermal decomposition of hydrated copper(II) sulfate.
17) How can anhydrous copper(II) sulfate be used to test for water?
18) True or false? All substances break down when heated.

# Reactions of Metals with Oxygen and Water

I don't know about you, but I'm ready for a violent reaction and a squeaky pop. Off we go...

## Reacting Metals With Oxygen

1) When a substance reacts and combines with oxygen, it's called an oxidation reaction.
2) Combustion (see page 76) and rusting (see next page) are both examples of oxidation reactions.
3) Most metals can react with oxygen to form a metal oxide.

**Metal + Oxygen → Metal Oxide**

4) The most reactive metals react violently when heated in oxygen, burning with a bright flame.
5) The less reactive metals react more slowly when heated in oxygen.
6) Metals will burn more brightly in pure oxygen than in air, since air is only about 20% oxygen.

EXAMPLES:

zinc + oxygen → zinc oxide

magnesium + oxygen → magnesium oxide

Magnesium produces a bright flame when it reacts with oxygen. See page 76.

## Reacting Metals With Water

**Metal + Water → Metal Hydroxide + Hydrogen**

OR: **Metal + Steam → Metal Oxide + Hydrogen**

1) Most metals will react with water or steam to produce hydrogen.
2) The more reactive metals react vigorously with cold water to produce hydroxides.
3) The less reactive metals will react with steam to make oxides.

EXAMPLES:

sodium + water → sodium hydroxide + hydrogen

magnesium + steam → magnesium oxide + hydrogen

PRACTICAL

Magnesium reacts very slowly with cold water but it reacts vigorously with steam.

Here is an experiment you may see:

1) Wet mineral wool is placed in the bottom of a boiling tube and the tube is clamped horizontally.
2) A piece of magnesium ribbon is added, and then the tube is sealed with a bung that has a glass tube through it.
3) The magnesium ribbon and mineral wool are heated — the magnesium glows brightly as it reacts with the steam coming from the mineral wool.
4) A lit splint can be used to show that hydrogen is produced — there should be a squeaky pop (see page 85).

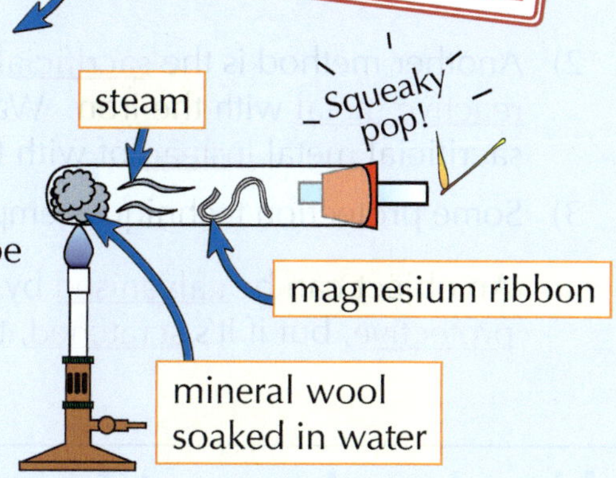

# Oxidation — Rusting

Here's a bit of chemistry that you can see evidence of in every day life — good old rust.

## Rusting is the Formation of Iron Oxide

1) Rusting is an example of an oxidation reaction.
2) Iron reacts with oxygen and water in the air to form iron oxide, i.e. rust.

$$\text{iron} + \text{oxygen} + \text{water} \longrightarrow \text{iron oxide (rust)}$$

Officially it's called hydrated iron(III) oxide.

3) Rust forms on the surface of iron materials, where it's exposed to air.
4) Unfortunately, rust is a soft crumbly solid that soon flakes off to leave more iron available to rust again. This means that, eventually, all the iron in an object corrodes away even if it wasn't initially at the surface.

Corrosion is where metals react with substances in their environment and are gradually destroyed. The word "rust" is only used when iron corrodes, not other metals.

## Both Air and Water are Needed for Iron to Rust

PRACTICAL

Experiments can show that both oxygen and water are needed for iron to rust.

1) If you put an iron nail in a boiling tube with just water, it won't rust. (The water is boiled to remove oxygen and oil is used to stop air getting in.)
2) If you put an iron nail in a boiling tube with just air, it won't rust. (Calcium chloride can be used to absorb any water from the air.)
3) However, if you put an iron nail in a boiling tube with air and water, it will rust.

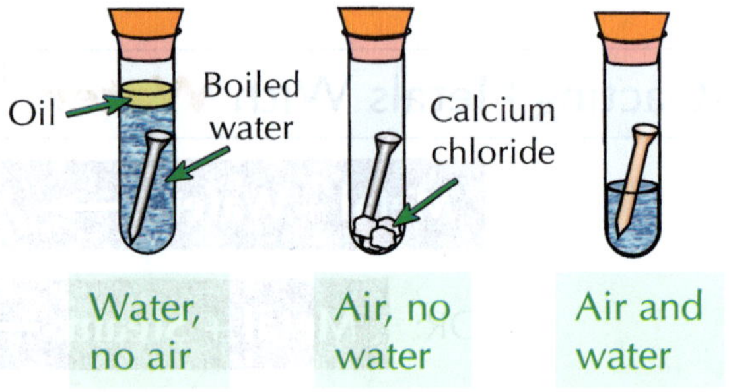


## There are Two Main Ways to Prevent Rusting

1) The obvious way to prevent rusting is to coat the iron with a barrier to keep out the water and oxygen. This can be done by:
   - Painting/Coating with plastic.
   - Coating the iron with a layer of a different metal that won't be corroded away.
   - Oiling/Greasing — this has to be used when moving parts are involved, like on bike chains.
2) Another method is the sacrificial method. This involves placing a more reactive metal with the iron. Water and oxygen then react with the sacrificial metal instead of with the iron.
3) Some protection techniques employ both the methods above. For example:

An object can be galvanised by spraying it with a coating of zinc. The zinc layer is firstly protective, but if it's scratched, the zinc around the site of the scratch works as a sacrificial metal.

### I just bought a rust-free car — they didn't charge me for the rust...

Rusting is a great example of a chemical reaction in action. Make sure you know what it is and that oxygen and water are needed. You'd be wise to get the two ways to prevent rusting lodged firmly in your brain too.

# Acids and Alkalis

The pH scale is what scientists use to describe how acidic or alkaline a substance is.

## The pH Scale Shows the Strength of Acids and Alkalis

1) The pH scale goes from 0 to 14.
2) Anything with a pH below 7 is an acid. The strongest acid has pH 0.
3) Anything with a pH above 7 is an alkali. The strongest alkali has pH 14.
4) A neutral substance has pH 7 (e.g. water).

These are the colours that Universal indicator solution (see below) turns in the presence of acids and alkalis.

An alkali is a base that will dissolve in water (see p.84 for more on bases).

## Indicators Are Special Dyes Which Change Colour

1) An indicator is something that changes colour depending on whether it's in an acid or in an alkali.
2) Litmus paper is quite a popular indicator. Acids turn blue litmus paper red and alkalis turn red litmus paper blue.
3) Universal indicator solution is a mixture of dyes which gives the range of colours shown above.

**Using Universal indicator**

1) Use a dropper to put a few drops of the solution on a white dimple tile.
2) Add a few drops of Universal indicator.
3) Match the colour to a pH chart.

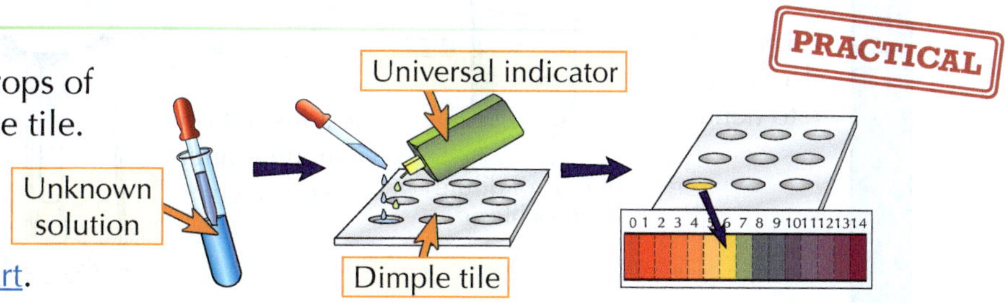


4) The colour change has to be obvious for an indicator to be useful.

## pH Meters Are More Accurate Than Indicators

1) A pH probe attached to a pH meter can also be used to measure pH electronically.
2) The probe is placed in the solution you are measuring and the pH is given on a digital display as a numerical value, so it's more accurate than an indicator.

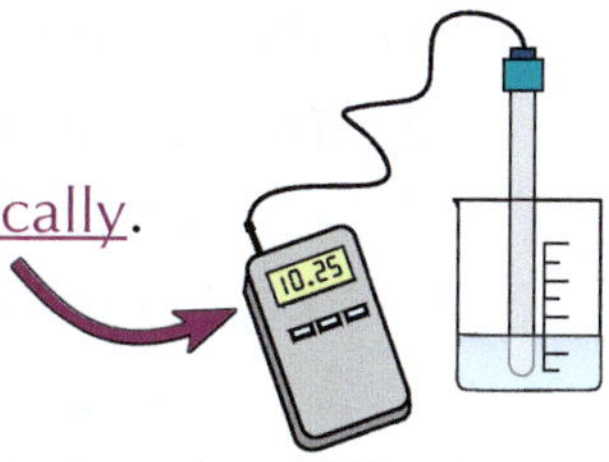


### pHew — the end of another page...

All of the items above are positioned below their actual pH on the pH scale. You see, pH is worth knowing about — you don't want to get acid rain mixed up with washing-up liquid. That sounds painful...

# Neutralisation

Make sure you learn all this stuff — it's pretty easy and a super-useful thing to know about.

## Acids and Bases Neutralise Each Other

1) A base is any substance that will react with an acid to form a salt and water:

**acid + base ⟶ salt + water**

2) This is known as a neutralisation reaction because the products have a neutral pH, i.e. a pH of 7.
3) There's a special case — if the base is a metal carbonate (like calcium carbonate) this reaction also produces carbon dioxide. Fizzing or bubbles show that carbon dioxide is being produced.

**acid + metal carbonate ⟶ salt + water + carbon dioxide**

## Making Salts by Neutralisation is Easy

PRACTICAL

1) Wearing eye protection, add a base to an acid 1 $cm^3$ at a time with a measuring cylinder (the base is soluble so it is an alkali).
2) After every 1 $cm^3$, remove a small sample to check if the pH is neutral (pH 7).
3) Keep adding base until the solution is neutral.
4) When it's neutral, put the solution in an evaporating dish and boil off about two-thirds of the liquid to make a saturated solution of the salt.
5) Leave this solution overnight for the rest of the water to evaporate and nice big salt crystals will form. The slower the crystallisation, the bigger the crystals.

**Example**

React sodium hydroxide with hydrochloric acid to make sodium chloride.

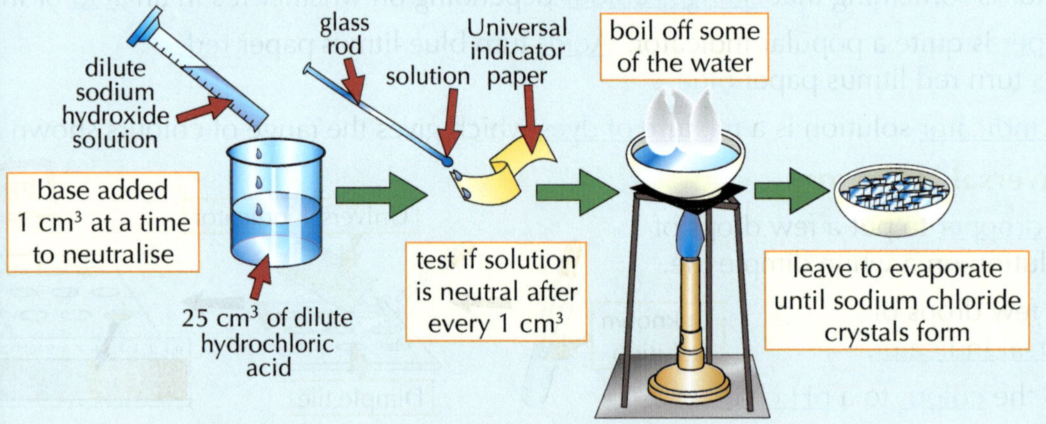


## To Change the Salt, You Must Change the Acid

1) The salt you get out of a neutralisation reaction depends on the acid you use.
2) The clue is normally in the name:

Hydrochloric acid reacts to make chloride salts... like sodium chloride.

Sulfuric acid reacts to make sulfate salts... like copper sulfate.

Nitric acid reacts to make nitrate salts... like sodium nitrate.

### It's fun making salts — but I wouldn't put them on yer chips...

Make sure you know which kinds of salts you get from which kind of acid. I could tell you that if you don't learn this stuff it'll come up at the worst possible opportunity, and that without knowing the simple stuff on this page you'll get nowhere... but that would just be rubbing salt into the wound.

# Reactions of Metals with Acids

On page 81 you learnt how metals react with oxygen, water and steam. Well here's another page on metals to test your mettle — this time you need to learn how metals react with acids.

## Reacting Metals With Dilute Acid

1) Most metals will react with acids to make a salt and hydrogen.

**metal + acid ⟶ salt + hydrogen**

All acids contain hydrogen — so the hydrogen here comes from the acid.

2) The speed of reaction is indicated by the rate at which the bubbles of hydrogen are given off.
3) The more reactive the metal, the faster the reaction will go.
4) Very reactive metals like potassium, sodium, lithium and calcium react explosively, but less reactive metals such as magnesium, zinc and iron react less violently.

### Example: magnesium and hydrochloric acid

magnesium + hydrochloric acid ⟶ magnesium chloride + hydrogen

$$Mg + 2HCl \longrightarrow MgCl_2 + H_2$$

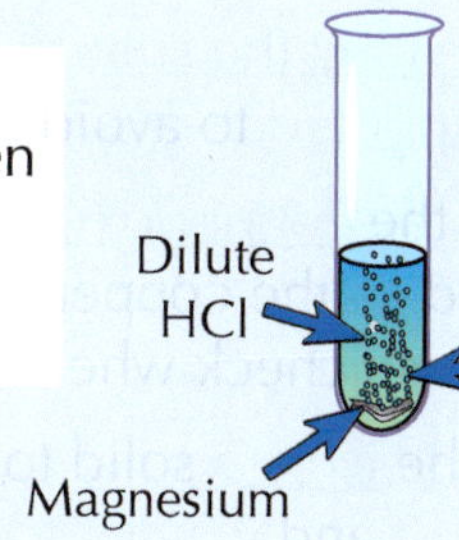


Magnesium reacts vigorously with dilute acids and produces loads of bubbles.

### Example: zinc and sulfuric acid

zinc + sulfuric acid ⟶ zinc sulfate + hydrogen

$$Zn + H_2SO_4 \longrightarrow ZnSO_4 + H_2$$

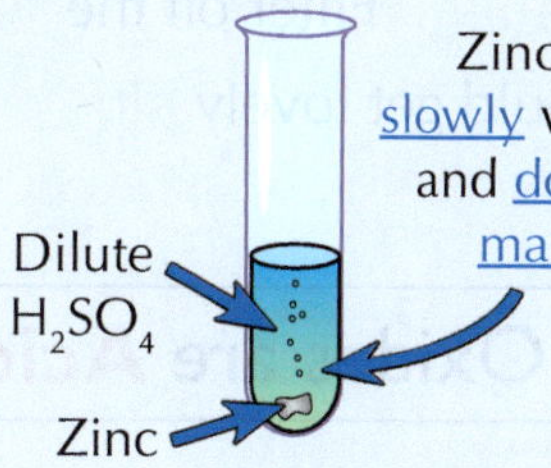


Zinc reacts more slowly with dilute acids and doesn't produce many bubbles.

## The Test for Hydrogen

You can easily check whether a gas produced in a reaction is hydrogen...

Hydrogen makes a "squeaky pop" with a lit splint. (The noise comes from the hydrogen burning with the oxygen in the air to form water.)

### You're probably bored of metals now — time to reactivate...

A metal reacts with an acid and produces a salt and some hydrogen, which fizzes and makes a lit splint go 'pop!'. Different metals react at different speeds and produce different salts, but it's all the same idea.

# Reactions of Oxides with Acids

Oxides are pretty self-explanatory — they've got oxygen in them somewhere.

## Metal Oxides are Alkaline

1) As you saw on page 81, metals react with oxygen to make metal oxides.
   E.g.
   magnesium + oxygen → magnesium oxide
2) Metal oxides in solution have a pH which is higher than 7 — i.e. they're alkaline.
3) So metal oxides react with acids to make a salt and water.

pH more than 7

**acid + metal oxide → salt + water**

PRACTICAL

**Example**

You can add copper oxide to warm sulfuric acid to make crystals of copper sulfate:

copper oxide + sulfuric acid → copper sulfate + water

All the acid has been neutralised when the excess copper oxide just sinks to the bottom.

1) Start by heating the sulfuric acid in a water bath. Do this in a fume cupboard to avoid releasing acid fumes into the room.
2) Then add the copper oxide to the sulfuric acid until all the acid has been neutralised — the copper oxide and acid will react to produce a salt (and water). (You can also check when it's been neutralised using the method on p.84).
3) Filter off the excess solid to get a solution containing only the salt and water.
4) Heat the solution gently, using a Bunsen burner, to slowly evaporate off some of the water. Leave the solution to cool and allow the salt to crystallise. Filter off the solid salt and leave it to dry.
5) You should get lovely blue crystals of copper sulfate.

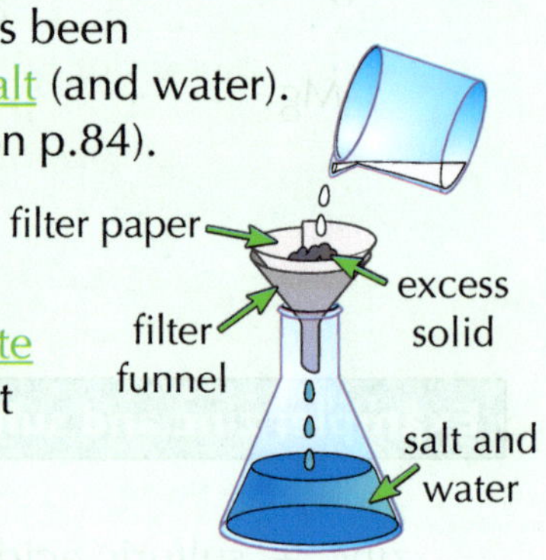


## Non-Metal Oxides are Acidic

1) Non-metals also react with oxygen to make oxides.
   E.g.
   sulfur + oxygen → sulfur dioxide
2) The oxides of non-metals have a pH below 7. This means they're acidic.
3) So non-metal oxides will react with alkalis to make a salt and water.

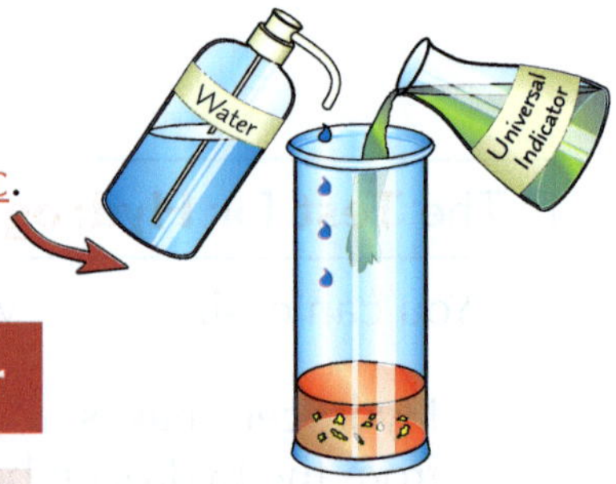

pH less than 7

**alkali + non-metal oxide → salt + water**

E.g. sodium hydroxide + silicon dioxide → sodium silicate + water

REVISION TIP

### Metal oxides are alkaline, non-metal oxides are acidic

Remember this key fact, and the word equation acid + alkali → salt + water (p.84). Then you can work out the word equations on this page for yourself (by sticking in either 'metal oxide' or 'non-metal oxide'), instead of having to remember three separate equations.

# Limestone

Limestone's often formed from sea shells, so you might not expect that it'd be a great building material...

## Limestone is Mainly Calcium Carbonate

Limestone is mainly calcium carbonate ($CaCO_3$), and is quarried out of the ground. It has lots of different uses in construction:

1) It's great for making into blocks for building with. Fine old buildings like cathedrals are often made purely from limestone blocks.
2) Limestone is used in the manufacture of cement, mortar, concrete and glass, as well as in the extraction of iron from iron ore.
3) It is also heated to produce quicklime (calcium oxide), which can be used as a building material.

St Paul's Cathedral is made from limestone.

## Limestone Reacts with Acids

1) Even though limestone is pretty sturdy stuff, don't go thinking it doesn't react with anything.
2) Limestone reacts with acids in the same way as other metal carbonates (see page 84). For example, limestone reacts with dilute hydrochloric acid to make a salt, water and carbon dioxide.

$$\text{calcium carbonate + hydrochloric acid} \longrightarrow \text{calcium chloride + water + carbon dioxide}$$

3) Unfortunately the reaction between calcium carbonate and acids means that limestone buildings can be damaged by acid rain (there's more about this on the next page).

## Limestone is Also Used in Agriculture

1) When limestone is heated it breaks down into calcium oxide and carbon dioxide.
2) The calcium oxide can be really useful for farmers.
3) If you add water to calcium oxide you get calcium hydroxide (also called slaked lime or agricultural lime).

$$\text{calcium oxide + water} \longrightarrow \text{calcium hydroxide}$$

4) Calcium hydroxide is an alkali which can be used to neutralise acidic soil in fields. Powdered limestone and calcium oxide can be used for this too, but the advantage of calcium hydroxide is that it works much faster.

### Limestone — high in Vitamin C-shells...

Don't give me that stony glare. That joke was sublime. Okay fine, I'll stop, there's no need to look so mortar-fied. Right, now it's lime — whoops, time — to get cracking with the learning. Practise writing out the page until it's cemented in your brain. Sorry, I'm done now. I've had my time in the limelight.

# Acids and the Environment

Whilst you may like a bit of acid on your chips, it's not quite so welcome in the rain.

## Rain is Naturally Acidic

1) Rain is naturally a bit acidic due to carbon dioxide in the air.
2) Carbon dioxide dissolves in rain water to make carbonic acid.
3) Gases such as sulfur dioxide in the atmosphere make rain even more acidic and create 'acid rain' (see page 77).

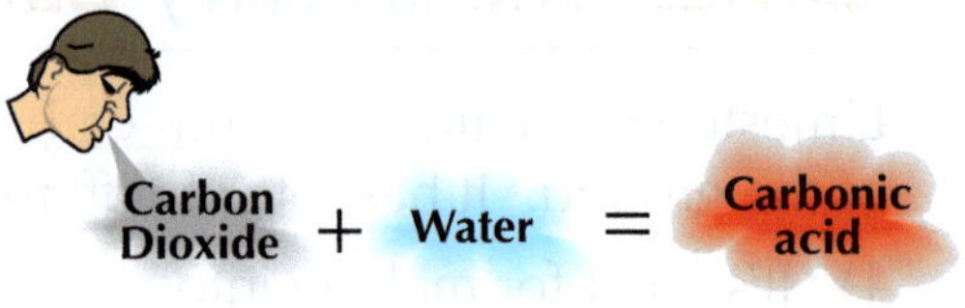


## Acids Attack Metals

1) When some metals are exposed to acids, they corrode by chemical reaction.
2) As you saw on page 85, the metal reacts with the acid to produce a salt and hydrogen:

metal + acid ⟶ salt + hydrogen

3) This weakens the metal with devastating effects. For example, acid rain attacks exposed metals in statues and bridges.

## Acid Rain can Eat Away at Limestone

1) Rocks like limestone, chalk and marble contain calcium carbonate.
2) If acid rain falls onto these rocks a chemical reaction turns them into a calcium salt, water and carbon dioxide.
3) This material is then washed away, damaging the rock. When rocks gradually wear away like this it's called chemical weathering.
4) The natural acidity in rainwater slowly hollows out caves in limestone rock and eats away at limestone cliffs.
5) Acid rain speeds up this weathering process.
6) Buildings and statues made of limestone are also damaged by acid rain.

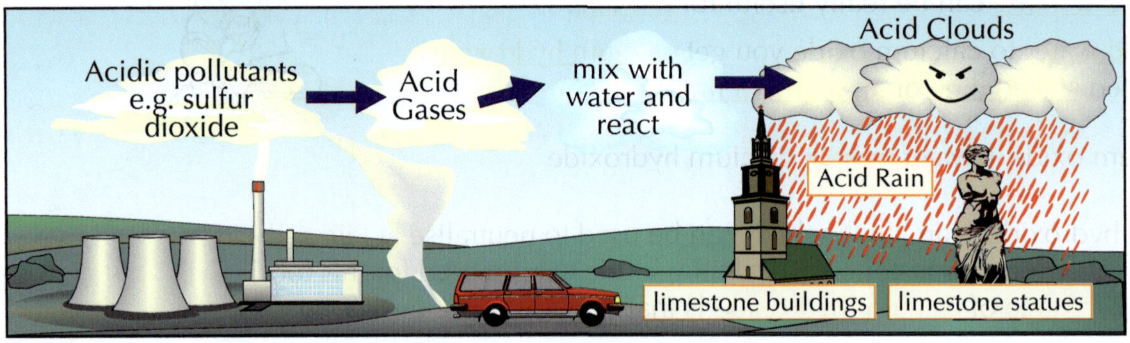


### It's acid raining, it's pouring, the statue is corroding...

REVISION TIP

This page has three sections — each one has a heading, several numbered points and a smattering of pictures. Learn them bit by bit. Keep testing how much you've learnt by covering the page and scribbling down what you've learnt. And I'll let you into a secret... this 'breaking it down into little chunks' trick works for all the other pages in this book too.

# Warm-Up & Practice Questions

Try these questions to see how rusty you are on the stuff in this section...

## Warm-Up Questions

1) What pH might an acid have? What pH might an alkali have?
2) What products are formed when an acid reacts with a metal carbonate?
3) What kind of acid would you use to make a sulfate salt?
4) Other than as a building material, give one use of limestone.

## Practice Questions

1 Use the pH chart below to answer this question.

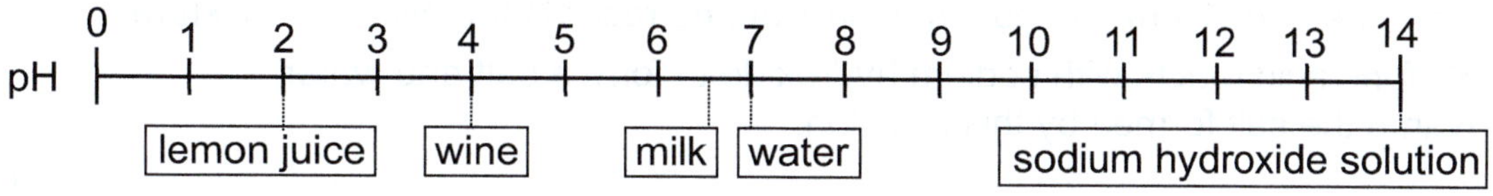


(a) Give **one** substance on the chart that is:

(i) acidic

*(1 mark)*

(ii) alkaline

*(1 mark)*

(b) Suggest **one** substance on the chart that could neutralise sodium hydroxide solution. Explain your answer.

*(2 marks)*

PRACTICAL

2 Ruby is investigating the rusting of an iron nail. She sets up the two test tubes shown on the right. Over time, rust develops on the nails in both test tubes.

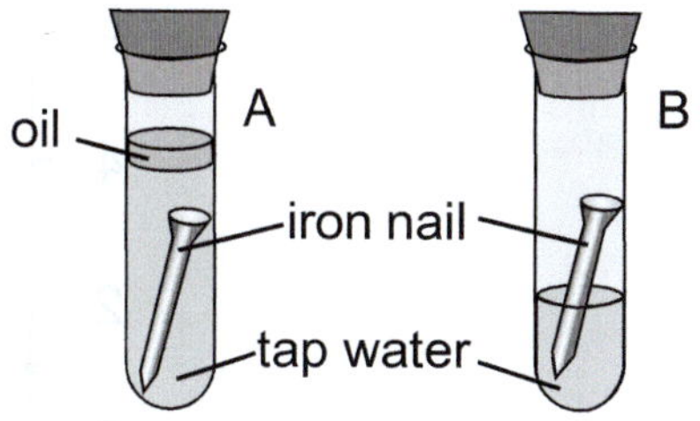


(a) Explain why the nail in test tube B starts to rust sooner than the nail in test tube A.

*(2 marks)*

(b) Suggest **one** change Ruby could make to her experimental set up for test tube A that would slow down the formation of rust on the nail.

*(1 mark)*

3 Nish is making sodium chloride by mixing sodium hydroxide solution with hydrochloric acid.

(a) Explain what Nish can do to find out whether the reaction is complete.

*(2 marks)*

(b) Copy and complete the general word equation for this kind of reaction:

acid + alkali ⟶ ............................ + ............................

*(1 mark)*

(c) Name the acid that Nish should use to make the salt sodium nitrate.

*(1 mark)*

# Practice Questions

4 The following table shows some reactions of different oxides.

| oxide | reaction with acids | reaction with alkalis |
|---|---|---|
| potassium oxide | reacts, making a salt and water | no reaction |
| sulfur dioxide | no reaction | reacts, making a salt and water |

A piece of red litmus paper is dipped into a solution containing one of the two oxides listed in the table. The paper turns blue. State which oxide is in the solution and explain your answer.

*(2 marks)*

5 Pete has 10 $cm^3$ of sulfuric acid in a beaker.
He adds sodium hydroxide solution to the beaker using a pipette.
Each time he adds 2 $cm^3$ of sodium hydroxide, he records the pH of the mixture.

(a) Sulfuric acid reacts with sodium hydroxide to form a salt and water.
Name the salt formed by this reaction.

*(1 mark)*

(b) Pete drew the graph below to show the results of his experiment.

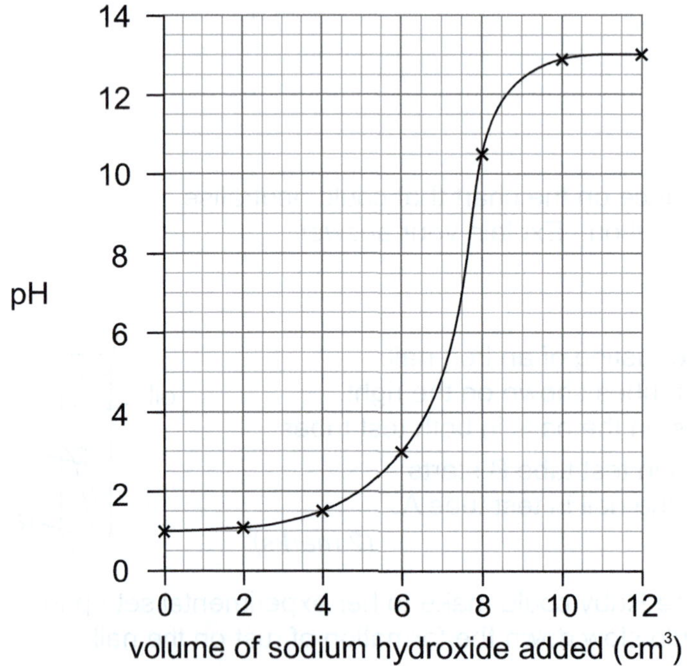


(i) Use the graph to find the pH of the mixture when Pete had added 6 $cm^3$ of sodium hydroxide.

*(1 mark)*

(ii) Use the graph to estimate how much sodium hydroxide Pete would need to have added to make a neutral mixture.

*(1 mark)*

# Summary Questions

You've reached the end of Section C5. Use these questions as an indicator of how much you remember.

- Try these questions and tick off each one when you get it right.
- When you've done all the questions for a topic and are completely happy with it, tick it off.

## Reactions of Metals and Oxidation (p.81-p.82) ☐

1) What is the general equation for the oxidation of a metal? ☐
2) Name the product formed when magnesium reacts with oxygen. ☐
3) What is produced when a metal reacts with cold water? ☐
4) What is produced when magnesium reacts with steam? ☐
5) Briefly describe a method to react magnesium with steam. ☐
6) What is rust? ☐
7) Give two things that are needed for rust to form. ☐
8) Describe one way that rusting can be prevented. ☐

## Acids and Alkalis (p.83-p.86) ☐

9) What pH does the strongest acid on a pH chart have? And the strongest alkali? ☐
10) What colour would Universal indicator go if it was mixed with a strong acid? ☐
11) Describe how pH can be measured electronically. ☐
12) Is Universal indicator, litmus paper or a pH meter more accurate? ☐
13) What is neutralisation? ☐
14) True or false? Hydrogen is one of the products of a reaction between an acid and a base. ☐
15) Outline a method you could use to make common salt (sodium chloride). ☐
16) What do metals produce when they react with an acid? ☐
17) Name the salt formed when magnesium reacts with hydrochloric acid. ☐
18) Describe the test for hydrogen. ☐
19) Are metal oxides acidic or alkaline? ☐
20) Are non-metal oxides acidic or alkaline? ☐

## Limestone and the Environment (p.87-p.88) ☐

21) What chemical is limestone mainly made up of? ☐
22) Give three building materials that limestone is used to make. ☐
23) What is acid rain? ☐
24) Explain why acid rain is a problem for limestone buildings and statues. ☐

# Energy Stores and Energy Transfers

Ah, energy transfer. Everything you do involves energy transfer, which makes this page very important.

## There are Six Main Energy Stores

### Chemical Energy Store

Food, fuels and batteries have energy in this store, which is released by chemical reactions.

### Gravitational Potential Energy Store

Anything in a gravitational field (i.e. anything that can fall) has energy in this store — the higher it goes, the more it has.

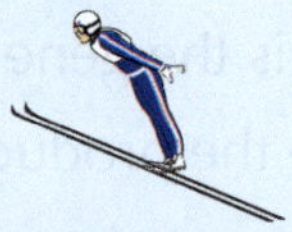

An internal energy store can also be called a heat or thermal energy store.

### Internal Energy Store

Everything has some energy in this store — the hotter an object is, the higher its temperature and so the more energy it has in this store.

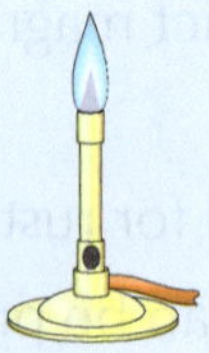

### Nuclear Energy Store

Atomic nuclei have energy in this store, which is released in nuclear reactions.

### Kinetic Energy Store

Anything that moves has energy in this store.

### Elastic Energy Store

When you deform an elastic object (apply a force to change its shape) it will build up energy in this store. Anything stretched or compressed has an elastic energy store — things like rubber bands, springs, etc.

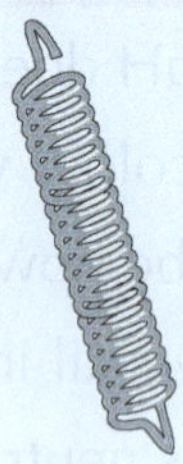

## Energy Can Be Transferred Between Stores

A system is just an object or group of objects you're looking at.

1) Whenever (pretty much) anything happens in a system, energy is transferred from one store to another — as the energy in one store increases, the energy in another store decreases.
2) Energy can be transferred from one store to another by one of these different pathways:
   - light
   - sound
   - heating
   - electricity
   - mechanical work (when an object moves due to a force acting on it)
3) For example:
   - When there's a temperature difference between two objects, energy will be transferred by heating from the internal energy store of the hotter object to the internal energy store of the cooler object (so the hotter object will cool down and the cooler one will heat up).
   - A ball gets faster as it falls towards the ground, as energy is transferred mechanically from its gravitational potential energy store to its kinetic energy store.
   - When the Sun shines on solar cells, some of its energy is transferred electrically to power a device, e.g. to light an LED (light emitting diode) or turn a motor.
4) Friction always causes energy to be dissipated (see next page) — e.g. it causes energy to be transferred to useless internal energy stores.

# Conservation of Energy

Get ready — here comes another page that's all about energy...

## The Law of Conservation of Energy

Scientists have only been studying energy for about two or three hundred years so far, and in that short space of time they've already come up with two "Pretty Important Principles" relating to energy: Learn them really well:

**The Law of Conservation of Energy:**

Energy can never be created nor destroyed — it's only ever transferred from one store to another.

That means energy never simply disappears — it always transfers into another store.
The other Pretty Important Principle:

Energy is only useful when it is transferred from one store to a useful store.

## Most Energy Transfers are Not Perfect

1) Useful devices can transfer energy from one store to a useful store.
2) However, some energy is always lost in some way, nearly always to internal energy stores by heating. When this happens, we say energy has been dissipated (or wasted) and become less useful.

When any object is moving through air, some energy will be dissipated due to air resistance (see p.106).

3) For example, a motor will transfer energy to its kinetic energy store (useful), but will also transfer energy to the internal energy stores of the motor and the surroundings (wasted).
4) This means that you never get as much useful energy out as you put in.
5) It also means that the amount of energy available as a useful resource is reduced, as it's difficult to transfer dissipated energy back into another, more useful store.
6) As the diagram shows, the energy input will always end up coming out partly as useful energy and partly as wasted energy — but no energy is destroyed:

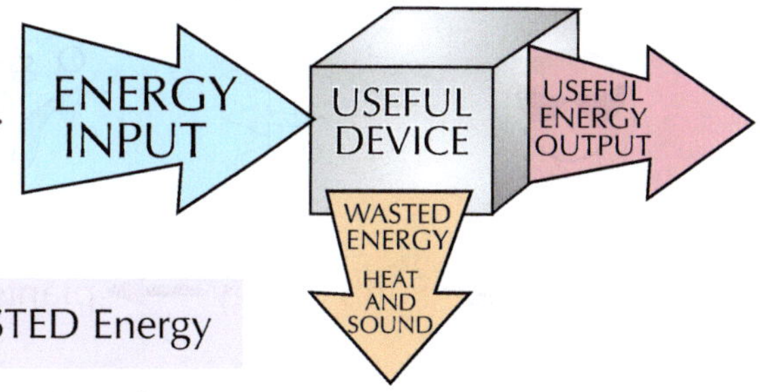


Total Energy INPUT = The USEFUL Energy + The WASTED Energy

7) You can measure energy transfers. Energy is measured in joules (J).
8) Energy is wasted in most day-to-day energy transfers. For example:

When power stations burn fossil fuels to generate electricity (see p.95), energy is lost to the environment by heating. When this electricity is transmitted to people's homes along power lines, energy is dissipated as the power lines heat up.

Car engines transfer energy from the chemical energy store of the petrol to the kinetic energy store of the car. During the transfer, a lot of energy is lost to the environment by heating and sound.

### No mum I'm not slacking — I'm just conserving energy...

So remember, energy's only ever transferred to other stores. No matter how hard you try, you can't ever create or destroy energy. It's just impossible. Futile. 100% completely out of the question.

# Fossil Fuels and Energy Resources

The Sun's a useful little critter. It provides us with oodles of energy and asks for nothing in return.

## We Burn Fuels for Energy

1) Most of the energy we use is stored in the chemical energy stores of fuels.
2) When we burn fuels, the energy is released and can be used, e.g. for heating or generating electricity.
3) Fuels include biomass (e.g. wood) and fossil fuels (e.g. coal, oil and natural gas).

## Fossil Fuels Come from Long-Dead Plants and Animals

1) Millions of years ago, plants on Earth were capturing the Sun's energy using photosynthesis (see page 33). There were also animals that got energy from eating plants (and other animals).
2) Some of this energy was stored up in the tissues of these plants and animals.
3) After they had died, their remains gradually got buried under layers of mud, rock and sand.
4) The remains slowly decayed and over millions of years the pressure turned them into fossil fuels. Coal is mainly made from dead plant matter, and oil and natural gas are mainly made from dead marine life.
5) These fuels contain the energy (in their chemical energy stores) that was originally stored in the tissues of the plants and animals.

## The Sun is the Source of Our Energy Resources

Most energy around us originates from the Sun. The Sun's energy is useful for supplying our energy demands. Often the Sun's energy is transferred into different forms before we use it. E.g.:

Sun → Sun's energy → photosynthesis → dead plants/animals → fossil fuels

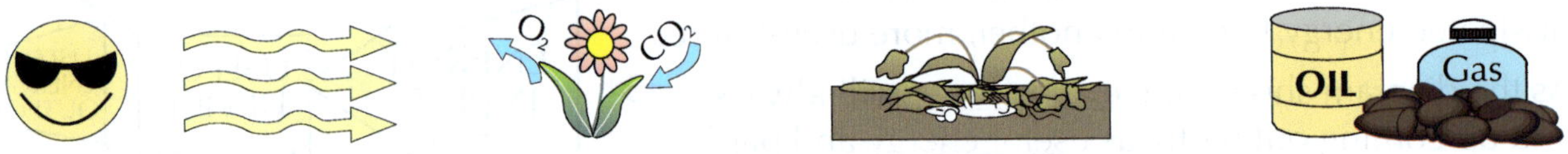


Sun → Sun's energy → plants → photosynthesis → biomass (e.g. wood)

Sun → Sun's energy → plants → photosynthesis → biomass (food)

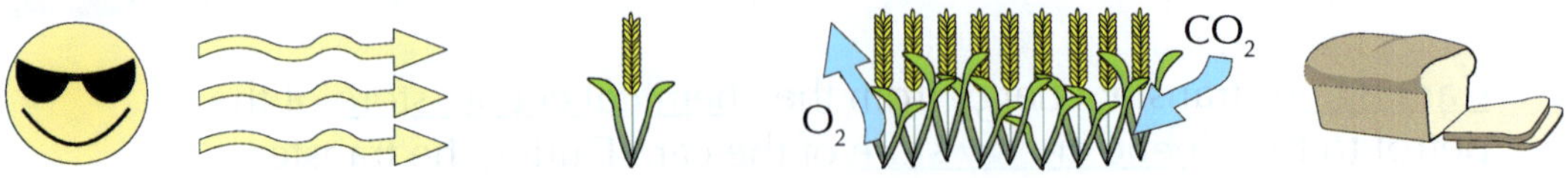


The Sun's energy also creates wind and waves, which we use as energy resources (see p.96).

### Three cheers for the Sun...

...hip hip... hip hip... hip hip... (I hope you're joining in, otherwise this is embarrassing). Don't take the Sun for granted because it supplies nearly all the energy we have here on Earth. Whether it's fossil fuels, biomass, food, wind power or wave power — in the end, it's the Sun behind them all. Awesome.

# Generating Electricity and More on Fossil Fuels

It takes millions of years for fossil fuels to form, but only a fraction of that time for them to burn. It seems kind of silly that we'd use them up so quickly, but we do use them for lots of different things...

## We Can Generate Electricity by Burning Fuels

1) At the moment we generate some of our electricity by burning fossil fuels (coal, oil and gas).

This diagram shows how it's done:

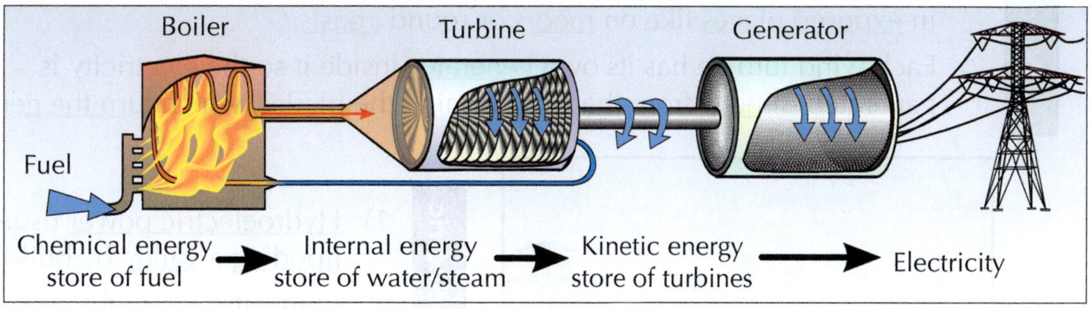


2) Fuels are burnt in the boiler which releases energy.
3) This is used to heat up water which then changes to high pressure steam.
4) The energy in the internal energy store of the steam is transferred to the kinetic energy store of the turbines (these are just like really big fans).
5) The turbines are attached to a generator, which spins and generates electricity.

Nuclear power stations also use steam to turn turbines and power a generator — but they split apart atoms of nuclear fuel (such as uranium) to heat up the water.

## Other Uses of Fossil Fuels

Fossil fuels aren't just used for generating electricity — they have other uses too:

**Oil**

Petrol and diesel powered vehicles use fuel created from oil.

**Coal**

1) Burnt in fireplaces as a source of heat.
2) Used in some old-fashioned steam trains to boil water and produce the steam needed to make the train move.

**Natural gas**

1) Used in boilers in people's homes. The gas is used to heat water, which then comes out of taps (for baths, washing-up, etc). The hot water can also be pumped into radiators to heat the home.
2) Used in some ovens and hobs for cooking food.

Fossil fuels are a reliable energy resource but there are many disadvantages of using them, so there's a lot of focus on finding alternative ways to generate the power we need. This often means using electricity, which can be generated without using fossil fuels (see next page). For example, we now have electric trains, cars, fires, heaters, ovens, etc.

See page 97 for the advantages and disadvantages of using fossil fuels.

# More on Generating Electricity

You saw on the previous page that fossil fuels and nuclear fuels can be used to generate electricity. Well, buckle up, as there are lots of other ways electricity can be generated.

## Here are Seven Ways of Generating Electricity...

**Wind**

1) This involves putting lots of windmills (wind turbines) up in exposed places like on moors or round coasts.
2) Each wind turbine has its own generator inside it so the electricity is generated directly from the wind turning the blades, which turn the generator.

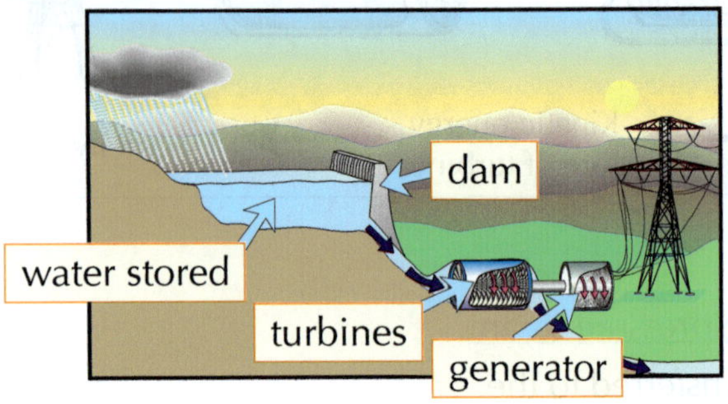


**Hydroelectric**

1) Hydroelectric power usually requires flooding a valley by building a big dam.
2) Rainwater is caught and allowed out through turbines, driving them directly. The turbines then drive generators to make electricity.

**Wave**

1) You need lots of small wave-powered turbines located around the coast.
2) As waves come into the shore they create an up and down motion that can be used to turn a turbine. The turbine drives a generator.

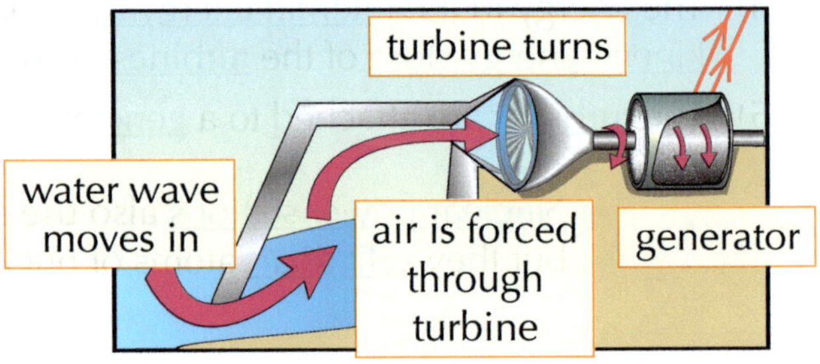


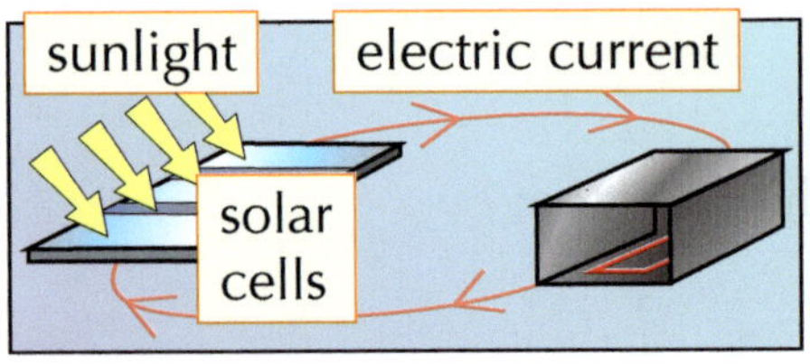


**Solar**

1) Solar cells generate electric currents directly from sunlight.
2) Solar cells can be used to generate electricity on a relatively small scale, e.g. powering individual homes.

**Geothermal**

1) This is only possible in certain places where hot rocks lie quite near to the surface.
2) Water is pumped in pipes down to the hot rocks and comes back up as steam to turn a turbine which drives a generator.

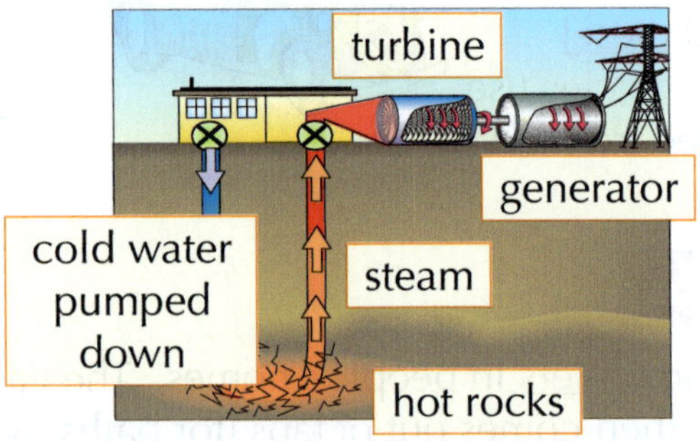


Water heated by sunlight or geothermal hot rocks can also be used to e.g. heat buildings.

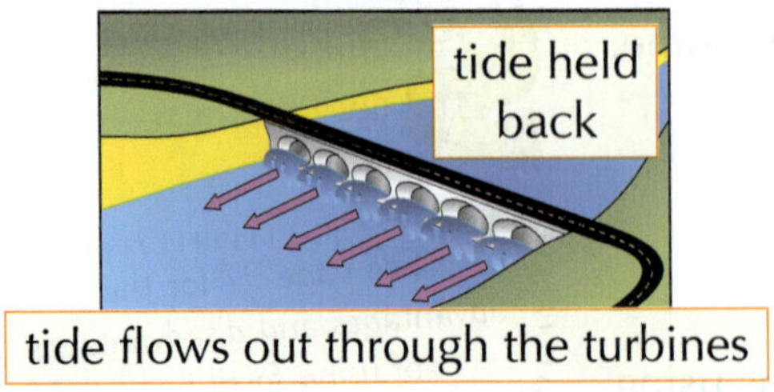


**Tidal**

1) Tidal barrages are big dams built across river estuaries, with turbines in them. As the tide comes in, water fills up behind the dam.
2) The water can then be allowed out through turbines, generating electricity.

**Biomass**

1) During photosynthesis plants generate biomass — organic matter that stores the Sun's energy.
2) Biomass can be burned like fossil fuels to generate electricity.

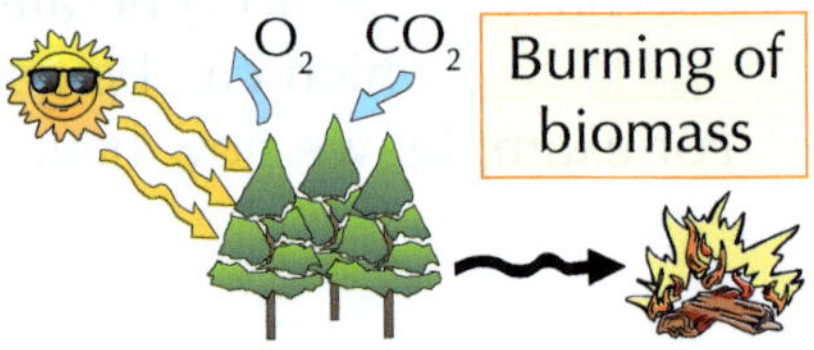

# Renewable and Non-Renewable Energy Resources

Electricity can be generated with non-renewable or renewable energy resources...

## Non-renewable Energy Resources Will Run Out

Non-renewable energy resources include fossil fuels and nuclear fuel. Fossil fuels can't be replenished within a lifetime — they took millions of years to come about so once they've been taken from Earth then that's it, they're gone. They have advantages and disadvantages:

### Advantages

1) Non-renewable energy resources produce a lot of energy.
2) They do not rely on the weather, unlike most renewable resources.
3) We have lots of fossil fuel power stations already, so we don't need to spend money on new technology to carry on using them.

### Disadvantages

1) There's a limited supply of them. We use them up much faster than they're produced so eventually our supply will run out.
2) Burning fossil fuels releases a lot of carbon dioxide into the atmosphere, which can contribute to global warming and climate change (see page 77).
3) Burning coal and oil also releases sulfur dioxide, which causes acid rain (p.77).
4) Nuclear power stations produce radioactive waste — this can be very dangerous and difficult to dispose of.

For the same amount of energy produced, coal releases the most $CO_2$, followed by oil, then gas.

## Renewable Energy Resources Won't Run Out

Renewable energy resources are ones which can be replaced in a person's lifetime. We say that they won't run out, e.g. biomass, wind, waves, etc. Just like non-renewable energy resources, they have advantages and disadvantages:

### Advantages

1) They will never run out — as long as the Sun shines we'll always have renewable energy resources (those on page 96).
2) They can damage the environment (see below), but often in less nasty ways than non-renewables.
3) Once the equipment has been set up, there are minimal running costs and the fuel is free.
4) Most create little or no pollution once they're up and running.

### Disadvantages

1) They don't provide as much energy as non-renewable resources.
2) They can be unreliable if they depend on the weather — e.g. wind turbines only work when it's windy, solar cells work best when it's sunny, etc.
3) They can change or sometimes damage the local environment. E.g. wind turbines can change a nice view and some hydroelectric power schemes need valleys to be flooded, which can destroy habitats for wildlife.
4) It can cost a lot at first to set up the equipment needed to generate power from renewables.

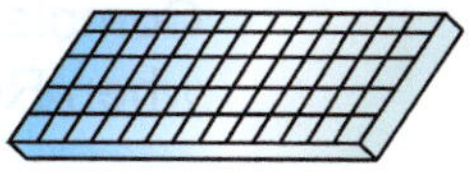

REVISION TIP

**Think on this — it'll affect all your generation...**

When revising, don't slip into the bad habit of calling renewable energy resources "re-usable". If a tree is burnt it can't be re-used, but it can grow again if replanted — it can be renewed.

# Warm-Up & Practice Questions

Have a good mull over everything you've learnt in this section, then have a go at these questions.

## Warm-Up Questions

1) Name six types of energy stores.
2) What is the Law of Conservation of Energy?
3) Where does most of our energy originate from?
4) Give one use of natural gas, other than generating electricity.
5) How is electricity generated from wave power?
6) Give one example of how a renewable energy resource can have a negative effect on the environment.

## Practice Questions

1 Ricky is on a caving holiday. He fixes his head torch onto his hat, to help him see when he is inside a dark cave. The torch is powered by a battery.

(a) The head torch is initially switched off.
Complete the sentence below using words from the box.

| | | | |
|---|---|---|---|
| **chemical** | **bulb** | **battery** | **kinetic** |

Energy is stored inside the ..........................

in its ......................... energy store.

*(2 marks)*

(b) Ricky climbs up the wall of the cave.
Complete the flow diagram to show some of the energy transfers that take place when Ricky climbs.

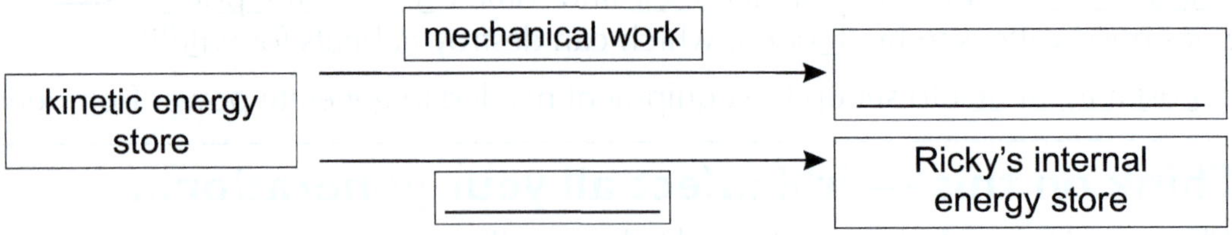


*(2 marks)*

# Practice Questions

2 Natural gas is an important fossil fuel used in power stations and in the home.

(a) Natural gas is described as a 'non-renewable energy resource'. Explain what this term means.

*(1 mark)*

(b) Give **two** other examples of non-renewable energy resources.

*(2 marks)*

3 During a useful energy transfer, energy is transferred from one store to another useful store.

(a) Complete the following table to show the energy transfers that take place in each scenario.

| Scenario | Energy store transferred from | Useful energy store transferred to |
|---|---|---|
| Coal being used to cook food on a barbecue | | Internal energy store of the food |
| A stretched rubber band on a catapult being released | | |

*(3 marks)*

(b) Describe and explain how the amount of energy that goes into an energy transfer compares to the amount of useful energy that comes out.

*(2 marks)*

4 The diagram below shows a way of generating electricity from a renewable source of energy.

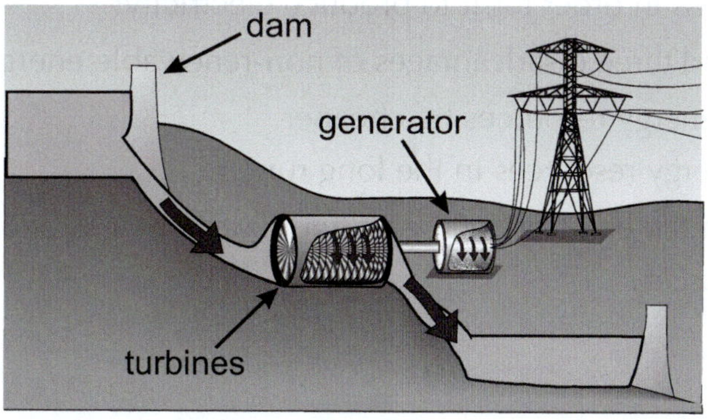


A dam is constructed to flood a valley and catch rainwater. The rainwater is released in order to drive the turbines, which in turn drives the generators to produce electricity.

(a) Name the renewable energy resource.

*(1 mark)*

(b) Give **two** other examples of renewable energy resources that use water.

*(2 marks)*

(c) Give **two** advantages of renewable energy resources over non-renewable energy resources.

*(2 marks)*

# Summary Questions

Congratulations! You've made it to the end of this section on energy and resources. Don't worry if it wasn't a walk in the park, there's lots of tricky information to wrap your head around here.

- Try these questions and tick off each one when you get it right.
- When you've done all the questions for a topic and are completely happy with it, tick it off.

## Energy Transfers (p.92-p.93)

1) Atomic nuclei release energy from what kind of energy store?
2) True or false? Stretching a spring transfers energy to its elastic energy store.
3) Energy can be transferred from one store to another via different pathways. Name five of these pathways.
4) Describe the energy transfers that take place as a ball falls towards the ground.
5) Describe how friction influences the transfer of energy between stores.
6) True or false? Energy can be created but never destroyed.
7) How is wasted energy usually dissipated during an energy transfer?
8) Describe one way in which energy is wasted in power stations.
9) Describe one way in which energy is wasted in cars.

## Energy Resources (p.94-p.97)

10) What are the three main fossil fuels? Describe how they form.
11) How does the Sun's energy get stored in fossil fuels?
12) Describe how we generate electricity from fossil fuels.
13) Give one example of how oil is used, other than for generating electricity.
14) Why can geothermal power plants only be set up in certain areas?
15) Explain how tidal barrages are used to generate electricity.
16) What happens to biomass in order for it to produce electricity?
17) Give two advantages and three disadvantages of non-renewable energy resources.
18) Why might renewable energy resources be cheaper than non-renewable energy resources in the long run?
19) Other than the effect on the environment, give two disadvantages of using renewable energy resources.

# Speed

Neeeoww... Yes, it's a page on speed. Make sure you can do these calculations. Don't zoom through.

## Speed is How Fast You're Going

1) Speed is a measure of how far you travel in a set amount of time.

$$\text{Speed} = \frac{\text{Distance}}{\text{Time}}$$

This line means divided by or shared by (÷).

2) A formula triangle is definitely the best way to do speed calculations.
3) Use the word SIDOT to help you remember the formula:

   SIDOT — Speed Is Distance Over Time.

Make sure you always use the correct units when you're doing a calculation.

4) There are three common units for speed. You can see that they're all kind of the same, i.e. distance unit per time unit. →
   - metres per second — m/s
   - miles per hour — mph or miles/h
   - kilometres per hour — km/h

1 hour = 60 minutes = 60 × 60 seconds = 3600 s. So...

(1) To convert from hours to seconds, multiply by 3600 → 3 hours = 3 × 3600 s = 10 800 s

(2) To convert from seconds to hours, divide by 3600 → 12 600 s = 12 600 ÷ 3600 = 3.5 hours

## Work Out Speed Using Distance and Time

To work out speed you need to know the distance travelled and the time taken.

**Example**

**A girl is skateboarding down a path. You notice it takes exactly 5 seconds for the girl to move between two fence posts, 10 metres apart. What is the girl's speed?**

Step 1: Write down what you know:
distance, d = 10 m   time, t = 5 s

Step 2: We want to find speed, s
from the formula triangle: s = d/t
Speed = Distance ÷ Time = 10 ÷ 5 = 2 m/s

Put your finger over "s" in the formula triangle — which leaves d/t (i.e. d ÷ t).

You need to make sure that all the units in your calculations match up too. For example, if you're asked to work out the speed of a car in km/h, you need the distance in km and the time in hours.

**Example**

**A campervan travels 15 miles in 30 minutes. What is its speed?**

Step 1: Write down what you know:
distance, d = 15 miles   time, t = 30 minutes = 0.5 of an hour.

Step 2: We want to find speed, s
from the formula triangle: s = d/t
Speed = Distance ÷ Time = 15 ÷ 0.5 = 30 miles/hour (mph)

For the answer to be in miles per hour you need the distance in miles and the time in hours so the 30 mins had to become 0.5 hr.

# More on Speed

This section started so well, let's keep up the pace. First up, how you can measure speed...

## You can Measure the Speed of a Trolley

PRACTICAL

1) Set up your apparatus as shown in the diagram below.
2) Measure the distance between the start of the runway and the finish line using a ruler.
3) Hold the trolley still at the start line, and then let go of it so that it starts to roll down the slope.
4) When it reaches the start of the runway, start your stopwatch.
5) When it reaches the finish line, stop your stopwatch.
6) The time it takes to travel between the start of the runway and the finish line can be used, along with the distance of the runway, to find the trolley's speed on the runway (using speed = distance ÷ time).

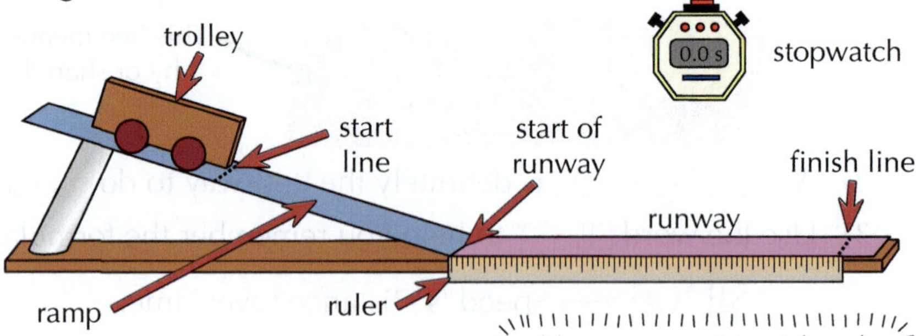


You can use a stopwatch and calculate the speed of most things (e.g. a falling ball, a runner on a track, a car on the road), providing you also know the distance the thing covers.

## You Get Relative Motion Between Two Moving Objects

1) When two vehicles are moving, it can be useful to know how fast they are moving together or apart — their relative motion.
2) If you were in one of the vehicles, the relative speed would be how fast the other vehicle appears to be moving towards or away from you.

### Add the Speeds of Two Objects Moving Towards Each Other

If two objects are approaching each other in opposite directions on the same straight line you can add their speeds together to calculate their relative motion. Look:

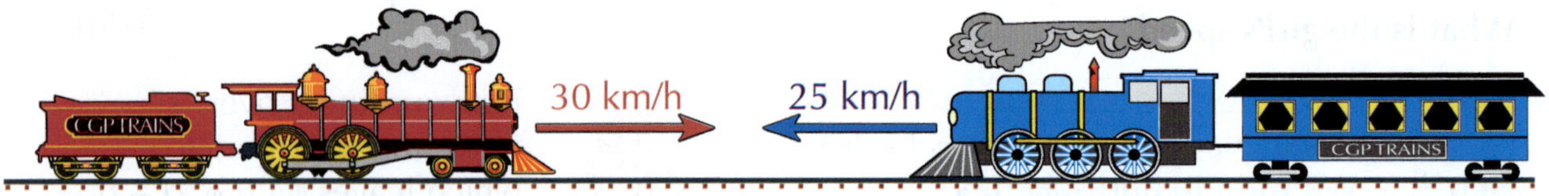


1) If you're sat on the red train, the blue train is getting closer much faster than if you were sat still at the side of the track. This is because it is moving towards you while you're moving towards it.
2) To work out the relative speed, just add the speeds together. 30 + 25 = 55 km/h, so if you were sat on the red train, it would look like the blue train was moving at 55 km/h.

### Subtract the Speeds of Two Objects Travelling in the Same Direction

1) If two objects are passing each other in the same direction on the same straight line you can subtract their speeds to calculate their relative motion.
2) For example, if you're moving at 60 mph in a bus on the motorway, and a car overtakes you at 70 mph, the speed of the car is 70 – 60 = 10 mph relative to the bus. If you look out the window, the car moves past you as quickly as if you were stationary and the car was moving at 10 mph.

## My speed increases when I see that biscuit tin...

This stuff about relative motion can be tricky. Make sure you've got your head around it before moving on.

# Stopping Distances

You don't need to learn the thinking, braking and stopping distances in the Highway Code, but you might be asked to research them while learning about speed and forces. And it's quite possible that those pesky examiners could use this stuff to test your physics knowledge, so we've treated you to a whole page on it...

## Many Factors Affect Your Total Stopping Distance

1) If you need to stop in a given distance, then the faster your vehicle's going, the bigger braking force it'll need.
2) Likewise, for any given braking force, the faster you're going, the greater your stopping distance.
3) The total stopping distance of a vehicle is the distance covered in the time between the driver first spotting a hazard and the vehicle coming to a complete stop.
4) The stopping distance is the sum of the thinking distance and the braking distance.

## 1) Thinking Distance

This is "the distance the vehicle travels during the driver's reaction time".

The reaction time is the time between the driver spotting a hazard and taking action.

It's affected by two main factors:

(1) How fast you're going — obviously. Whatever your reaction time, the faster you're going, the further you'll go.

(2) How aware you are — this is affected by tiredness, drugs, alcohol and a careless attitude.

The figures below for typical stopping distances are from the Highway Code. It's frightening to see just how far it takes to stop when you're going at 70 mph.

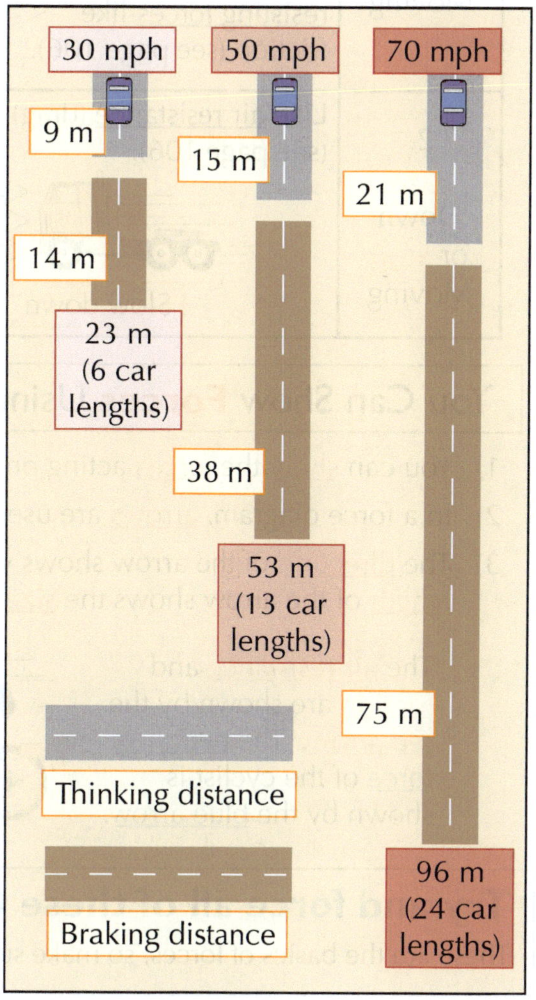


## 2) Braking Distance

This is "the distance the car travels under the braking force".

It's affected by four main factors:

(1) How fast you're going — the faster you're going, the further it takes to stop.

(2) How good your brakes are — all brakes must be checked and maintained regularly. Worn or faulty brakes will let you down badly just when you need them the most, i.e. in an emergency.

(3) How good the tyres are — tyres should have a minimum tread depth of 1.6 mm in order to be able to get rid of the water in wet conditions. Leaves, diesel spills and muck on the road can greatly increase the braking distance, and cause the car to skid too.

(4) How good the grip is — this depends on three things: 1) road surface, 2) weather conditions, 3) tyres.

Wet or icy roads are always much more slippy than dry roads, but often you only discover this when you try to brake hard. You don't have as much grip, so you travel further before stopping.

# Forces

Well, I can't force you to read this page — but if I were you, I'd push on with it...

## Forces are Nearly Always Pushes and Pulls

1) Forces are pushes or pulls that occur when two objects interact.
2) Forces can't be seen, but the effects of a force can be seen.
3) Forces are measured in newtons — N.
4) They always act in a certain direction.
5) A force meter (known as a newton meter) is used to measure forces.
6) Objects don't need to touch to interact. For example, forces between magnets (page 131) and gravity (page 136).

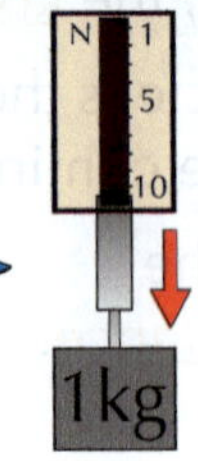

## Forces Can Make an Object do Five Things

| | |
|---|---|
| 1. Speed Up or Start Moving | Like kicking a football. To start something moving, a push force must be larger than resisting forces like friction (see page 106).   |
| 2. Slow Down or Stop Moving | Like air resistance (drag) or friction (see page 106).   |
| 3. Change Direction | Like hitting a ball with a bat or gravity causing footballs to come back down to Earth.   |
| 4. Turn | Like turning a spanner.   |
| 5. Change Shape | Like stretching and compressing (see p.107).   |

## You Can Show Forces Using Arrows

1) You can show the forces acting on an object in a force diagram.
2) In a force diagram, arrows are used to represent all the forces acting on an object.
3) The direction of the arrow shows you the direction of the force, and the length of the arrow shows the size of the force. Here are two examples:

The air resistance and friction are shown by the red arrow. The peddling force of the cyclist is shown by the blue arrow.

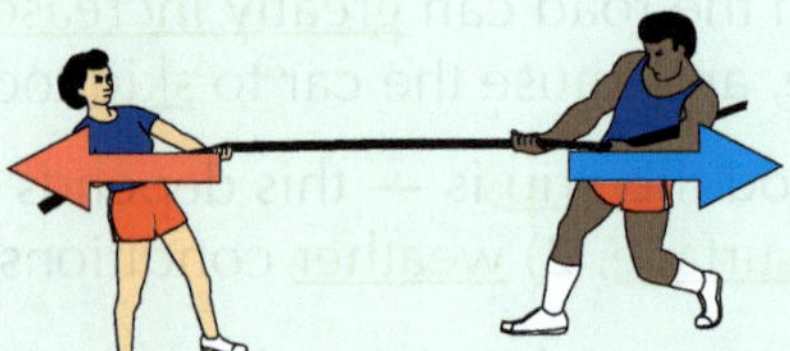

The pulling force of each person acts on either end of the rope.

### Try and force all of these facts into your brain...

These are the basics of forces, so make sure you learn 'em. Remember — learn, cover, scribble, check...

# Balanced and Unbalanced Forces

Oh would you look at that — another page on forces. Life's a drag, eh?

## Forces Can be Balanced or Unbalanced

BALANCED FORCES produce No Change in Movement.

The arrows are the same length, showing same-sized forces.

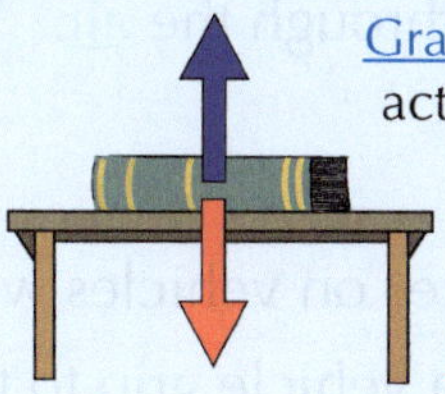

Gravity (see page 136) acting on the book is balanced...

...by the upward force of the table.

UNBALANCED FORCES Change the Speed and/or Direction of Objects.

The arrows are different lengths, showing different-sized forces.

The force from the boat's motor is greater...

...than the resistance from the water, so the boat speeds up.

## The Overall Force Tells You if an Object is Balanced

1) If all the forces on an object are acting along the same line (e.g. forwards and backwards OR up and down), the overall force is found by adding or subtracting the forces.
2) If the forces are acting in opposite directions, you subtract the forces to get the overall force. If they're acting in the same direction, you add the forces together to get the overall force.
3) If the overall force is equal to zero, the forces are balanced.
4) If the overall force is non-zero, then the forces are unbalanced and the speed and/or direction of the object's motion will change.
5) Have a look at these examples:

Forces acting along the same line are said to be acting in one dimension.

Overall force:
200 + 50 – 20 = 230 N
Non-zero force
— unbalanced

Overall force:
100 – 100 = 0 N
Zero force
— balanced

## Unbalanced Forces in the Lab

PRACTICAL

Recognise this? It's the practical from page 102.
You can use the same set-up to investigate unbalanced forces...

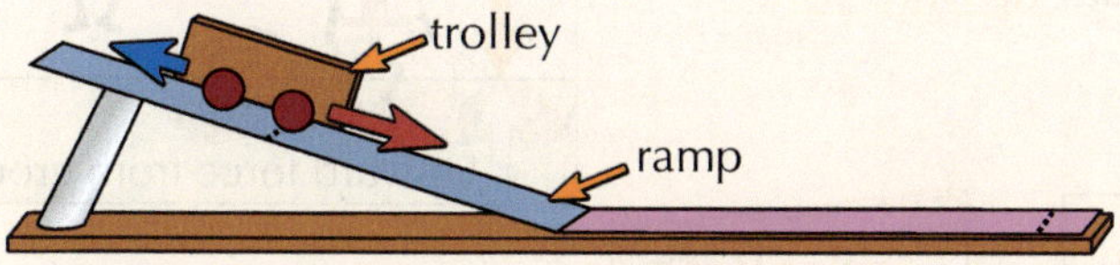


When the trolley is initially released, the forces are unbalanced — the force pulling the trolley down the ramp is larger than the friction that acts between the trolley and the ramp, so the trolley speeds up.

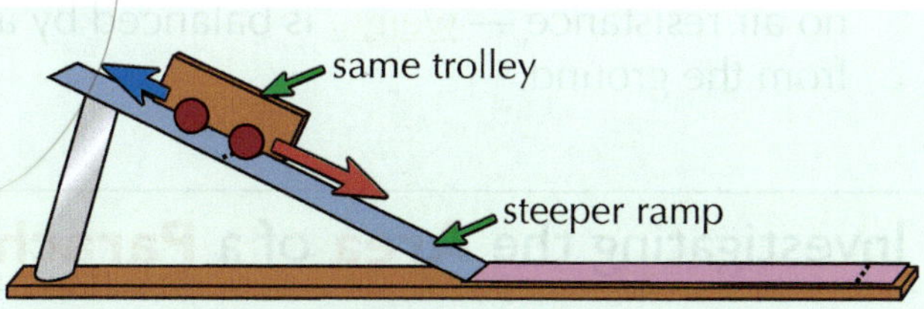


If you make the ramp steeper, the forces are initially more unbalanced — there is a greater force pulling the trolley down the ramp, so the trolley speeds up more.

### All this revision — it's a balancing act...

"Balanced forces" doesn't necessarily mean "no movement". Objects moving at a steady speed in the same direction have balanced forces acting on them (as there is no change in their movement).

# Friction and Air Resistance

Friction and air resistance act in the opposite direction to moving objects. They're actually pretty handy most of the time — if you've ever tried running on ice (where there's little friction) you'll get what I mean.

## Frictional Forces Act on Moving Objects

Friction and air resistance are two types of frictional forces. Friction acts between two surfaces (e.g. tyres on a road) and makes it harder for objects to slide past each other. Air resistance (or "drag") pushes against objects moving through the air.

Frictional forces always act in the opposite direction to movement.

### Advantages of Frictional Forces

1) Friction allows things to stop, start and slow down — the brakes on vehicles work due to friction.
2) Friction also allows things to grip to a surface — the tyres on a vehicle grip to the road surface — without this grip you couldn't make the vehicle move forward or come to a stop.
3) Air resistance slows down falling objects — this helps skydivers land safely with a parachute (see below).

Parachutes can't be used in space as there's hardly any air in space (and no air means no air resistance).

### Disadvantages of Frictional Forces

1) They always waste energy (usually by heating).
2) They limit your top speed. This is why current cars and planes could never reach, say, a billion mph.

## Air Resistance and Sheep Jumping Out of Planes

1) At the start, the sheep only has the force of its weight (i.e. gravity) pulling it down — so it starts to move faster.
2) Air resistance begins to act to balance the force of weight.
3) When the parachute opens air resistance increases enormously — because there's a much larger area trying to cut through the air. The sheep loses speed and slows down gratefully.
4) Very quickly the air resistance becomes equal to the weight — the two forces are balanced. The sheep now moves at a steady speed.
5) Once safely on the ground, the sheep is not moving so there is no air resistance — weight is balanced by an equal upward force from the ground.

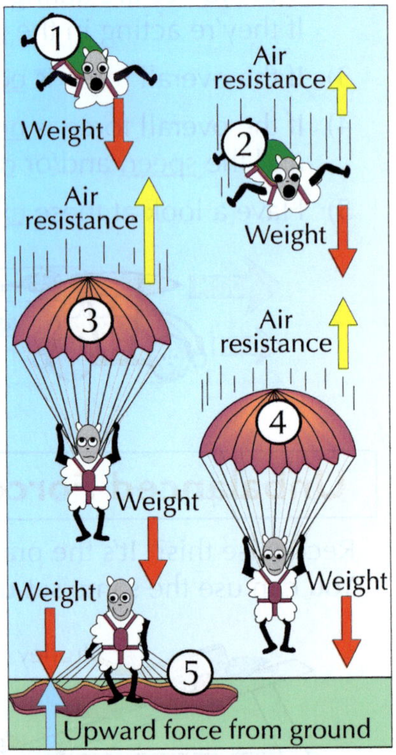


## Investigating the Area of a Parachute

PRACTICAL

The larger the canopy area of a parachute, the greater the air resistance that acts on it, and so the longer it takes the parachute (and the object attached to it) to fall. You can investigate this...

1) Make a model parachute using plastic or paper.
2) Attach a light object to the parachute and drop it from a sensible height (e.g. from a window or balcony).
3) Using a stopwatch, measure the time it takes to reach the ground.
4) Repeat this for parachutes with different canopy areas and compare your results.

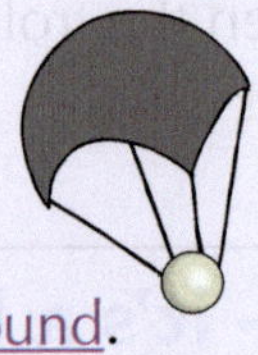

Remember to control the variables in this experiment — e.g. always drop the object from the same height, use the same object each time, make all parachutes from the same material, etc.

# Springs

It's not just about pushing and pulling — forces are also able to stretch or squash things.

## You Can Deform Objects by Stretching or Squashing

1) You can use forces to stretch or compress (squash) objects, e.g. when you stomp on an empty fizzy pop can.
2) The force you apply causes the object to deform (change its shape).
3) Springs are special because they usually spring back into their original shape after the force has been removed — they are elastic.

It's not just springs that are elastic. E.g. foam mattresses compress when you're in bed, but return to their original shape after you get up.

## You Can Investigate the Stretching of a Spring

PRACTICAL

1) First set up the equipment as in the diagram.
2) Record the position of the bottom of the spring, first without the weight and then with the weight attached. The difference between the two positions is the extension.

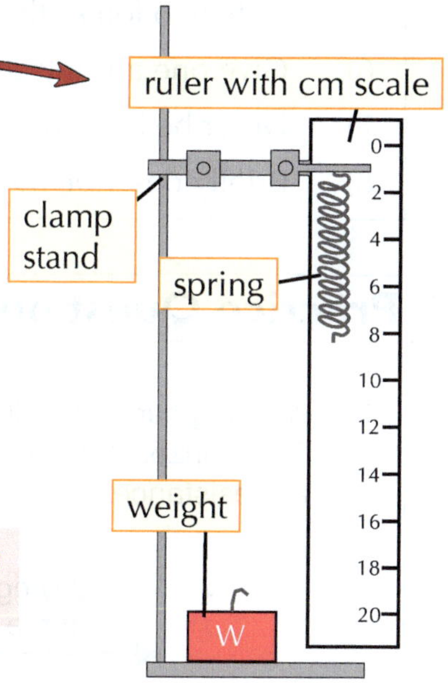


**extension = position with weight – position without weight**

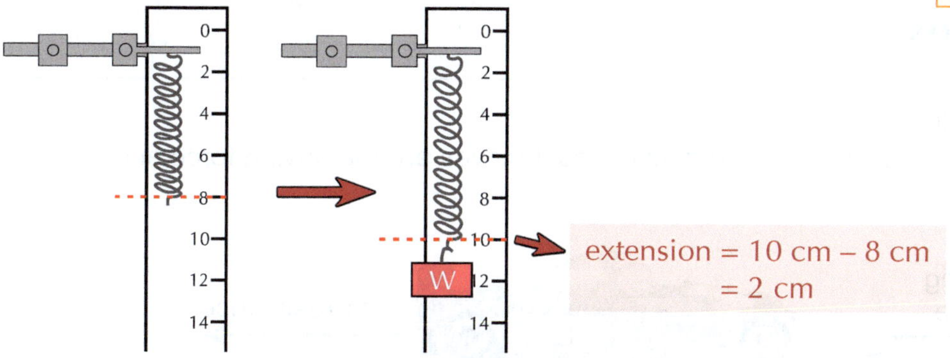


3) Repeat with different weights to see how the force of weight changes the extension.
4) You should see that extension and force are directly proportional — i.e. if you double the force, the extension will double too.

This only works up to a certain force.

### You Can also Investigate the Compression

1) Move the clamp to the bottom of the stand and adjust the spring and ruler accordingly.
2) Record the position of the top of the spring, first without the weight and then with the weight added on top.
3) The difference between the two positions is the compression:

**compression = position without weight – position with weight**

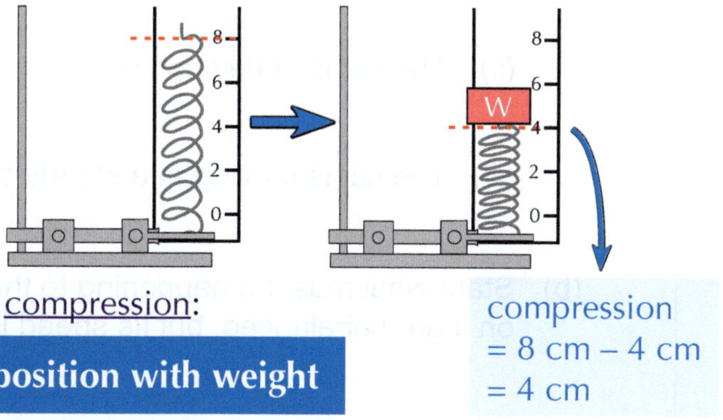


4) Like extension above, if you repeat with different weights you should find that compression is directly proportional to the force.

**REVISION TIP**

### This page will stretch your understanding...

The compression formula is just the extension formula... but the other way round. Just learn one and remember to reverse it if you need the other. Hey presto — revision cut in half!

# Warm-Up & Practice Questions

Here's another set of Warm-Up and Practice Questions. Take time to give these questions a good go — they'll help you to find out which pages you've understood really well, and which pages could do with a bit more attention. Go on, you know you want to...

## Warm-Up Questions

1) What is the equation for speed?
2) Why does a car driving in the opposite direction to you look like it's moving faster than a car driving at the same speed in the same direction?
3) What unit are forces measured in?
4) Draw a force diagram for a car moving at a steady speed.
5) State two forces that always act in the opposite direction to movement.
6) Give one advantage of friction.
7) Describe how the canopy area of a parachute affects how much air resistance acts upon it.
8) Briefly describe how you could measure the extension of a spring when a weight is added.

## Practice Questions

1 A racing car is travelling around a circuit.
Two horizontal forces that act on the racing car as it moves are the driving force and air resistance:

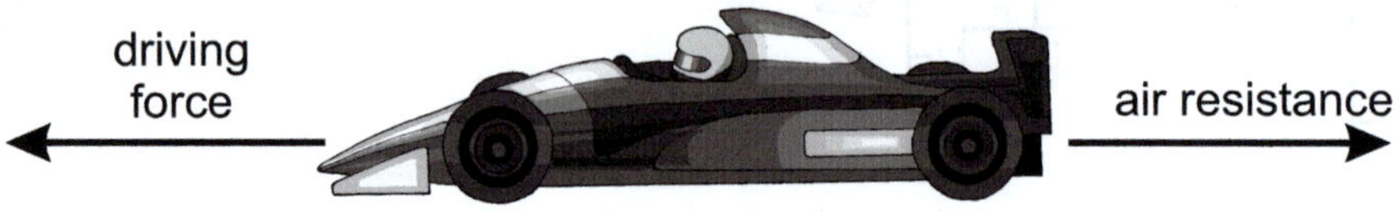


(a) Compare the sizes of the driving force and the air resistance when:

(i) The car is slowing down.

*(1 mark)*

(ii) The car is speeding up.

*(1 mark)*

(iii) The car is moving at a steady speed.

*(1 mark)*

(b) State what must be happening to the car if the forces acting on it are unbalanced, but its speed is remaining the same.

*(1 mark)*

(c) Suggest **two** disadvantages of air resistance when it comes to race car driving.

*(2 marks)*

(d) The car contains springs that help to absorb shock forces from bumps in the road.
Suggest **two** ways these forces may deform the springs.

*(2 marks)*

# Practice Questions

2 Three aircraft are taking part in a display.

(a) In one part of the display, two of the aircraft fly towards each other as shown:

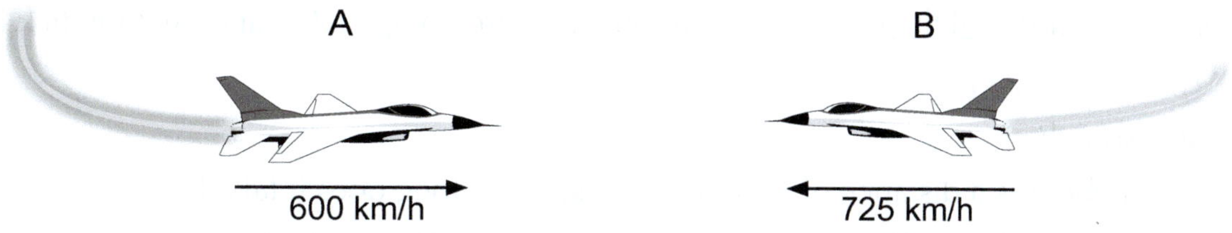


Calculate the speed of aircraft B relative to aircraft A.

*(1 mark)*

(b) The third aircraft is travelling in the same direction as aircraft A.
Describe how you could calculate its speed relative to aircraft A.

*(1 mark)*

**PRACTICAL**

3 Tamwar wants to measure how fast a ball will fall when he drops it from different heights. He measures 50 cm up the wall and makes a mark. Then he drops the ball from the mark and starts his stopwatch at the same time. He stops the stopwatch when the ball hits the floor. Tamwar repeats this for a number of different heights. His results are shown in the table below.

| height up the wall (cm) | time (s) | speed (m/s) |
|---|---|---|
| 50 | 0.45 | 1.1 |
| 100 | 0.51 | 2.0 |
| 150 | 0.58 | 2.6 |
| 200 | 0.60 | |

(a) Calculate the missing value in the table using the formula:
speed = distance ÷ time.

*(3 marks)*

(b) (i) Due to the ball's speed, Tamwar doesn't always stop the stopwatch at the exact time the ball hits the floor.
State what type of error this introduces into Tamwar's results for time.

*(1 mark)*

(ii) Suggest how Tamwar could make his results for time more reliable.

*(2 marks)*

(c) Explain whether the forces acting on the ball are balanced or unbalanced just after it is dropped.

*(1 mark)*

(d) Tamwar attaches a small model parachute to the ball and then repeats the experiment. Suggest and explain how this will affect his results.

*(3 marks)*

# Summary Questions

Section P2 is all about speed and forces — the questions below will test whether you've learnt the basic facts. Soon you'll be ready to face any question that gets forced your way...

- Try these questions and tick off each one when you get it right.
- When you've done all the questions for a topic and are completely happy with it, tick it off.

## Speed (p.101-p.103) ☐

1) What is speed? ☐
2)* A girl skateboards a distance of 150 m at 3 m/s. How long does it take her? ☐
3)* When a car is going at 40 mph, how far will it travel in 15 minutes? ☐
4) Briefly describe how you could calculate the average speed of a runner around a track. ☐
5)* A cyclist, travelling at 15 km/h, is overtaken by a car travelling at 23 km/h. Calculate the speed of the car relative to the cyclist. ☐
6) What is meant by: a) thinking distance, b) braking distance, c) stopping distance? ☐

## Forces (p.104-p.105) ☐

7) What is a force? ☐
8) What five things can forces make objects do? ☐
9) What does the length of an arrow on a force diagram tell you? ☐
10) What do balanced forces produce? What do unbalanced forces do to an object? ☐
11) Is the car in the diagram travelling at a steady speed, speeding up or slowing down? ☐

## Friction and Air Resistance (p.106) ☐

12) Name the frictional force that makes it harder for objects to slide past each other. ☐
13) Which way do frictional forces always act? ☐
14) Give a useful application of air resistance. ☐
15) True or false? The larger the area of a parachute, the longer an object attached to it takes to fall. ☐

## Springs (p.107) ☐

16)* Without any weights attached, the bottom of a spring is level with the 10.2 cm mark on a ruler. When a weight is added, the bottom of the spring extends so it is level with the 11.4 cm mark. Calculate the extension of the spring. ☐
17) What will happen to the extension of a spring if the force causing it to stretch is doubled? ☐
18) Describe how you could measure the compression of a spring when a weight is added. ☐



*Answers on page 148.

# Pressure

Don't let pressure get you down — here's a lovely page that explains it. That's a load off your mind.

## Pressure is How Much Force is Put on a Certain Area

Pressure, force and area are all kind of tied up with each other — as the formula shows. The formula can also be put in a triangle, which is nice.

Pressure is a ratio of force over area.
So a given force acting over a big area means a small pressure (and vice versa).

$$\text{Pressure} = \frac{\text{Force}}{\text{Area}}$$

## Pressure is Measured in N/m² or N/cm²

If a force of 1 newton is spread over an area of 1 m$^2$ (like this) then it exerts a pressure of 1 N/m$^2$. Simple as that.

The units of pressure are N/cm$^2$ or N/m$^2$.
1 N/cm$^2$ = 10 000 N/m$^2$.

Force acts normal (at 90°) to area.

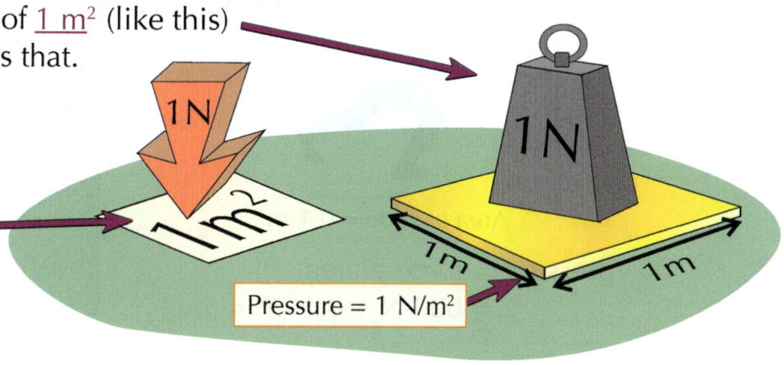


**Example**

**A bird is standing on one foot. It weighs 30 N and exerts a pressure of 20 000 N/m$^2$ on the ground. Calculate the area of one of the bird's feet.**

Pressure = force ÷ area
Area = force ÷ pressure
= 30 N ÷ 20 000 N/m$^2$ = 0.0015 m$^2$

You need to rearrange the pressure formula using the formula triangle at the top of the page.

## You Can Measure the Pressure Exerted by Different Objects

PRACTICAL

1) Weigh the object using a Newton meter to find the force.
2) Calculate the area of the face of the object that is touching the surface that pressure is exerted on. (E.g. if a rectangular box is on the floor, this is the area of the box face that is touching the floor. Calculate the area by measuring the length of the sides of this face and then using width × length.)
3) Now use the formula: Pressure = force ÷ area

Area is measured in cm$^2$ or m$^2$.

**Example**

**A wooden box weighs 18 N. Its base is a rectangle with sides 0.80 m and 0.90 m long.**
**Calculate the pressure exerted by the box on the floor.**

Area = 0.80 m × 0.90 m = 0.72 m$^2$
Pressure = force ÷ area
= 18 N ÷ 0.72 m$^2$ = 25 N/m$^2$

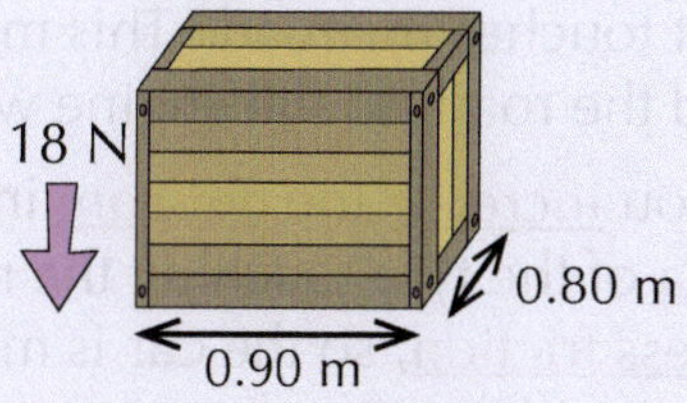


## I was under 500 N/m² of pressure to come up with a good joke...

First things first, get that formula learnt. When there is a set force, increasing the area will decrease pressure and decreasing the area will increase pressure. You'll need that on the next page...

# More on Pressure

If you've been waiting for a page about skis, blades and tyres, you're in luck...

## Changing the Area Increases or Decreases Pressure

1) Sometimes, if you've got a set force, it's helpful to decrease the pressure of something by increasing its area.
2) E.g. when people walk on snow, their feet sink down into it because the pressure is too high.
3) That's where skis come in — they increase the area of the foot, so they decrease the pressure on the snow. This makes moving in the snow much easier — the skis slide over the top of it.

Here's an example...

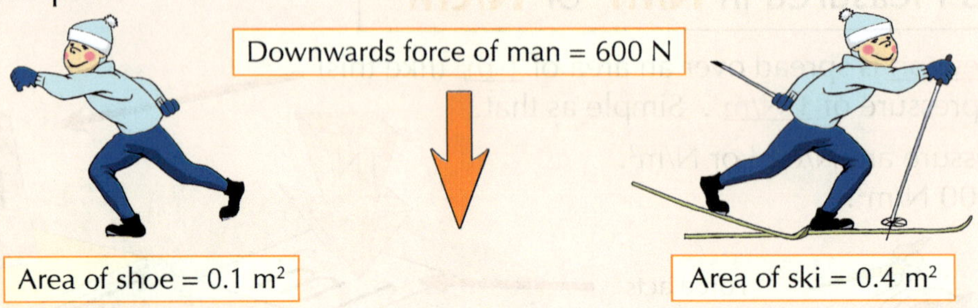


Snowboards have the same effect as skis.

pressure = force ÷ area
= 600 N ÷ 0.1 m² = 6000 N/m²

pressure = force ÷ area
= 600 N ÷ 0.4 m² = 1500 N/m²

4) Sometimes it's helpful to increase the pressure of something by decreasing the area.
5) For example, blades need to exert large pressures to cut through materials. To do this, they have edges with a small area (sharp edges).

For pressure calculations, check carefully whether the numbers are in N/m² or N/cm².

**Example**

**An axe needs to exert a pressure of 35 000 N/cm² to chop through a log. Jack can swing the axe with a force of 3500 N. How small does the area of the blade have to be to chop through the log?**

Area = force ÷ pressure
= 3500 N ÷ 35 000 N/cm² = 0.1 cm²

## Changing the Pressure in a Car Tyre Changes the Area

1) Just like increasing the area of something decreases the pressure, increasing the pressure of something decreases the area.
2) If you decrease the pressure in a car tyre, it increases the area of the tyre that touches the road. This means there's more friction between the tyre and the road, so the engine will use more energy to overcome the friction.
3) If you increase the pressure in a car tyre, it decreases the area of the tyre touching the road. This means that there is less friction, so the car is more likely to skid.

Some people decrease their tyre pressure to drive in a desert — the weight of the car is more spread out so it's less likely to sink into the sand.

### I need to spread out for a bit, take a bit a pressure off myself...

Next time it snows or you find yourself in a sandy spot with a choice of footwear, try this out... Walk around with some flat shoes on, then do the same with some heeled shoes. You'll find that you sink down further when you have the heeled shoes on because there's a smaller area of shoe in contact with the ground.

# Density

You should be a whizz at formula triangles by now. Show this page who's boss.

## Density is Mass per Unit Volume

1) Density is a measure of the 'compactness' of a substance. It relates the mass of a substance to how much space it takes up.
2) The units of density are g/cm³ or kg/m³. 1 g/cm³ = 1000 kg/m³.
3) Solids, liquids and gases (like air) are made up of particles (page 52) so they all have mass and volume.
4) You can find the density of any object or substance as long as you know its mass and volume...

$$\text{Density} = \frac{\text{mass}}{\text{volume}}$$

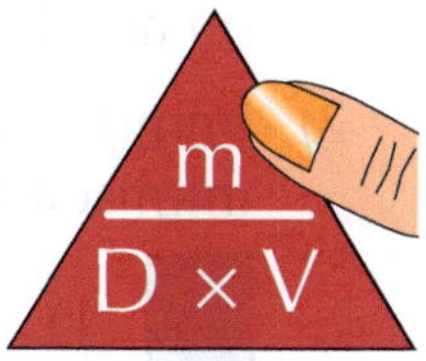


## Measuring the Density of...

PRACTICAL

### ...Regularly-Shaped Objects

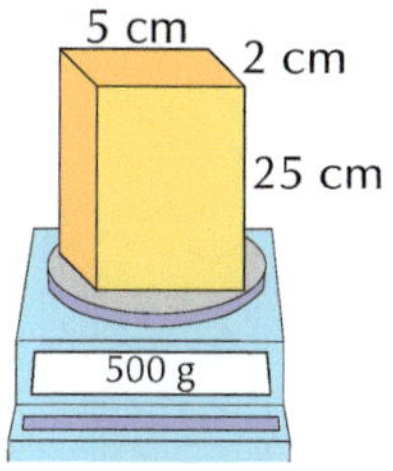


Find the mass and volume and use the formula above like this...

Use the right volume formula. E.g. volume of a cuboid = length × width × height

Volume of object = 25 cm × 5 cm × 2 cm = 250 cm³

Mass of object (from mass balance) = 500 g

Density = mass ÷ volume = 500 g ÷ 250 cm³ = 2 g/cm³

Volume is measured in cm³ or m³.

### ...Irregularly-Shaped Objects

1) First find the mass of the object using a mass balance. Then it gets a bit more tricky...
2) Find the volume by dropping the object into a measuring beaker of water. The change in water level is equal to the volume of the object.

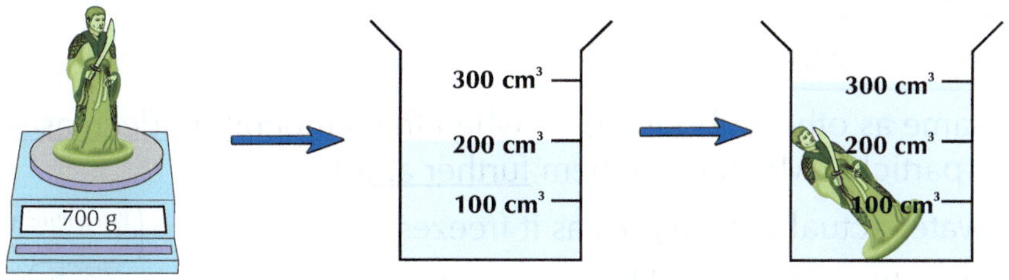


Change in water level
= volume after – volume before
= 300 cm³ – 200 cm³
= 100 cm³

3) Now use the formula: Density = mass ÷ volume = 700 g ÷ 100 cm³ = 7 g/cm³

### ...Liquids

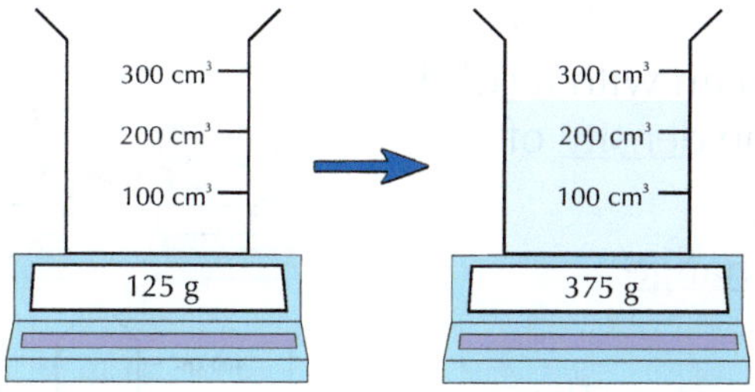


1) Find the mass of a liquid by measuring the mass of an empty beaker, then the mass of the beaker and liquid. The mass of the liquid is the same as this change in mass. From the diagram, mass = 375 g – 125 g = 250 g
2) Find the volume of the liquid by reading off the scale. Volume = 250 cm³
3) Now use the formula: Density = mass ÷ volume = 250 g ÷ 250 cm³ = 1 g/cm³

## Density — Not a settlement of foxes (oh my sides)...

This is another 'get this formula learned page', so I'd do that if I were you. Make sure you know the different ways to calculate volume for different objects and liquids, as it's easy to get caught out here.

# More on Density

Just in case you thought you were done with density, here's another whole page for you. Yey.

## A Less Dense Liquid will Float on a More Dense Liquid

1) Whether or not an object will float depends on its density. A substance will float on another substance if it has a lower density. If it has a higher density it will sink.
2) Immiscible liquids are liquids that don't mix together. If two liquids are immiscible, the one with a lower density floats on top of the other one.

PRACTICAL

**Example**

1) Add equal amounts of water and olive oil to a measuring beaker.
2) After a few seconds the liquids will have formed different layers because they are immiscible.
3) The water is more dense than the oil, so the oil will float on top of the water.

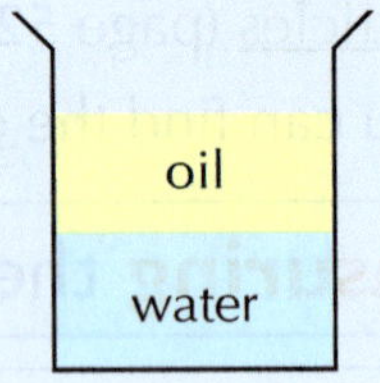


## Temperature Affects the Density of Substances

1) Usually, solids are more dense than liquids, and liquids are more dense than gases.
2) The density is affected by how the particles are arranged — the particles are packed tightly together in solids and very far apart in gases (see page 52).
3) When you heat a substance, the particles move around more and move further apart. This can cause a substance to change state, e.g. from a solid, to a liquid, to a gas. As the particles move apart, the substance expands and becomes less dense.
4) For example, warm water is less dense than cold water. So, if you very carefully pour some warm water into the beaker of cold water, the warm water will float in a layer on top of the cold water.

You can see this if you use food colouring to make the cold and warm water different colours.

### Ice is Less Dense Than Liquid Water

1) Water doesn't behave the same as other substances — when the temperature decreases, bonds form between water particles which push them further apart.
2) This means the density of water actually decreases as it freezes.
3) That's why ice floats on water. It seems normal because water is so common, but you'd usually expect a solid to sink in a pool of its liquid form.

## The Density of Air Can be Measured

PRACTICAL

You can measure the mass and volume of a gas, just like you can with a solid or liquid, to find its density. Here's one way you can estimate the density of air:

1) Find the mass of a deflated balloon using a mass balance. Then blow up the balloon and find the mass again. The change in mass shows the mass of the air inside the balloon.
2) Then find out its volume by pushing it into a container of water. The change in water level is roughly equal to the volume of the air inside the balloon.
3) Now use the formula: Density = mass ÷ volume.

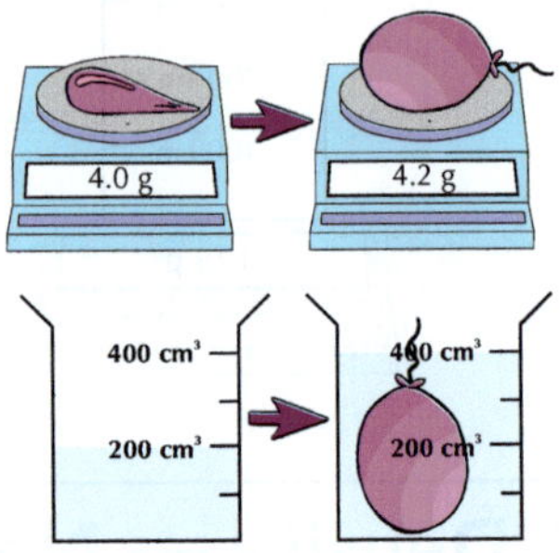


The density of air is approximately 0.001 g/cm³. You might not get very accurate results from this experiment because it doesn't take into account factors like the pressure of the air inside the balloon, or the volume of the balloon without air in. With more complex methods and equipment, scientists can accurately measure the density of air or any other gas.

# Warm-Up & Practice Questions

Well, that was a pretty dense section. Have crack at these Warm-Up Questions, then when you're confident you know your stuff and can handle a bit more pressure, move on to the Practice Questions.

## Warm-Up Questions

1) State two units of pressure.
2) Describe how to measure the pressure exerted by an object on the floor.
3) What happens to the area of a tyre that's touching the road if you decrease its pressure?
4) State two units of density.
5) Describe how to measure the density of a regularly-shaped object.

## Practice Questions

PRACTICAL

1 Akwesi wants to find out the density of a liquid he has.
He puts a measuring beaker on a mass balance and pours in some of the liquid.

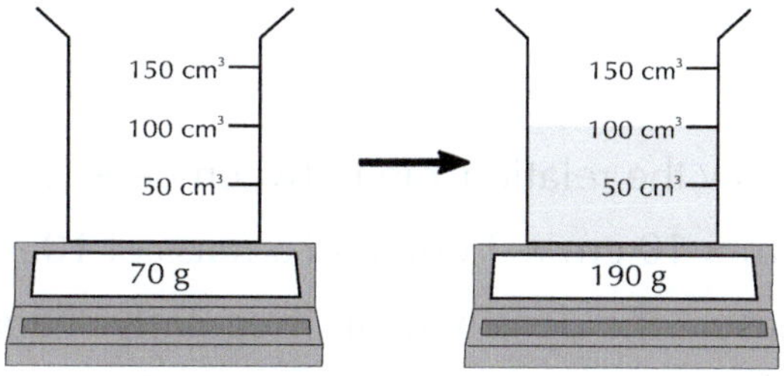


(a) (i) Calculate the mass of the liquid in the measuring beaker.

*(2 marks)*

(ii) The formula for calculating density is: Density = mass ÷ volume.
Calculate the density of the liquid.

*(2 marks)*

(b) Next Akwesi pours 50 cm$^3$ of another liquid into the beaker. The liquids are immiscible, and Akwesi observes that the second liquid floats on top of the first.
Explain why the second liquid floats on the first.

*(1 mark)*

2 Martin's mother wears shoes with a pointed heel. After she has walked across the floor, Martin notices that her heels have left dents in the floor.
Martin didn't leave any dents when he walked across the floor in his trainers.
Martin weighs 700 newtons and his mother weighs 600 newtons.

(a) Explain why his mother has dented the floor, even though she weighs less.

*(2 marks)*

(b) His mother's shoe heels have a total area of 0.0002 m$^2$. She leans back on her heels so that all of her weight acts through them onto the floor.

(i) State the formula for calculating pressure.

*(1 mark)*

(ii) Calculate the total pressure that his mother is putting on the floor when she is leaning back on her heels.

*(2 marks)*

# Summary Questions

Wow, Section P3 was pretty cool — all of that stuff on pressure and density is enough to get anyone excited... OK, maybe I'm trying a bit hard there. But I'm sure you'd love to see how much you know.

- Try these questions and tick off each one when you get it right.
- When you've done all the questions for a topic and are completely happy with it, tick it off.

## Pressure (p.111-p.112) ☐

1) What is pressure? ☐
2) If the force increases but the area it's applied over stays the same, what happens to the pressure? ☐
3)* A force of 200 N acts on an area of 2 $m^2$. Calculate the pressure. ☐
4)* A tomato weighs 1.2 N and exerts a pressure of 0.6 $N/cm^2$ on a table. Calculate the area of tomato touching the table. ☐
5) Explain why skis help people to walk on snow without sinking. ☐
6) Explain why blades need sharp edges to cut through some materials. ☐
7) Explain why a car may be more likely to skid if the pressure in its tyres in increased. ☐

## Density (p.113-p.114) ☐

8) What is density? ☐
9) Draw a formula triangle to show the relationship between density, mass and volume. ☐
10)* A brick has dimensions 10 cm × 10 cm × 3 cm, and a mass of 1050 g. What is its density? ☐
11) Describe how you could measure the density of an irregularly-shaped object. ☐
12)* An empty beaker has a mass of 100 g. The same beaker with 200 $cm^3$ of liquid in it has a mass of 350 g. What is the density of the liquid? ☐
13) Explain why oil floats on top of water when the two are poured into the same container. ☐
14) Which of these is usually the least dense — solid, liquid or gas? ☐
15) Describe how you could show that warm water is less dense than cold water. ☐
16) Describe what happens to the density of ice as it melts. ☐
17) Describe how you could estimate the density of air. ☐



*Answers on page 149.

# Sound

Time for a section on waves — first up, sound waves. Enter stage right...

## Sound Can't Travel Through a Vacuum

1) A sound wave is a wave of vibrating particles.
2) Sound waves are produced by a vibrating object.
3) Any substance that sound (or another wave, e.g. light) travels through is called a medium.
4) Sound needs a medium to travel through because something has to pass on the sound vibrations.
5) Sound can travel through solids, liquids and gases.
6) Sound takes time to travel. It has a finite speed in different mediums. How fast it travels depends on the medium it's in...
    1) Sound travels quickly in solids, because the particles of a solid are very close together (p.52). So it's easy for the particles to knock into each other and pass on the vibrations.
    2) Sound travels more slowly in water, as the water particles are further away from each other.
    3) Sound travels even more slowly in air, because the air particles are even further apart.
7) A vacuum is where there is nothing at all — no air, no particles, nothing. So sound can't travel through a vacuum.

Space is mostly a vacuum.

## You Can Measure the Speed of Sound

PRACTICAL

### Using an Echo Method:

An echo is heard when a sound is reflected from a surface.

1) Stand a long distance away from a wall (e.g. 100 m) and bang a drum.
2) Ask a friend to stand next to you and measure (using a stopwatch) the time taken between you making the noise and them hearing the echo.
3) You can calculate the speed of sound using the formula:

$$\text{speed} = \frac{\text{distance}}{\text{time}}$$

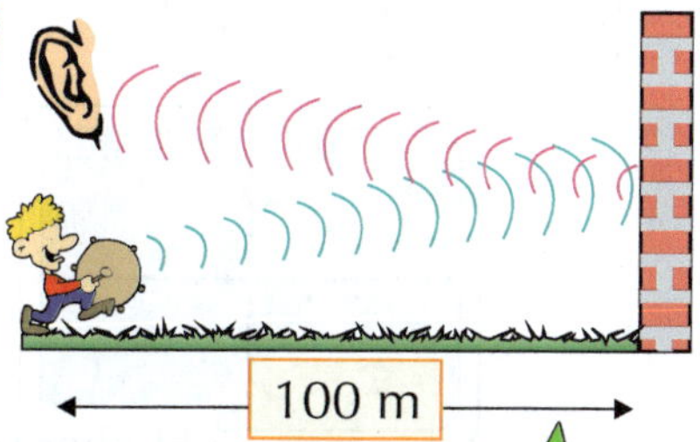


**Example**

**Calculate the speed of sound in this example, if it takes 0.6 seconds from banging the drum to hearing the echo:**

Distance = 200 m
Time = 0.6 seconds

Speed = 200 ÷ 0.6 = 333.33 m/s

The distance travelled is twice the distance between the people and the wall.

### Using Microphones:

1) Set up two microphones several metres apart. Measure the distance between them.
2) Set up the data logger so that it records the time taken for a sound to reach each microphone.
3) The sound could be made by a speaker or you could clap your hands.
4) Calculate the difference between these times. This gives the time taken for the sound to travel the measured distance between the microphones.
5) Use the formula speed = distance ÷ time to give you the speed of sound.

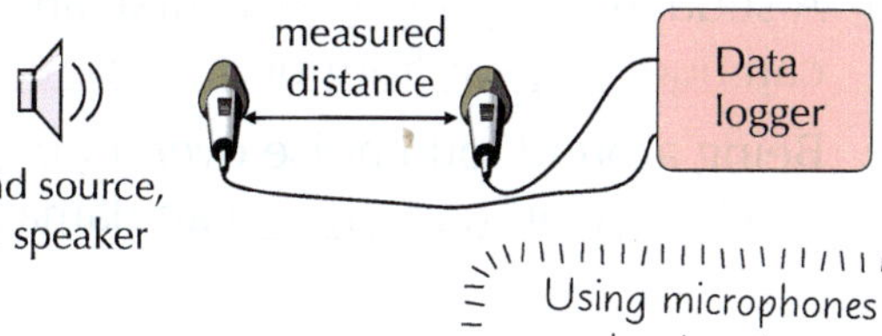


Using microphones and a data logger measures the speed of sound directly and is more accurate than using an echo method.

# More on Sound

Listen up — it's time to get noisy with another page on sound...

## Amplitude is the Loudness of Sound

An oscilloscope is an instrument that can display wave forms.

1) If sound is 'seen' on an oscilloscope it looks like this — a wave.
2) The amplitude of sound is the height of the wave.
3) The amplitude shows how much energy the sound has.
4) A large amplitude means the wave has lots of energy.
5) A large amplitude also means the sound is louder. So a wave with more energy has a bigger amplitude and is louder.
6) A whisper has a low amplitude — a shout has a large amplitude.

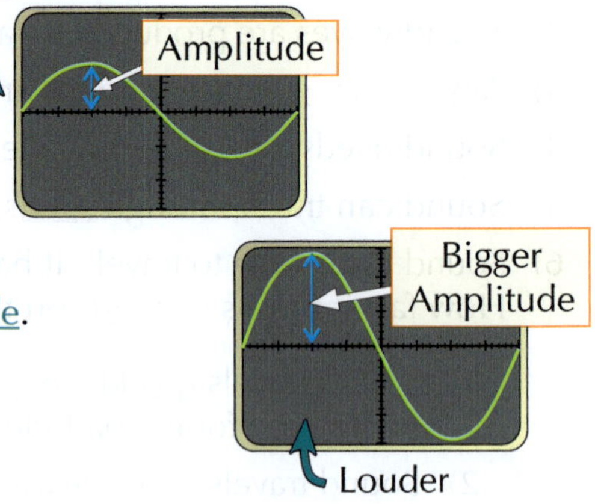


## Frequency is the Pitch of Sound

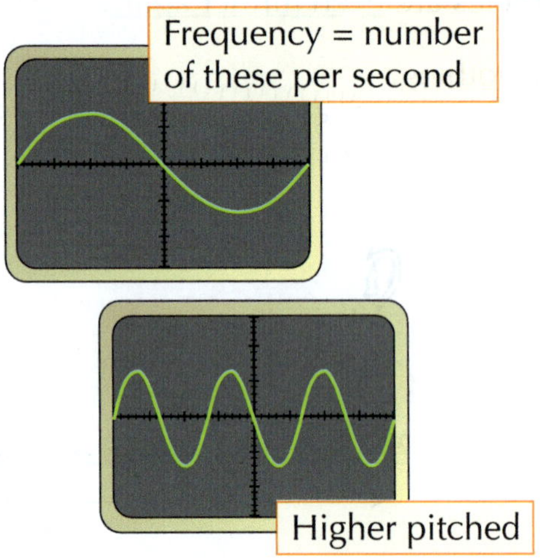


1) The frequency of sound is the number of complete waves that pass a point per second — it's a measure of how high pitched the note is.
2) A high frequency means more waves per second. More waves per second means the sound gets higher pitched.
3) So the higher the frequency, the higher the pitch.
4) A mooing cow produces low frequency sounds whilst screeching teenagers produce high frequency sounds. (All too frequently...)
5) Frequency is measured in hertz (Hz). So when you're chatting away, the frequency of your voice will be around 100-300 Hz.

## Loud Noises Can Damage Hearing

1) The vibrations in a sound wave cause your eardrum, then ear bones, then tiny hair cells deep inside your ear to vibrate. These vibrations result in messages being sent to your brain, so you hear the sound.
2) Loudness is measured in decibels (dB).
3) Hearing can be damaged by noises above 85 dB.
4) A sudden really loud noise (like an explosion) can burst the eardrum or damage ear bones.
5) Being around loud noise over a long period of time (such as noisy machinery or loud music can damage the hair cells in the ear.

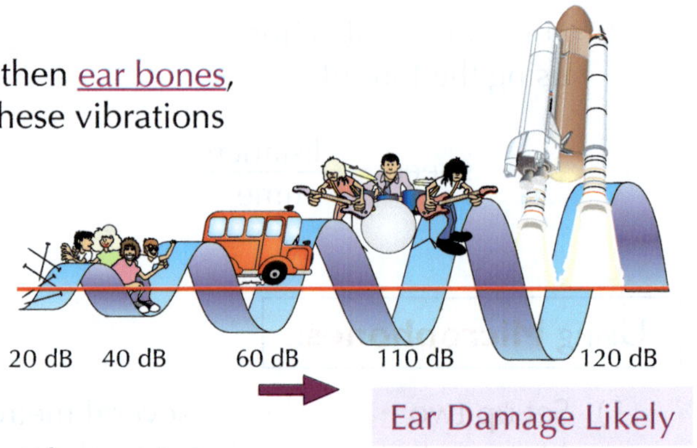


### Hopefully this is all music to your ears...

You may think that sound is a pretty harmless thing, but trust me, it can cause your ears real damage. Maybe think twice before turning your music up to full volume. Hopefully you heard me loud and clear.

# Hearing

They say gags about mishearing don't work in books. I think that's silly — I'm not fearing anything.

## People Have Different Auditory Ranges

1) Your auditory range is the range of frequencies (vibrations per second) that you can hear.
2) The auditory range of humans varies a lot — but it's typically 20-20 000 hertz (Hz).
3) This means we can't hear low-pitched sounds with frequencies of less than 20 Hz or high-pitched sounds above 20 000 Hz.
4) As you get older, the upper limit decreases, and sounds may need to be louder for you to hear them.
5) You can investigate how age affects the upper limit of the auditory range using a signal generator connected to a loud speaker...

PRACTICAL

   1) Start by playing a sound with a low frequency (20 Hz).
   2) Gradually increase the frequency, recording the point at which you can no longer hear the sound.
   3) Repeat this experiment with people in different age ranges.
   4) You should find similar results to these.

| Age Range (years) | Upper Limit (Hz) |
|---|---|
| 18 and under | 17 500 |
| 19 to 40 | 15 000 |
| 41 to 50 | 13 000 |
| 50 and over | 8 000 |

6) Some people can't hear higher pitched sounds for reasons other than age. Poor hearing like that can be caused by:
   1) Wax blocking ears.
   2) Nerve damage.
   3) Damage caused by illnesses and infections.

## Animals Have Different Auditory Ranges

1) Different types of animal have different auditory ranges.
2) Some animals like dogs, bats and dolphins can hear much higher frequencies than humans, as the chart shows.

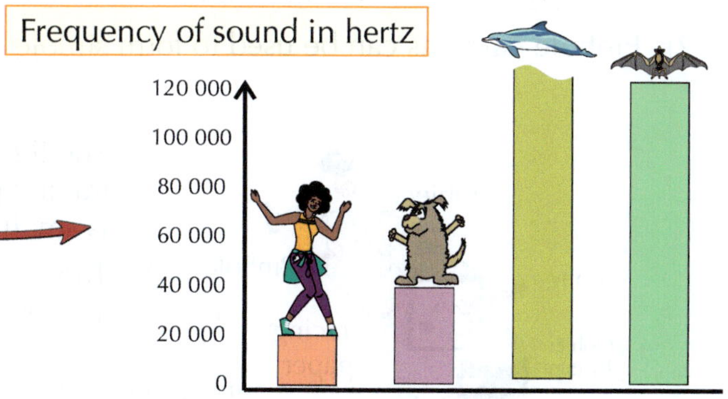


You could use the internet or books to research the different auditory ranges of animals.

### Hear me out...

REVISION TASK

Why not make a poster covering everything you need to know about sound? Make sure you include how sound is produced, the speed of sound and ways you can measure it, and what determines the loudness and pitch of a sound. Don't forget the stuff on hearing damage and auditory ranges too. Ooo, I can tell it's going to look just lovely stuck on the front of the fridge...

# Light

Light's fantastic — it's super-fast for a start. Here's a page all about light...

## Light is a Wave of Energy

1) Light comes from luminous sources such as the Sun, candles, light bulbs, flames and glow worms.
2) Light is a wave, which always travels in a straight line.
3) A light wave is also known as a light ray.

## Light Travels Faster Than Sound

1) Light travels very fast — much much faster than sound.
2) When a starting pistol is fired (some distance away), you see the smoke first — and hear the bang afterwards.
3) This is because the light reaches you before the sound does.

## Light Travels Fastest in a Vacuum

1) Light waves can travel through a vacuum (but sound waves can't — see page 117).
2) Nothing travels faster than light in a vacuum — it's the ultimate speed.
3) Although light is slower when it has to travel through matter (like air or water), it's still so fast that its movement appears instant to the human eye.

## The Pinhole Camera is a Simple Camera

1) A pinhole camera is a box with a tiny hole at one end. It doesn't have a lens or any electronics.
2) Pinhole cameras can be used to form simple images on a paper screen.

1) The light travels in a straight line from the sheep to the tracing paper screen through the pinhole. Because the hole is small, only one ray gets in from each point on the sheep.
2) The image of the sheep is upside down and crossed over. This is because the light rays cross over inside the camera:

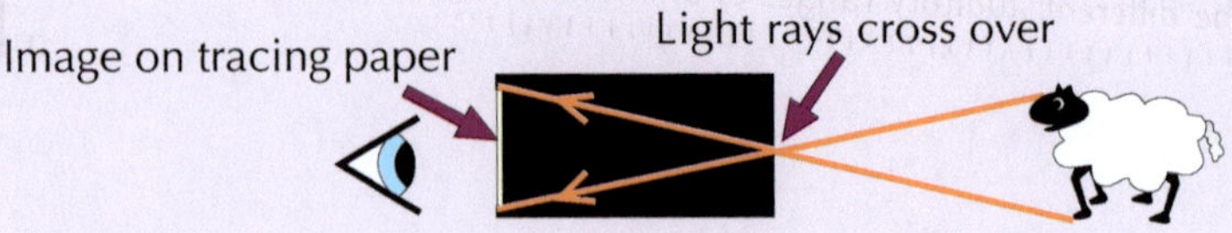


Take a look at the next page for more on light rays.

**Pinhole camera? Check. Sheep? Che...wait, what?**

Light travels fast — I mean really fast. "Faster-than-Usain-Bolt-running-away-from-a-bear" kind of fast.

# Reflection

Take a moment and reflect on what you're about to learn...

## Mirrors Have Shiny Surfaces Which Reflect Light

1) Light rays reflect off mirrors and most other things.
2) Plane (flat) mirrors have a very smooth shiny surface, which allows each light ray to reflect off it at the same angle, giving a clear reflection.
3) You can draw a ray model diagram by remembering the law of reflection:

Angle of incidence = Angle of reflection
Angle i = Angle r

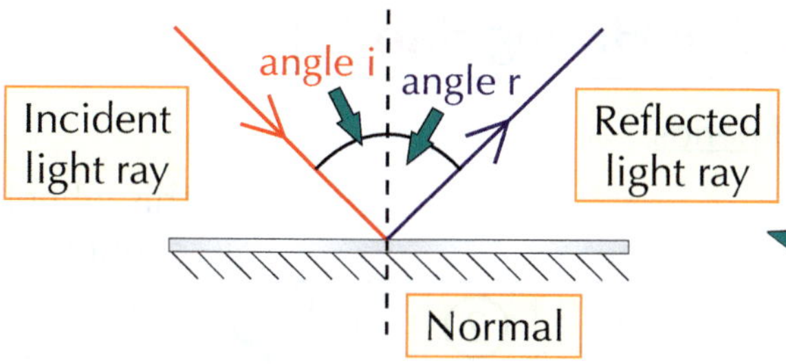


4) The angle of incidence and the angle of reflection are always measured between the light ray and the normal.
5) The normal is a line at a right angle (90°) to the surface.

The reflected light rays that reach Charlene makes it look like Scott is in the mirror.

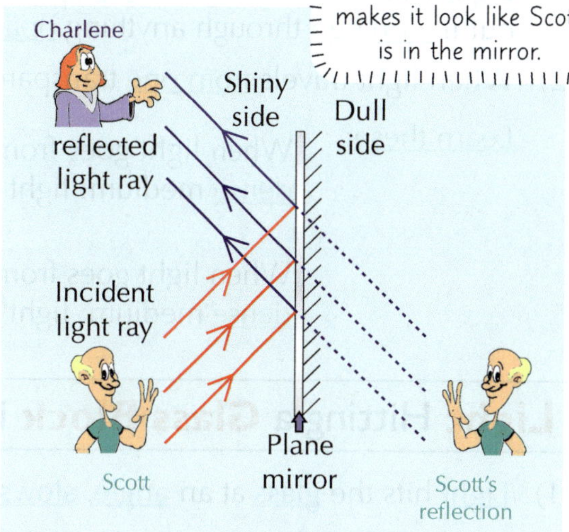


This is a ray diagram. Make sure you draw straight lines and get the angles the same when drawing ray diagrams (use a ruler and a protractor).

## Periscopes Are Really Useful

Periscopes use mirrors to let you see around an obstacle. They can be used in submarines, etc.

A simple periscope is made up of two mirrors held in a tube — each mirror is angled at 45° so that light reflects into the user's eyes.

This example of a simple periscope only uses flat mirrors. However, periscopes on submarines use a more complex system of lenses and mirrors.

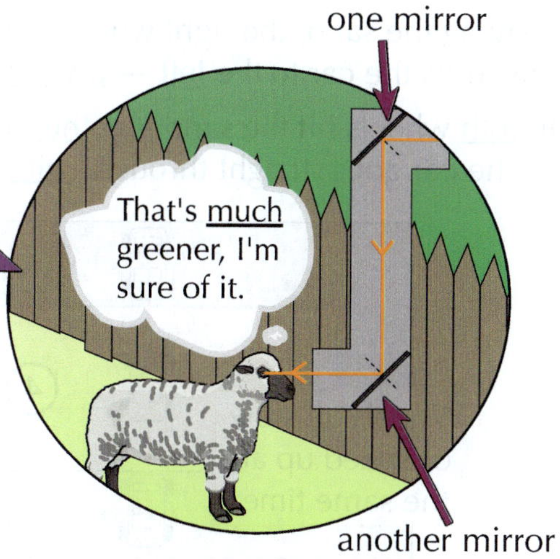


### Mirror mirror on the wall, you reflect light rays, that is all...

REVISION TASK

Why not try explaining to a friend how a periscope works? Draw them a picture of a periscope including ray diagrams to show how the light reflects off the two mirrors. If you're feeling especially ambitious you could even make a periscope to assist your explanation — they'll love it.

# Refraction

Refraction is all about light bending — nothing to do with redoing your maths homework.

## Refraction is When Light Bends as it Crosses a Boundary

1) Light will travel through transparent (see-through) materials, but it won't go through anything opaque (not see-through).
2) When light travels from one transparent medium to another, it bends or refracts.

There's more about light travelling through a material on the next page.

Learn these:

When light goes from a less dense medium to a more dense medium: light bends towards the normal. — Example: air to glass.

When light goes from a more dense medium to a less dense medium: light bends away from the normal. — Example: glass to air.

## Light Hitting a Glass Block is Like a Car Hitting Sand

1) Light hits the glass at an angle, slows down and bends.

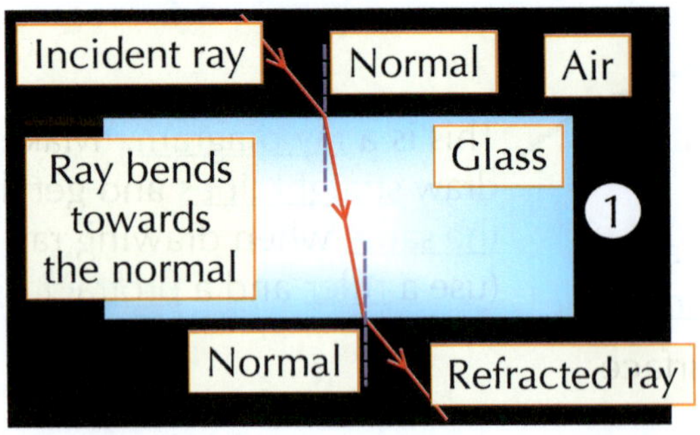


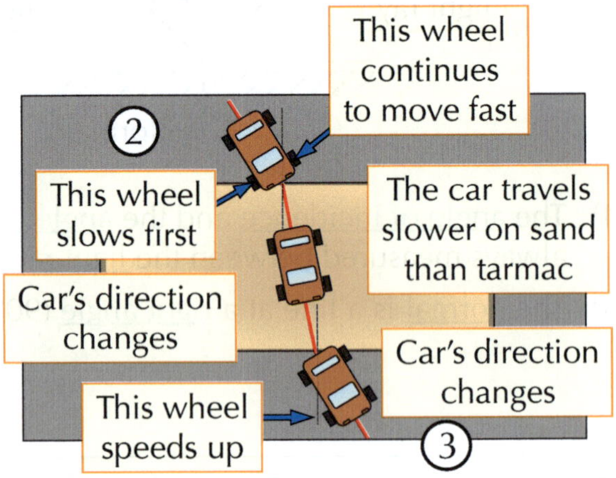


2) It's a bit like a car hitting sand at an angle. The right wheel get slowed down first and this turns the car to the right — towards the normal.
3) Leaving the sand, the right wheel speeds up first and this turns the car to the left — away from the normal.
4) If both wheels hit the sand together they slow down together, so the car goes straight through, without turning.

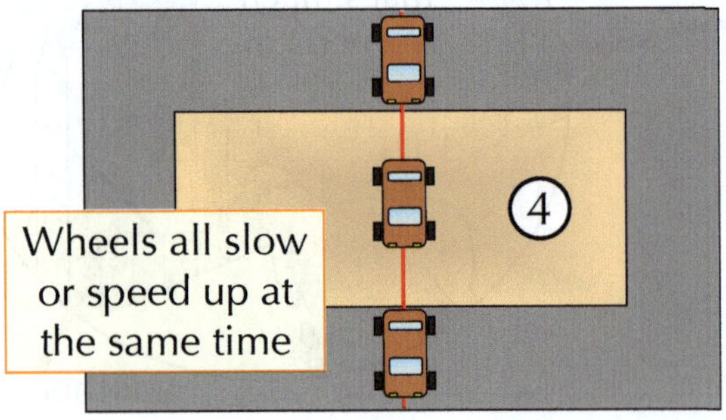


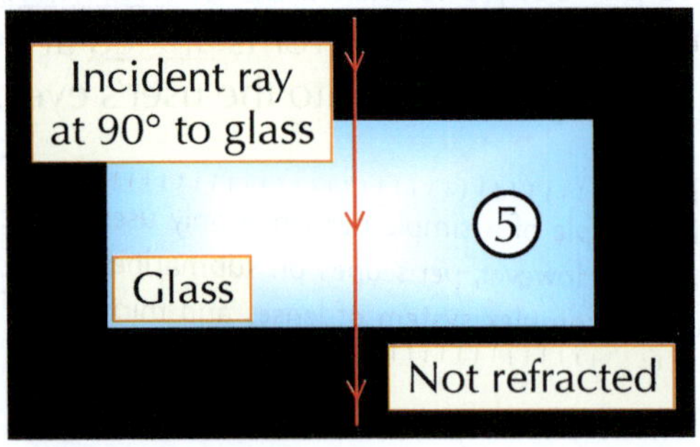


5) Light does exactly the same when it hits the glass block straight on.

**REVISION TIP**

### Don't get reflection and refraction mixed up...

Refraction — the first thing you've got to do is spot that it's a different word to reflection. Watch, I'll do it again: ref-l-e-c-tion and ref-r-a-c-tion. Now all you need to do is learn what they are, and all the details about how they work. It really helps to learn the patterns of the light rays — reflected rays form a V-shape, and refracted rays form a badly drawn Z- or S-shape.

# Light and Materials

Light can be transmitted or absorbed by a material. And if it's transmitted, you could get a rainbow...

## Some Materials Transmit Light

1) Materials that don't absorb light are called transparent — the light is transmitted through them.
2) When light travels through a transparent material, it can be refracted (see previous page).
3) Glass windows are an example of a transparent material.

## Some Materials Absorb and Scatter Light

1) Some materials are translucent, e.g. tracing paper. Some light passes through them but not all of it.
2) Some of the light is absorbed by the material, and some is scattered (reflected back in lots of different directions).
3) The result is that light can be seen through the material, but it does not give a clear picture like transparent materials do.

## White Light is Not Just a Single Colour

1) White light is actually a mixture of colours. This shows up when white light is transmitted through a prism or a raindrop. It gets dispersed (i.e. split up) into a full rainbow of colours.
2) Each of the different colours of light has a different frequency.
3) As white light travels through a prism, the different frequencies are refracted by different amounts causing the light to disperse (i.e. split up), which gives you the rainbow of colours, called a spectrum.

**PRACTICAL**

- You can try this out for yourself using a ray box and a glass prism.
- A ray box produces thin rays of light which, when pointed at a prism, will disperse to create a spectrum.
- It's best to do this in a dimly lit room so you can clearly see the light rays.

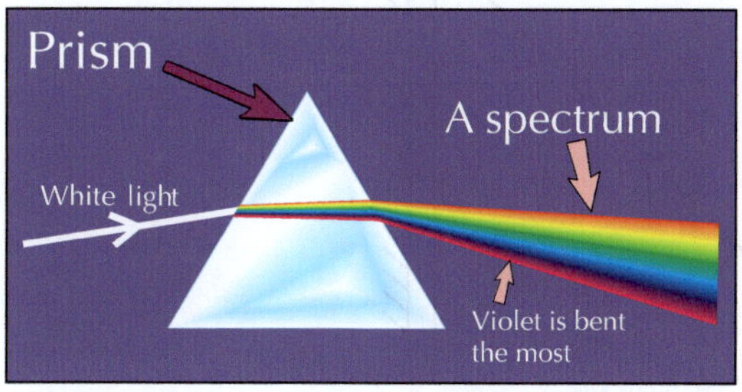


4) A similar thing happens for a natural rainbow — different colours are refracted by different amounts in raindrops.

5) Learn the order that the colours come out in: Red Orange Yellow Green Blue Indigo Violet
6) Remember it with this historical jollyism: Richard Of York Gave Battle In Velvet

### Oooh pretty colours...

You'll only get a rainbow in the sky if it's sunny and raining — the rainbow is always on the opposite side of the sky to the Sun. And it's not magic that makes them, it's good ol' white light and refraction.

# Warm-Up & Practice Questions

Have a bash at these questions, and see how far you get. If you can't answer some of the questions, or get an answer wrong, go back and read the relevant pages again. Then have another go at these questions until you can do them all.

## Warm-Up Questions

1) Name one thing that sound can't travel through.
2) Explain what is meant by the 'amplitude of sound'.
3) What determines the pitch of sound?
4) Which travels faster: light or sound?

## Practice Questions

1 Bruno is carrying out some investigations using light.
First, he shines a ray of light at a mirror.
The ray diagram below shows the ray of light hitting the mirror.

(a) Complete the diagram to show how the ray of light is reflected from the mirror.

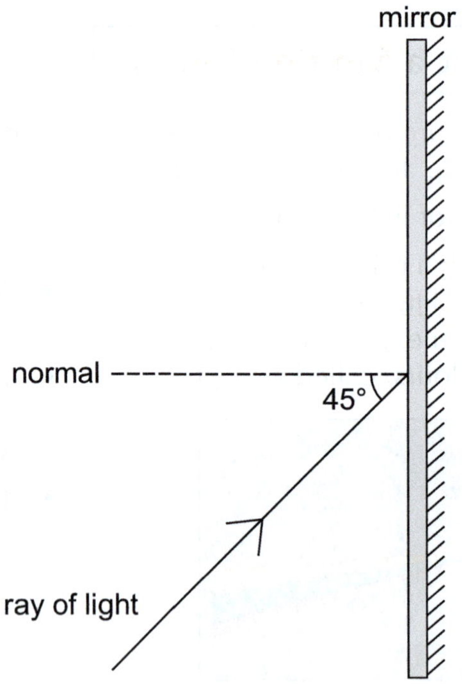


*(2 marks)*

(b) Next, Bruno shines a ray of white light at a prism.

(i) Describe what Bruno will see.

*(1 mark)*

(ii) Explain why this happens.

*(3 marks)*

# Practice Questions

(c) Bruno then places a block of glass with parallel sides in the path of the ray of light. He notices that the light bends when it enters the glass block, and bends again when it exits the far side of the glass block.

(i) The glass block is much more dense than air. In which direction does the light bend when it enters the glass block?

*(1 mark)*

(ii) Draw a ray diagram to show the light entering and leaving the block.

*(2 marks)*

**PRACTICAL**

2 Amber is investigating the speed of sound using an echo method.
She stands 125 m away from a wall and asks a friend to stand next to her.
She then asks her friend to measure the time between Amber sounding a horn and the point when they hear the echo.
It takes 0.78 seconds for them to hear the echo of Amber's horn.

(a) Calculate the speed of sound using the formula:
speed = distance ÷ time

*(1 mark)*

(b) Give an appropriate unit for the answer to this calculation.

*(1 mark)*

3 Guy is investigating sound waves.
He is making sounds and recording them using a microphone.
Below are three of the sound waves as seen on an oscilloscope.

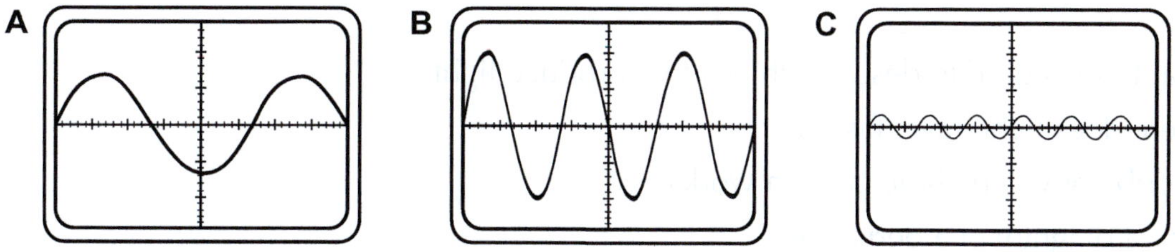


(a) Which sound wave has the largest amplitude?

*(1 mark)*

(b) Which sound wave has the highest frequency?

*(1 mark)*

(c) Guy makes the sound recorded in diagram **A** again, but with a higher amplitude. Describe how the sound heard would differ from the original.

*(1 mark)*

(d) Guy makes the sound recorded in diagram **C** again, but with a lower frequency. Describe how the sound heard would differ from the original.

*(1 mark)*

# Summary Questions

Section P4 tells you everything you need to know about sound and light. There are quite a few words in there — and some pretty important diagrams too. Science isn't always a complete doddle, so you're bound to find some of the facts a bit tricky to learn. Never fear! As somebody famous once said, "Nothing can take the place of persistence" — in other words, if you want to achieve anything worthwhile or difficult, all you have to do is keep on slogging away at it. Better get cracking with this lot then...

- Try these questions and tick off each one when you get it right.
- When you've done all the questions for a topic and are completely happy with it, tick it off.

## Sound and Hearing (p.117-p.119) ☐

1) What is a sound wave? ☐
2) How is a sound wave produced? ☐
3) Why do sound waves need a medium to travel through? ☐
4) Why can't you hear a ringing bell in a vacuum? ☐
5) What is an echo? ☐
6) How could you measure the speed of sound directly? ☐
7) If you were to 'see' a sound wave on an oscilloscope, which bit would show the amplitude? ☐
8) Which would have a larger amplitude — a shout or a whisper? ☐
9) Which would have a higher frequency — a high pitched note or a low pitched note? ☐
10) Describe how a sudden loud noise might damage the ear. ☐
11) Describe how being around loud noise over a long period of time might damage the ear. ☐
12) What does auditory range mean? ☐
13) True or false? Humans can hear the same range of sounds as all other animals. ☐

## Light and Reflection (p.120-p.121) ☐

14) What term is used to describe things that produce light? ☐
15) Where does light travel fastest? ☐
16) Describe how a pinhole camera works. ☐
17) Draw a diagram of a periscope. ☐

## Refraction and Light and Materials (p.122-p.123) ☐

18) What is refraction? ☐
19) What happens when light goes from a more dense medium to a less dense medium? ☐
20) What is meant by:
    a) a transparent material, b) a translucent material? ☐
21) Write down the order of the colours in a spectrum, starting from red. ☐

# Electrical Circuits

First up in this section, a page that covers all the basics of electricity...

## Electric Current is the Flow of Charge

1) Electric current is the flow of charge around a circuit.
2) It can only flow if a circuit is complete.
3) The moving charges are negatively charged particles called electrons.
4) It's vital that you realise that current is not used up by any components as it flows through a circuit. The total current in the circuit is always the same.
5) The more cells (or batteries) in a circuit, the higher the current.

A component is anything you put in a circuit.

A cell is a single electrical energy source. A battery is two or more cells put together.

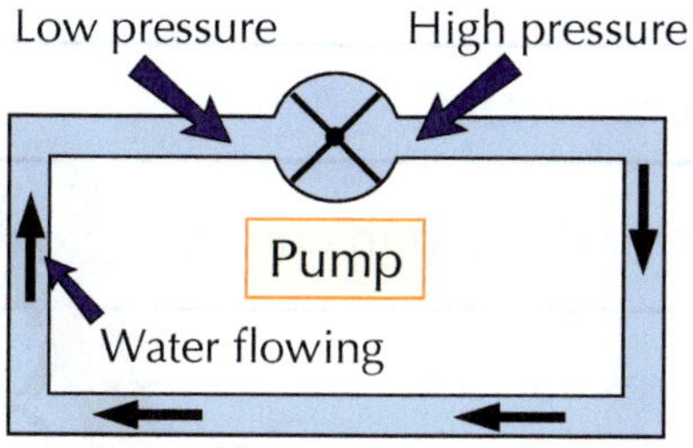


**Current is a bit like water flowing...**

The pump drives the water along like a power supply. The water is there at the pump and is still there when it returns to it — and just like the water, electric current in a circuit doesn't get used up either.

## Resistance is All About How Easily Electricity Can Flow

1) Resistance is anything in a circuit that slows down the flow of current.
2) The lower the resistance of a component, the better it is at conducting electricity.
3) So the lower the resistance of a component, the greater the current through it.
4) Components and materials that electricity can easily travel through (e.g. metals) are called conductors — they have low resistance.
5) Components and materials that electric charges don't easily pass through (e.g. wood/plastic) are called insulators — they have high resistance.

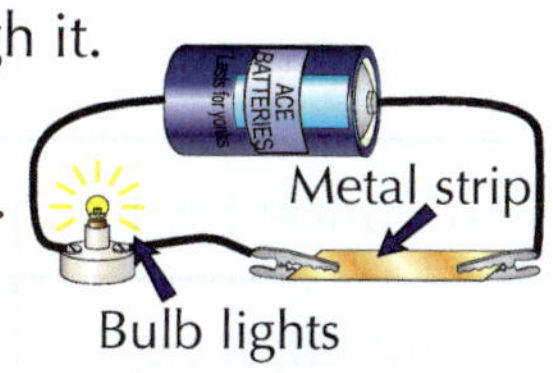


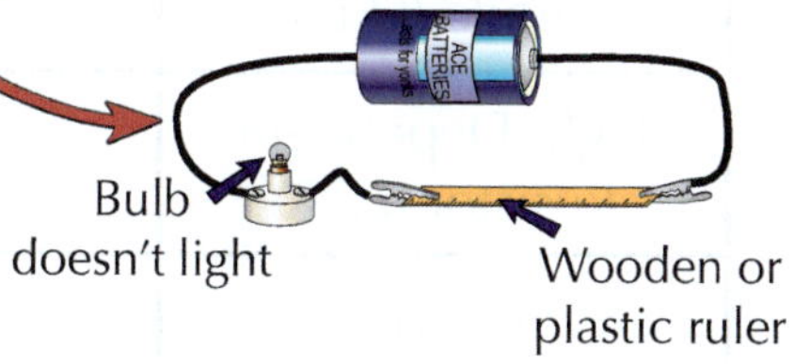


### Ammeters Measure Current

1) Ammeters measure electric current. It's measured in amperes (or amps, A, for short).
2) You measure the current through a circuit by inserting the ammeter into the circuit in series (see p.129), like this:
3) The ammeter can be inserted anywhere along the circuit, the current measured will be the same.
4) Remember — current doesn't get used up, so the current through the ammeter is the same as through the bulb.

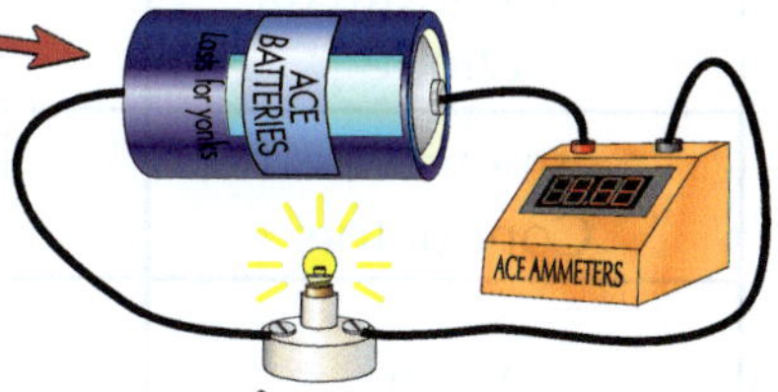


**Investigating the Resistance of Different Materials**

Replace the bulb with any material, and measure the current using the ammeter. Repeat for different materials. The lower the current recorded, the higher the material's resistance.

## I have a low resistance to cakes and biscuits...

We use electricity for a lot these days — just look around you and you'll likely see something electric. Back in my day it was all candlelight and horse-drawn carriages (that's right, I'm er... 200 years old...).

# More on Electrical Circuits

Whether you're constructing circuits or drawing circuit diagrams, knowing these symbols is essential.

## Lots of Components can be Put in Circuits

You'll have already come across circuit diagrams before — simplified diagrams of real circuits showing components as symbols. Well, here are some components you need to know about and their symbols:

The symbol for a cell (see p.127) is: 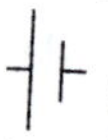

| Component | Symbol | Function |
|---|---|---|
| Battery | 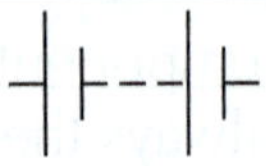 | Power source |
| Bulb/lamp | 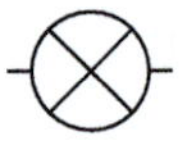 | Lights up when a current is passed through |
| Resistor |  | Reduces current |
| Variable Resistor | 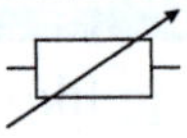 | Gives control over reduction in current |
| Ammeter | 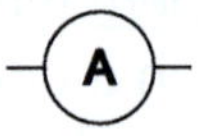 | Measures current |
| SPST |  | Simple on-off switch |
| Reed Switch |  | Switch controlled by a magnetic field |
| Electromagnet | 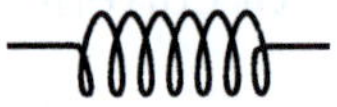 | Coil of wire with magnetic field |
| Motor | 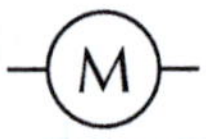 | Spins when a current is passed through |
| Push Button Switch |  | Switch controlled by button |
| Light Emitting Diode (LED) | 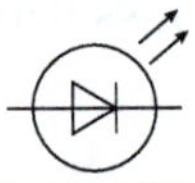 | Lights up when a current is passed through |
| Light Dependent Resistor (LDR) | 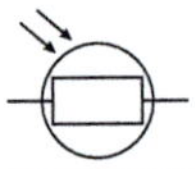 | Resistance decreases when light is shone on it |
| Buzzer |  | Makes a buzzing sound when current is passed through |
| Semiconductor Diode | 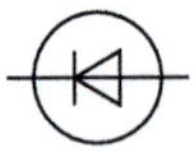 | Only lets current flow in one direction |
| Junction of Conductors |  | Point where current has a choice of multiple paths |
| Relay | 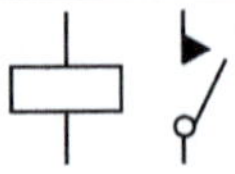 | Switch controlled by an electromagnet |
| Fuse | 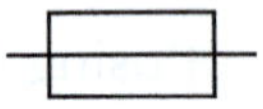 | Breaks the circuit if current is too high |

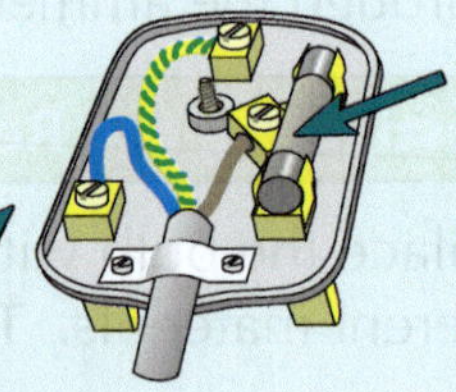

Fuses are often found in plugs.

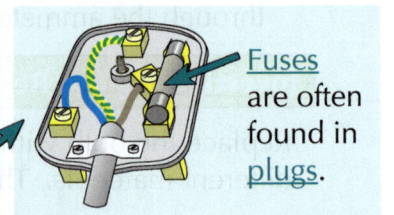

### If you like drumming, then you'll love symbols...

REVISION TASK

Try covering up the circuit symbols above and draw out as many you can. Then go back over them and learn the ones you forgot. Cover them again and repeat until they're in your head.

# Series Circuits

In a series circuit, every part of the circuit is on the same path. This may all sound nice and simple, but if one bulb within the circuit blows, it breaks the entire circuit. What a pain.

## Series Circuits — Current has No Choice of Route

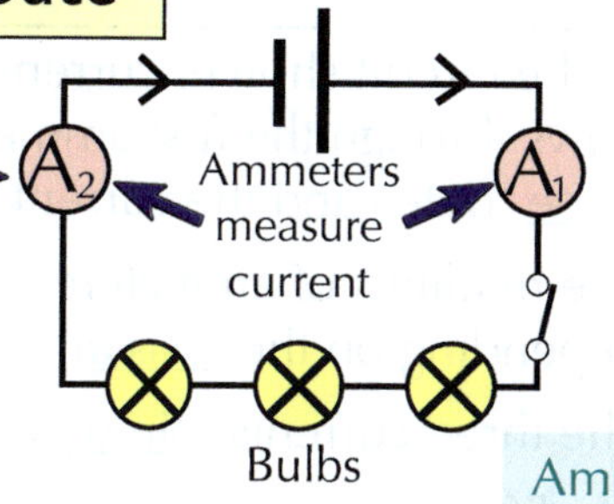


Ammeter readings: $A_1 = A_2$

1) In the circuit on the right, current flows out of the cell, through the ammeter, the switch, the bulbs, then through the other ammeter and back to the cell. As it passes through, the current gives up some of its energy to the bulbs.
2) The current is the same anywhere in this circuit as the current has no choice of route. Remember — current isn't used up.
3) In series circuits the current is either on or off — the switch being open or any other break in the circuit will stop the current flowing.
4) The number of components in a series circuit can affect the current — more components increase the resistance and reduce the current.
5) The type of component will also affect the current. High resistance components will reduce the current in the circuit more than low resistance components.
6) Changing the number of cells in a series circuit also affects the current (see p.127).

Circuits can be used in so many applications. For example, the circuit on the right is a very basic alarm circuit — by switching it on, the buzzer will make a sound.

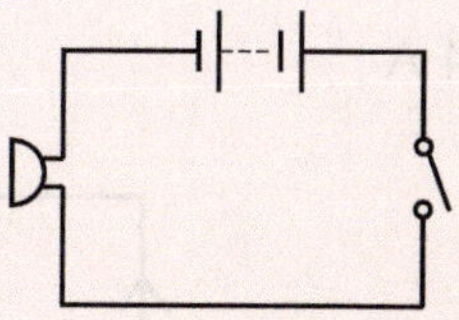

## You Need to be Able to Construct Series Circuits

PRACTICAL

Circuit diagrams are basically instructions for how to build a circuit from scratch. Make sure you know all the symbols on p.128 (I won't remind you again), so you can look at a circuit diagram and construct the circuit it shows.
To give you an idea, here's an example of a circuit diagram and the circuit it represents...

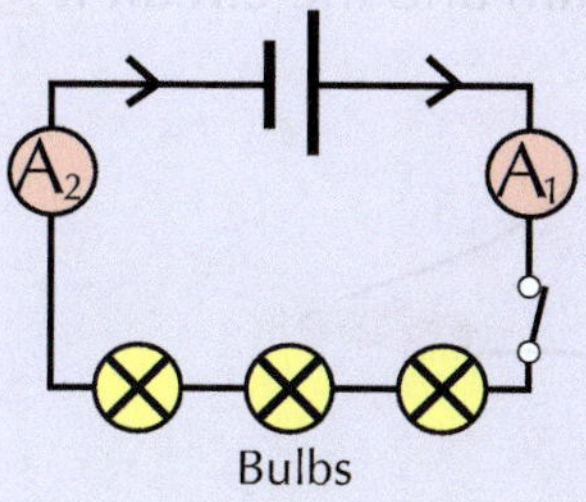


=

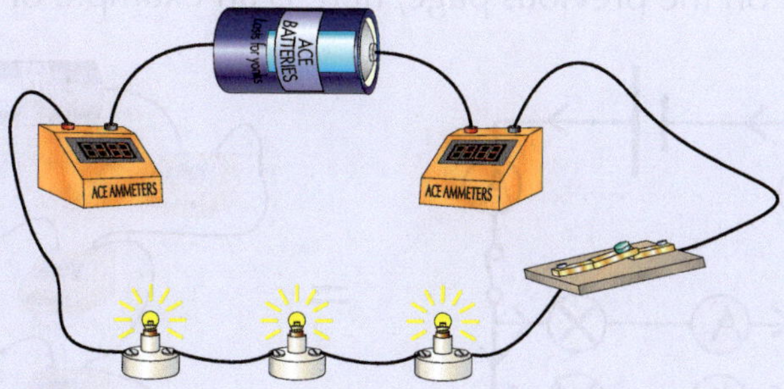


Ammeter readings: $A_1 = A_2$

### Why don't you wire your house lights in series?

REVISION TIP

If a bulb breaks, all the lights in a series circuit would go off, leaving you in total darkness.
If you're struggling with series circuits, try using the water analogy from page 127. The same 'water' flows through everything, so the current through all of the components is the same.

# Parallel Circuits

The big difference between series and parallel circuits is that in parallel circuits, current can take different routes around the circuit. And the charges don't even need a map or a GPS to do it...

## Parallel Circuits — Current has a Choice

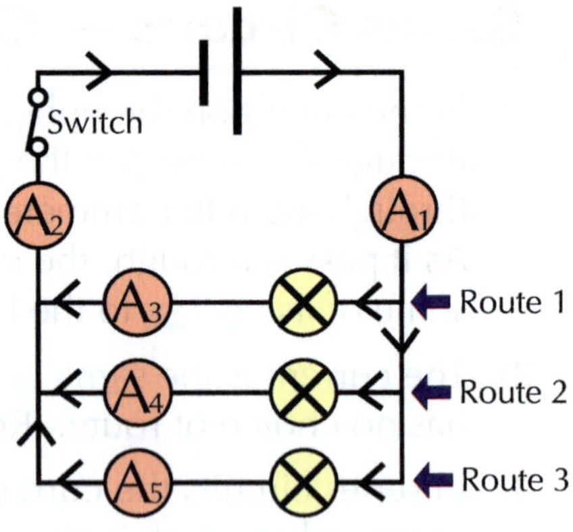


1) In the circuit shown, current flows out of the cell and it all flows through the first ammeter $A_1$. It then has a "choice" of three routes and the current splits down routes 1, 2 and 3.
2) The readings of ammeters $A_3$, $A_4$ and $A_5$ will usually be different, depending on the resistances of the components — i.e. the bulbs.
3) The three currents join up again on their way back to the cell.
4) It's difficult to believe I know, but the current through $A_1$ is the same as the current through $A_2$ — the current is not used up. (I may have told you that once or twice already.)
5) So the readings of $A_3 + A_4 + A_5$ added together will be equal to the reading for current on ammeter $A_2$ (which will also equal $A_1$).

The current splits here, so the readings on $A_2$ and $A_3$ should add up to $A_1$.

**Example**

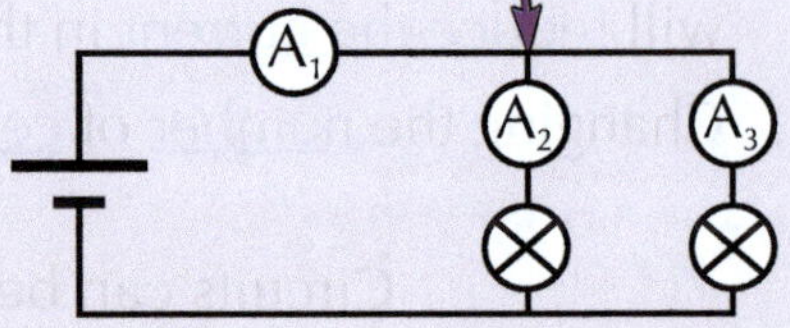


**In the circuit on the right, the ammeter reading on $A_1$ is 12 A and the reading on $A_2$ is 8 A. What will the reading on $A_3$ be?**

$A_3 = 12 - 8 = 4$ A

Switch 2 is open so current CAN'T flow through that bulb

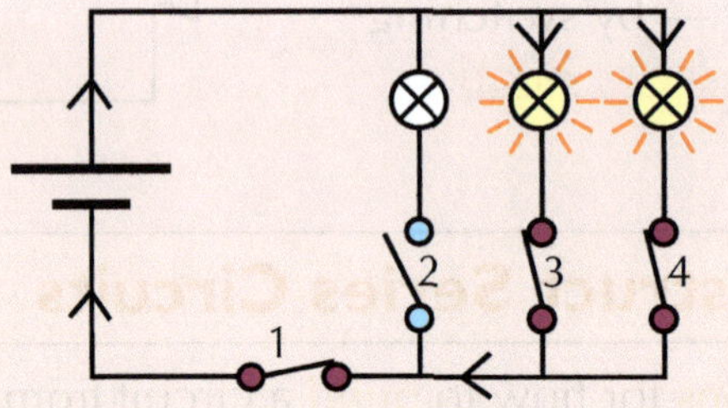


Parallel circuits are useful because part of them can be on while other bits are off. In the circuit here, two bulbs are on and the other one is off.

## You Need to be Able to Construct Parallel Circuits

PRACTICAL

It's not just series circuits you need to know how to construct — it's parallel ones too.
Just like on the previous page, here is an example of a circuit diagram and the circuit it represents...

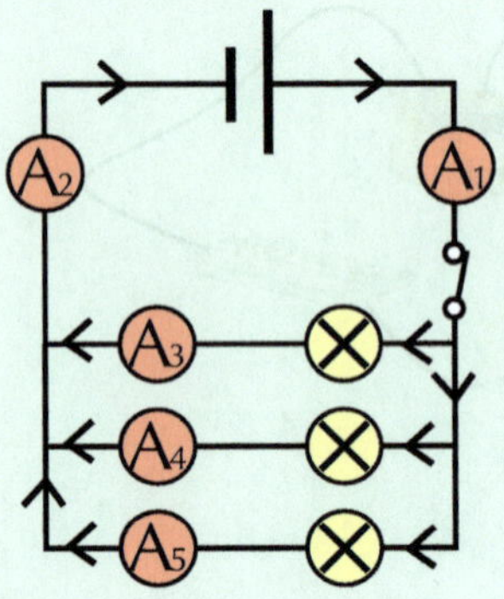


=

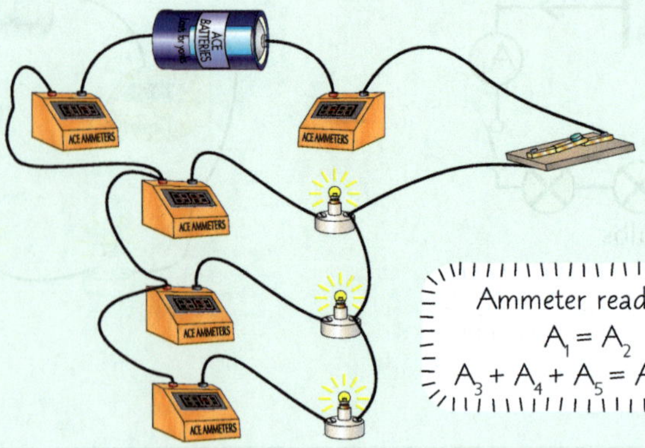

Ammeter readings:
$A_1 = A_2$
$A_3 + A_4 + A_5 = A_1 = A_2$

### Get your hard hat on — it's time to do some constructing...

Circuits can be tricky as you can't actually see the current flowing, so it's very difficult to appreciate what's going on. Give these last few pages a proper read though, and you should be seeing some physics progress.

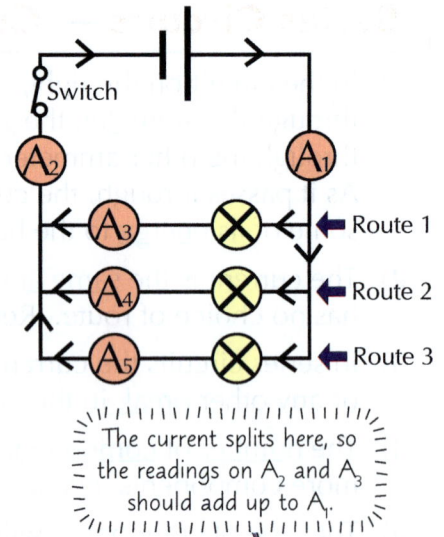

# Magnets

Magnets can push and pull each other without touching. Sounds like magic, eh? Nah, it's just science.

## Magnets are Surrounded by Fields

1) Bar magnets are (surprisingly enough) magnets that are in the shape of a bar. One end of the bar magnet is called the North pole (or North-seeking pole) and the other end is called the South pole (or South-seeking pole).
2) All bar magnets have invisible magnetic fields round them. A magnetic field is a region where magnetic materials (e.g. iron) experience a force.
3) You can draw a magnetic field using lines called magnetic field lines. The magnetic field lines always point from the N-pole to the S-pole.
4) As well as showing the direction of the magnetic field, they also show its size — the closer the field lines are to each other, the stronger the magnetic field at that point. The further you get from a magnet, the weaker the field.

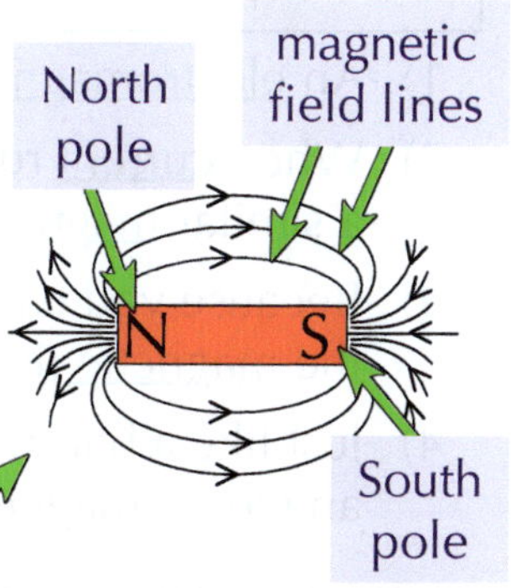


The magnetic field is strongest at the poles.

## Unlike Poles Attract — Like Poles Repel

Magnets don't need to touch for there to be a force between them.

Unlike poles are different poles i.e. a North and a South pole. Like poles are two of the same poles.

**Attraction**

North poles and South poles are attracted to each other.

**Repulsion**

If you try and bring two of the same type of magnetic pole together, they repel each other.

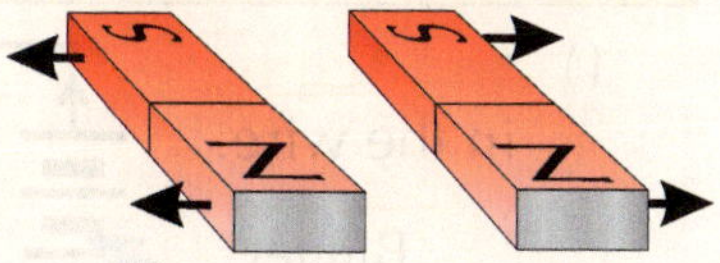


## Testing for a Magnet Using Repulsion

The only way to check if a material is a magnet is to hold it next to a known magnet to test for repulsion. Start by bringing each end of the material close to a known magnet...

...if either end REPELS, it must be a MAGNET.

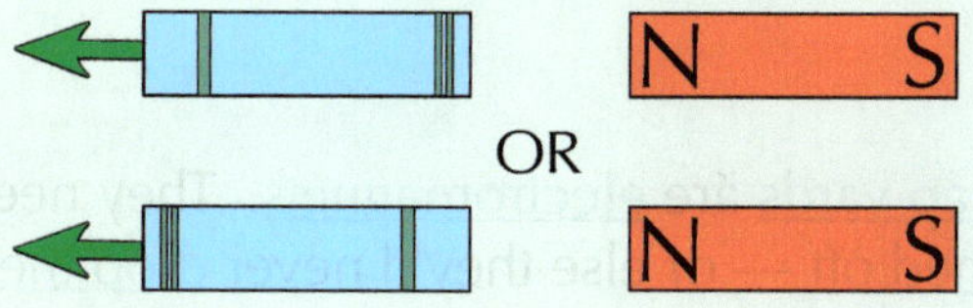


...if both ends ATTRACT, it is NOT A MAGNET (but it is magnetic).

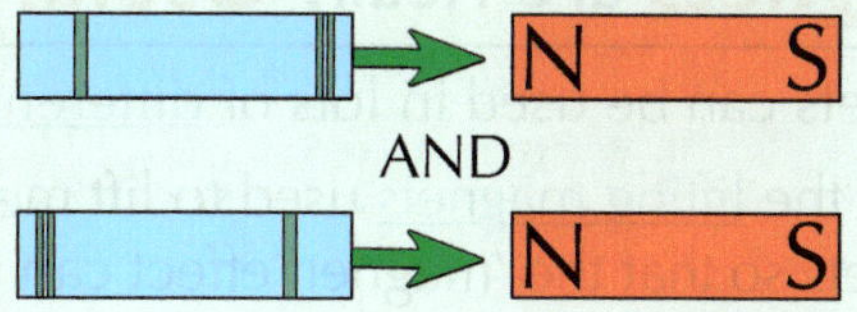


If it does nothing (no attraction or repulsion) it is not magnetic.

## The Earth has a Magnetic Field

1) The Earth has a magnetic field. It has a North pole and a South pole, just like a bar magnet.
2) A freely suspended (hanging) bar magnet will always align itself north-south in line with the Earth's magnetic field (unless it's really close to another magnet).
3) The needle of a compass (also known as a plotting compass) is a small bar magnet. It aligns with the Earth's magnetic field, and so always points North.

If you put a compass near a magnet, the needle will align itself with the magnet's magnetic field. So you can use a compass to find the shape of the magnetic field around a magnet.

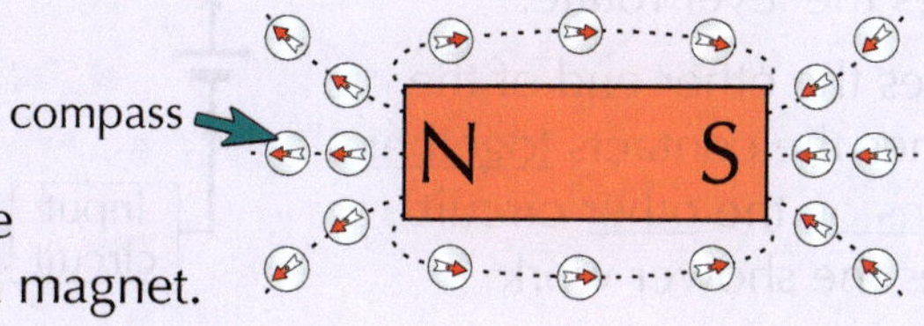


Pouring iron filings around a bar magnet also reveals the shape of its magnetic field.

# Electromagnets

Bar magnets are always magnetic. Electromagnets are fancy magnets which you can turn on and off.

## A Wire With a Current in it Has a Magnetic Field Round it

1) An electromagnet is made from a coil of insulated wire with a current passing through it.
2) When current runs through the coil of wire, it has a similar magnetic field pattern to a bar magnet.
3) Because you can turn the current on and off, the magnetic field can be turned on and off.
4) Just like a bar magnet, you can test for the magnetic field of an electromagnet using iron filings or a plotting compass...

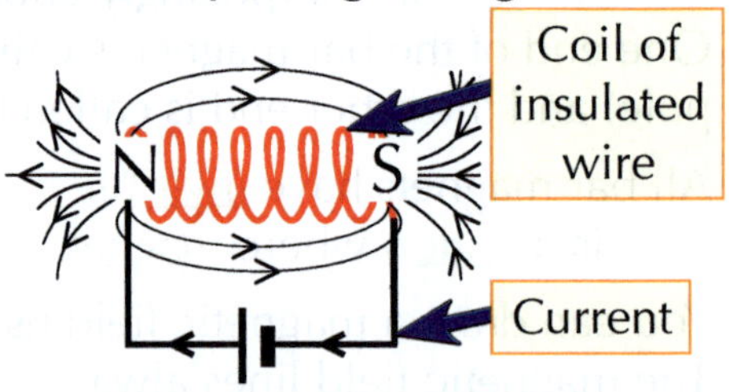


The iron filings will align along the field lines which looks quite jolly.

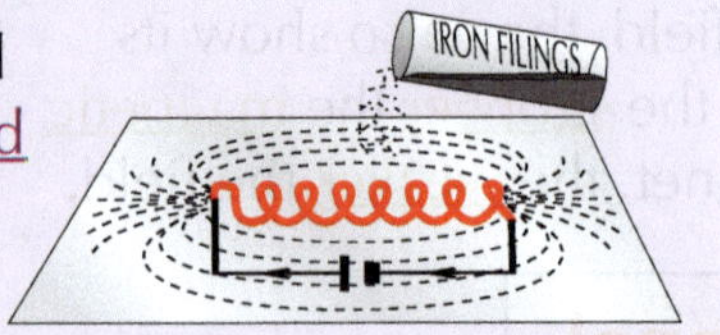


The plotting compass will always point from N to S along the field lines wherever it's placed in the field.

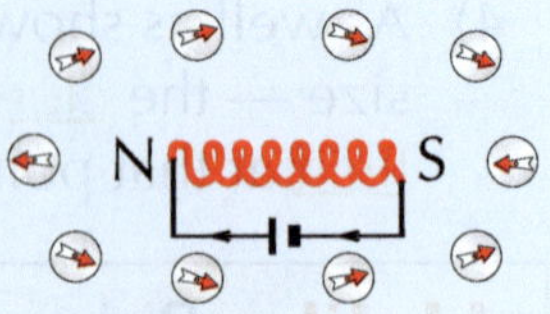


5) To make an electromagnet, wrap an insulated wire around an iron core. When current flows though the wire, the iron becomes magnetised.

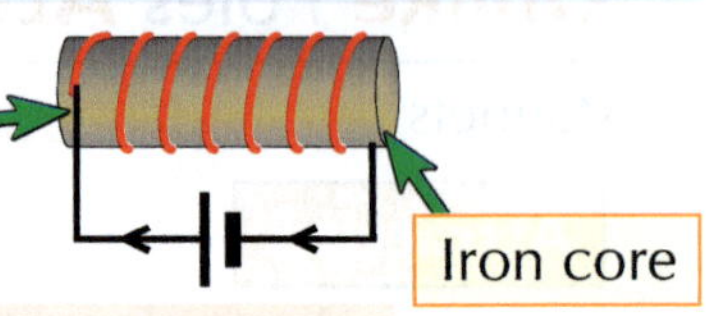


**You can increase the strength of an electromagnet by adding:**

1) More current in the wire.

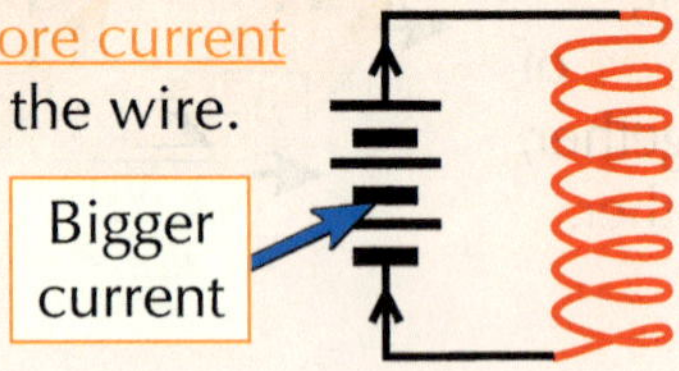


Doubling the current will double the strength of the magnet.

2) More turns on the coil.

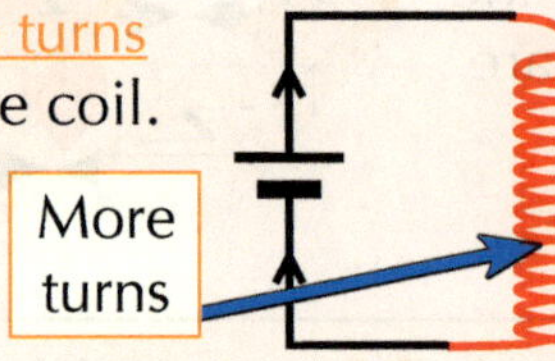


You can try this out by recording the distance at which a light magnetic object (e.g. a paperclip) is first attracted to an electromagnet. You should find that if you increase the strength of the electromagnet (by increasing the current, or the number of turns on the coil) the distance at which the attraction is first felt increases.

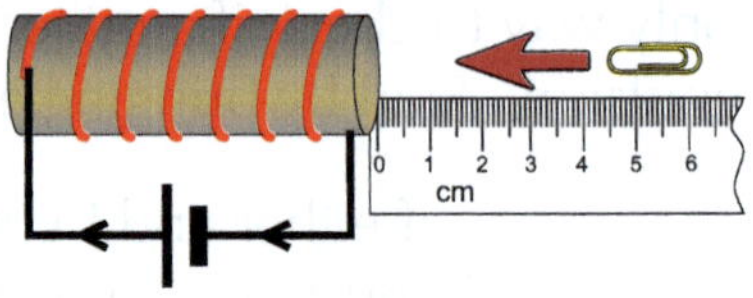


## Electromagnets are Really Useful

1) Electromagnets can be used in lots of different ways.
2) For example, the lifting magnets used to lift metal in scrap yards are electromagnets. They need to be electromagnets so that the 'magnet' effect can be switched off — or else they'd never drop the metal.

### Electromagnets are also Used in Relays

1) Relays link together two circuits, so that turning on one circuit causes the other to turn on too.
2) They are used to turn on very high-current circuits using a lower-current circuit, as they help to stop the user from coming into contact with the high current.

**Example — shower**

1) When the small current is switched on the electromagnet activates and the iron lever is attracted to it. This makes the lever rotate.
2) As it rotates the other end of the lever pushes the contacts together which turns on the other circuit and makes the shower work.

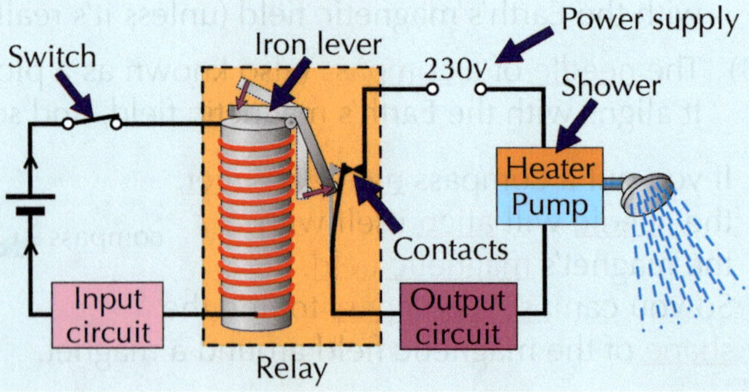

# Warm-Up & Practice Questions

There's a good mix of Warm-Up Questions here to get yourself started. Once they're done, you can launch yourself into the more difficult Practice Questions. What a great way to spend an evening.

## Warm-Up Questions

1) What is electric current?
2) What is an insulator? Give an example.
3) What do ammeters measure?
4) Draw the circuit symbols for: a) a resistor b) a fuse c) an ammeter.
5) Suggest why it can be useful to connect bulbs in a parallel circuit rather than a series circuit.
6) What is a magnetic field?

## Practice Questions

1 Look at the following circuit diagram.

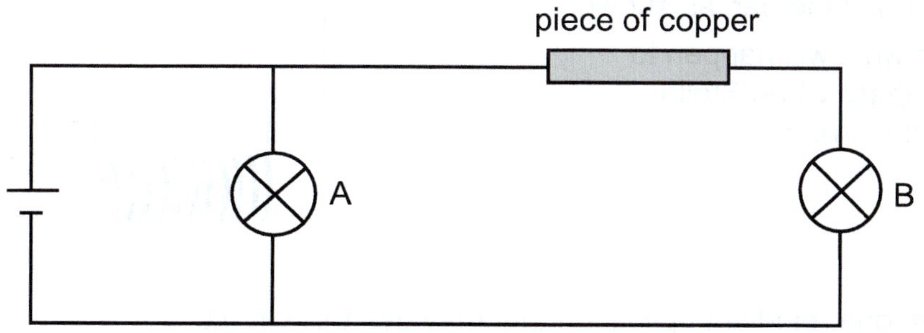


(a) Choose the correct name for this type of circuit, from the words below:

**parallel** **power** **double** **series**

*(1 mark)*

(b) In the circuit, both bulbs are on.
If the piece of copper was replaced with a piece of wood, describe what would happen, if anything, to:

(i) Bulb A.

*(1 mark)*

(ii) Bulb B.

*(1 mark)*

(c) Explain your answers to (b)(i) and (b)(ii).

*(3 marks)*

2 In the diagram below, the poles have not been marked on the magnets.
The magnetic field lines are shown.

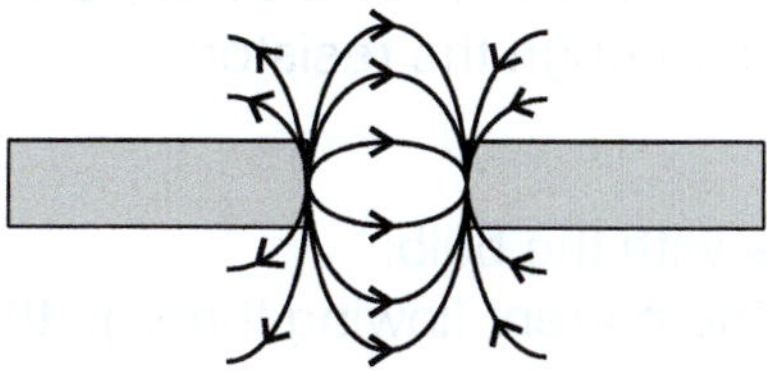

Copy the diagram, marking the poles of each magnet (use N = North, S = South).
Give a reason for your choices.

*(2 marks)*

# Practice Questions

3 Stella wraps a piece of insulated wire around an iron bar and connects it to a simple circuit.

(a) When Stella switches on the circuit she finds she can pick up three steel paper clips using the wire coil.
Suggest **one** change to the apparatus to make the coil pick up more paper clips at once.

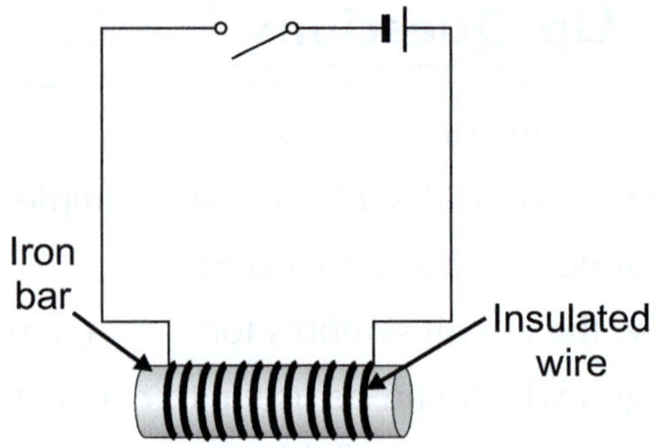


*(1 mark)*

(b) Stella opens the switch and places a small compass next to the end of the bar, as shown.
Explain what will happen to the compass when Stella closes the switch.

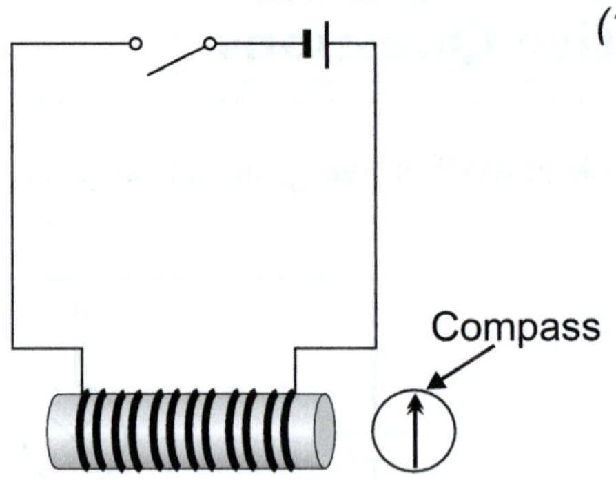


*(2 marks)*

(c) Suggest one real-life application that may use this circuit.

*(1 mark)*

4 Jade builds a simple electrical circuit.
The circuit diagram for Jade's circuit is shown below.

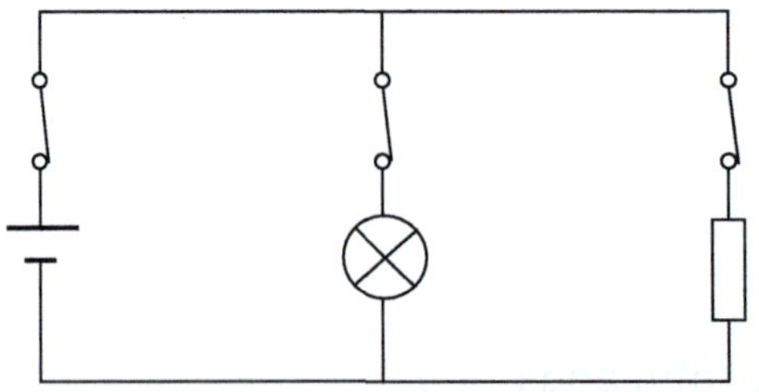

(a) Jade measures the current that is flowing through the bulb in her circuit.
The current flowing through the bulb is 0.60 A.
The current flowing through the cell in Jade's circuit is 1.90 A.
Calculate the current flowing through the resistor.

*(1 mark)*

(b) Jade adds a motor in series with the bulb.
Explain how this will affect the current flowing through the bulb.

*(2 marks)*

# Summary Questions

Phew. Circuits and Magnets — it's no holiday, that's for sure. There are certainly quite a few grisly bits and bobs in this section. Then again, life isn't all bad — just look at all these lovely questions.

- Try these questions and tick off each one when you get it right.
- When you've done all the questions for a topic and are completely happy with it, tick it off.

## Electrical Circuits (p.127-p.130)

1) True or false? Current can't flow in an incomplete circuit.
2) What happens to the current in a circuit if you add more batteries to the circuit?
3) What is resistance?
4) What is the difference between a conductor and an insulator?
5) Give an example of a material with a low resistance.
6) Give an example of a material with a high resistance.
7) What is the unit of current?
8) What is a circuit diagram?
9) Draw the symbol for all of these components:
   a) a battery b) a buzzer c) a reed switch
   d) an SPST (open) e) a light emitting diode f) a variable resistor.
10) Describe the function of each of these components:
   a) a fuse b) a motor c) a resistor.
11)* A series circuit contains 3 bulbs. A current of 3 A flows through the first bulb. What current flows through the third bulb?
12) Which circuit would have a larger current — one with three high resistance components, or one with three low resistance components?
13) True or false? The current in a parallel circuit cannot split, and so the current always follows the same route.
14) Which type of circuit allows part of the circuit to be switched off?

## Magnetism (p.131-p.132)

15) In which direction do field lines always go in a magnetic field?
16) Name two magnetic poles that will: a) attract each other b) repel each other.
17) What is the only true test for determining if a material is a magnet or not?
18) Explain why the needle of a compass will always point North if it's not close to another magnet.
19) What is an electromagnet?
20) Draw a diagram showing how a plotting compass points around an electromagnet.
21) Give two ways to increase the strength of an electromagnet.
22) Name two uses of electromagnets.

* Answer on page 150.

# Gravity

It's not magic, superglue or heavy shoes that keep your feet on the ground — it's gravity.

## Gravity is a Force that Attracts All Masses

1) Anything with mass will attract anything else with mass. In other words, everything in the Universe is attracted by the force of gravity to everything else. (But you only notice it when one of the things is really big, like a planet.)

A planet is something which orbits around a star.

2) You're attracted to the Earth by gravity. Gravity's a constant force, pulling you towards the centre of the Earth at all times.
3) The more massive the object (or body), the stronger the force of gravity is (so planets with a large mass have a large gravitational pull).

4) The further the distance between objects, the weaker the gravitational attraction becomes.

## Gravity Gives You Weight — But Not Mass

To understand this you must learn all these facts about mass and weight:

1) Mass is just the amount of 'stuff' in an object. The mass of an object never changes, no matter where it is in the Universe.
2) Weight is caused by the pull of gravity.
3) An object has the same mass whether it's on Earth or on another planet (or on a star) but its weight will be different. For example, a 1 kg mass will weigh less on Mars than it does on Earth, simply because the force of gravity pulling on it is less.

Weight is a force measured in newtons (N). It's measured using a spring balance (known as a newton meter). Mass is not a force. It's measured in kilograms (kg) with a mass balance.

### Learn this Important Formula...

**Weight = mass × gravitational field strength**

$$W = m \times g$$

(Weight in N, mass in kg, gravitational field strength in N/kg)

1) The letter "g" represents the strength of the gravity and its value is different for different planets. On Earth g = 10 N/kg. On Mars, where the gravity is weaker, g is only about 3.7 N/kg.
2) You can use this formula to work out how much an object weighs:

**Example**

**What is the weight, in newtons, of a 5 kg mass on Earth?**
On Earth, g = 10 N/kg, so:
Weight = mass × gravitational field strength = 5 × 10 = 50 N
So, on Earth, an object with a mass of 5 kg weighs 50 N.

If the object was on Mars, it would weigh less, because Mars' gravity is weaker.

REVISION TIP

**Just make sure you appreciate the gravity of all this...**
Make sure you really know your units — weight is measured in newtons, and mass is measured in kilograms. If you write the wrong one in the exam, you'll lose marks.

# The Solar System

Ahh. This is going to be a nice page, I can tell. Look at all those lovely big pictures for a start.

## Gravity Keeps the Solar System Together

1) The Sun (at the centre of our Solar System) is a star. The Earth is one of eight planets which orbit the Sun.
2) The further a planet is from the Sun, the less of the Sun's energy is transferred to it, so the colder it is. E.g. it's about –200 °C on the surface of Neptune. (An exception to the rule is Venus, which is actually hotter than Mercury due to its thick atmosphere).
3) The planets in our Solar System all move in elliptical orbits (stretched circles) around the Sun.
4) The Sun has a huge mass, so its gravity is very strong.
5) The pull from the Sun's gravity is what keeps all the planets in their orbits.
6) It's not only planets that are kept in place by gravity — the pull from Earth's gravity keeps the Moon and satellites (see p.140) in orbit around the Earth.

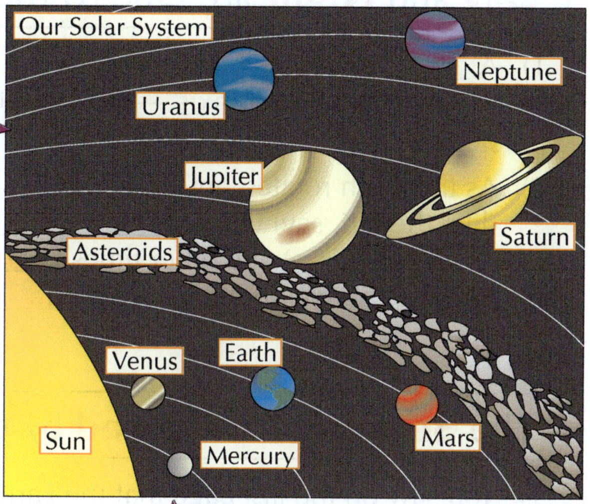


Make sure you know the order of the planets from the Sun.

## Orbits Come in All Different Shapes and Sizes

1) It takes the Earth 365 ¼ days to fully orbit the Sun. That's what a year actually is — the time it takes to complete one full orbit. So there are 365 ¼ days in an 'Earth year'.
2) The time it takes for one object to fully orbit around another is also called it's orbital period.
3) The further a planet is from the Sun, the longer it takes to complete one full orbit. The same is true for satellites — the further a satellite is from a planet or star, the longer its orbital period.

## Telescopes Let Us See the Solar System

Scientists use large, powerful telescopes to study the Moon and the planets in our solar system. Here are some examples of images taken through telescopes:

Telescopes can be used to see much further than just our own galaxy (the Milky Way) — some can even see stars in galaxies that are billions of light years away.

The Sun and other stars are light sources — they give out light. But the planets and the Moon are not light sources — we can only see them because they reflect the Sun's light.

### Galaxies, the Milky Way — physicists must like chocolate...

REVISION TASK

See if you can get a parent or a teacher to set you up on an online telescope so you can have a good nosey at space. You might get a bit freaked-out seeing what's hanging round up there, but viewing space in real life should hopefully make you more interested in revising all things space.

# The Movement of the Earth

In years to come, this stuff will come up in a quiz and you'll be able to wow your teammates with the answer. You also need to know it for your exam. So get cracking...

## Day and Night are Due to the Steady Rotation of the Earth

1) A day is how long it takes a planet to rotate once on its axis — the Earth does one complete rotation in 24 hours.
2) As the Earth rotates, any place on its surface (like the UK, say) will sometimes face the Sun (in the day time) and other times face away into dark space (in the night time).

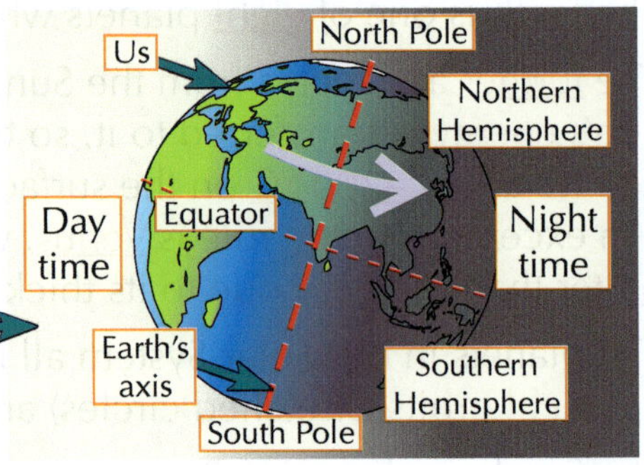


## The Seasons are Caused by the Earth's Tilt

1) You saw on the last page that the Earth takes 365 ¼ days to orbit once around the Sun. That's one year of course. (The extra ¼ day is sorted out every leap year.)
2) Each year has four seasons. The seasons are caused by the tilt of the Earth's axis.

A leap year has an extra day added. We have one every 4 years.

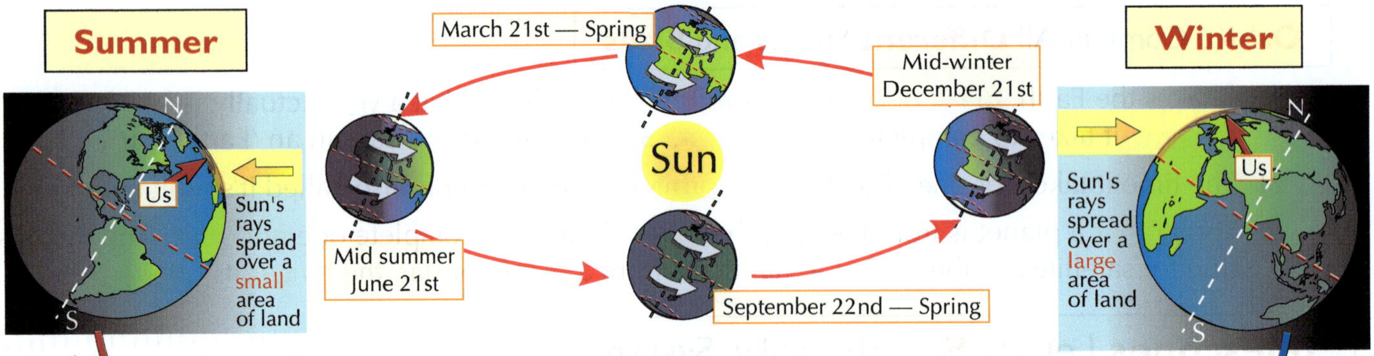


1) When it's summer in the UK, the northern hemisphere (everything above the equator) is tilted towards the Sun.
2) The northern half of the Earth spends more time in sunlight than it does in darkness, i.e. days are longer than nights. Longer days mean more hours of sunshine — so the land heats up.
3) Not only that, but the Sun's rays cover a small area of land. This means that the heat is focused on a small area. So it gets warm and we have summer — hoorah.

1) When it's winter in the UK, the northern hemisphere is tilted away from the Sun.
2) The northern half of the Earth now spends less time in sunlight so days are shorter than nights.
3) Also, the Sun's rays cover a larger area of land so the heat is more spread out. So it gets colder and we have winter.

When it's summer in the northern hemisphere, it's winter in the southern hemisphere — and vice versa.

REVISION TASK

### This page is jam-packed with fascinating facts

There's a lot to learn on this page, so you might like to try the mini-essay method. Scribble down a mini-essay that covers all the details on this page. Then check to see what you missed.

# The Movement of the Earth

People used to think the Earth stayed still and everything else moved around it. How wrong they were...

## The Sun Doesn't Move Round the Earth — the Earth Rotates

1) The Sun "rises" in the EAST and "sets" in the WEST. It seems like this to us because the Earth is rotating.
2) The Sun is highest in the sky at midday. (12.00 noon in winter, but 1.00 pm in British Summer Time.)
3) So shadows are always shortest at midday. This is because the Earth is tilted on its axis.
4) The tilt of the Earth causes the seasons (see p.138) and the height of the Sun in the sky changes from season to season.
5) The Sun is highest in the sky during summer and lowest during winter.
6) So shadows are shorter in summer than winter.

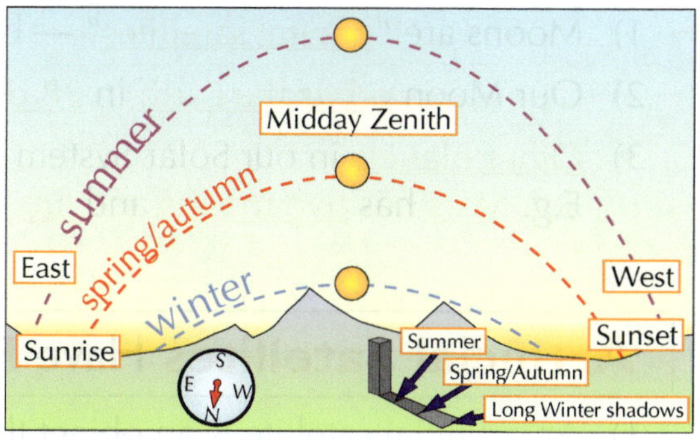


## The Stars Look Like They Move in Circles — But They Don't

1) The picture on the right is like a long exposure taken over several hours at night. It shows that the stars seem to move in circular paths around the night sky.
2) This is all simply caused by the rotation of the Earth.
3) The Pole Star in the north of the sky stays "fixed" and the other stars "rotate" slowly around it. This is because the Pole Star is directly above the Earth's axis of rotation. This makes it really handy for navigation.

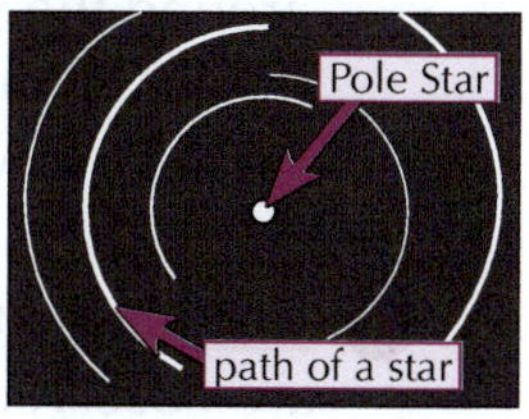


## Eclipses Happen When Light From the Sun is Blocked

During a total solar eclipse, it's darker and colder than normal day time.

### Solar Eclipse — an Eclipse of the Sun

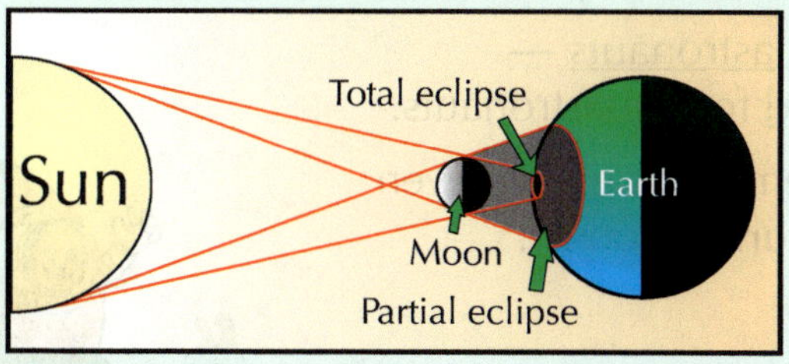


1) A solar eclipse is when the Moon passes between the Sun and the Earth, blocking the Sun's light from reaching Earth.
2) Some places will see a total eclipse (when all of the Sun's light is blocked) and some will see a partial eclipse (when only some of the light is blocked).

### Lunar Eclipse — an Eclipse of the Moon

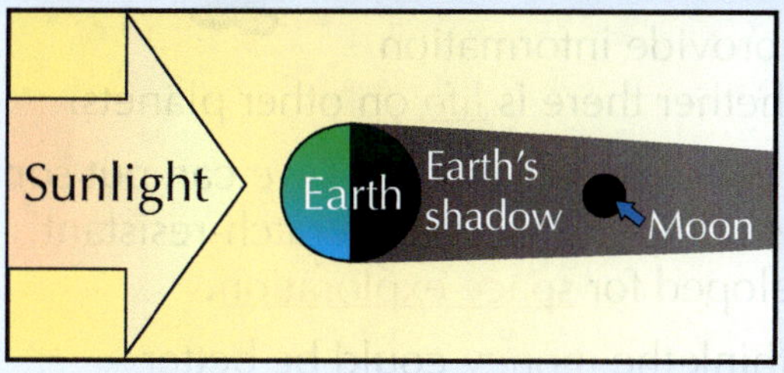


1) A lunar eclipse is when the Earth passes between the Sun and the Moon, blocking the Sun's light from reaching the Moon.
2) This means the Moon is less visible.
3) Lunar eclipses can be total or partial.

## Aaaargh — the Sun's been eaten by a giant sky monster...

Seeing a total solar eclipse* is amazing, but if you want to see one in the UK, you'll have to wait 'til 2090...

*If you ever get the chance to see one, don't look directly at the Sun, it can damage your eyes.

# Satellites

Everyone's heard of satellite TV but did you know the Moon is also a satellite?

## A Satellite is Something Which Orbits Round a Planet or Star

1) Moons are "natural satellites" — because they're natural objects which orbit around planets.
2) Our Moon orbits the Earth in 28 days — that's its orbital period.
3) Other planets in our Solar System have moons.
   E.g. Mars has two moons and Jupiter has 79 (talk about being greedy).

## Artificial Satellites Have Four Main Uses

1) An artificial satellite is an object that people have put into orbit around a planet.
2) There are thousands of artificial satellites orbiting round Earth. These are the four main things that they're used for:

1. Communication and Navigation — Radio, TV and telephone signals are relayed around the world. Satellites are also used for GPS (Global Positioning System) — what sat navs use to pinpoint their location.
2. Monitoring the Weather — Weather systems are observed to help weather forecasting.
3. Observing the Earth — Spy satellites have military uses and satellite imaging helps to map the land and monitor the environment.
4. Exploring the Solar System — E.g. the Hubble telescope orbits Earth. From there it gets a clear look at the Universe without our atmosphere getting in the way.

## Probes are Unmanned Spacecraft

1) Scientists send unmanned spacecraft called probes to explore other parts of our Solar System.
2) It's a cheaper and safer way to explore space than sending astronauts — for example, you don't have to worry about oxygen or food for the astronauts.
3) So far probes have visited all the planets in our Solar System. Some have even landed on the surface of Mars, Venus and Titan (one of Saturn's moons).

## The Pros and Cons of Space Exploration

1) There are many advantages of scientists exploring space. E.g. data collected from the surface of other planets could provide information about the origins of the Solar System, or help determine whether there is life on other planets.
2) Also, scientists and engineers need to invent new technology to explore space — we can put some of that new technology to good use on Earth. For example, computer mouses, scratch-resistant glasses and camera phones all result from technology developed for space exploration.
3) However, space exploration is expensive — some people think the money could be better spent on solving problems on Earth, such as reducing human suffering (e.g. by finding cures for diseases, or making sure there is enough food for everyone).
4) Also, launching satellites and rockets into space creates a lot of pollution, so there is concern about its impact on climate change.

# Warm-Up & Practice Questions

Is your head spinning with all this talk of orbits? Set things straight by answering these questions...

## Warm-Up Questions

1) Write the equation that links weight, mass and gravitational field strength.
2) Describe what a solar eclipse is.
3) Describe four uses of artificial satellites orbiting round Earth.

## Practice Questions

1 The diagram below shows the two motions of the Earth.

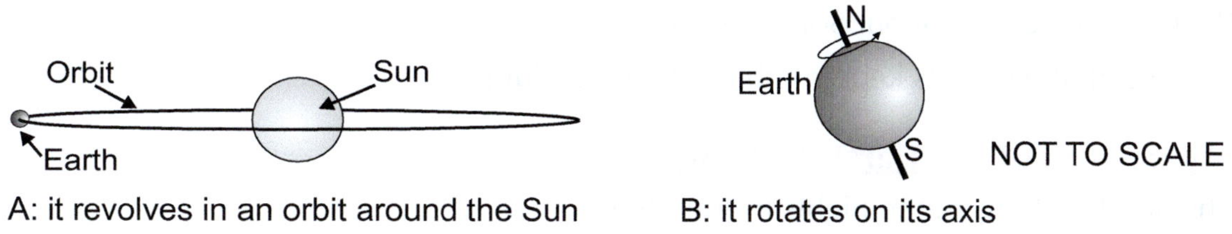


(a) Explain which of the above motions causes day and night.

*(2 marks)*

(b) State how many hours it takes the Earth to rotate once on its axis.

*(1 mark)*

(c) State how many times the Earth will rotate on its axis during one complete orbit of the Sun.

*(1 mark)*

2

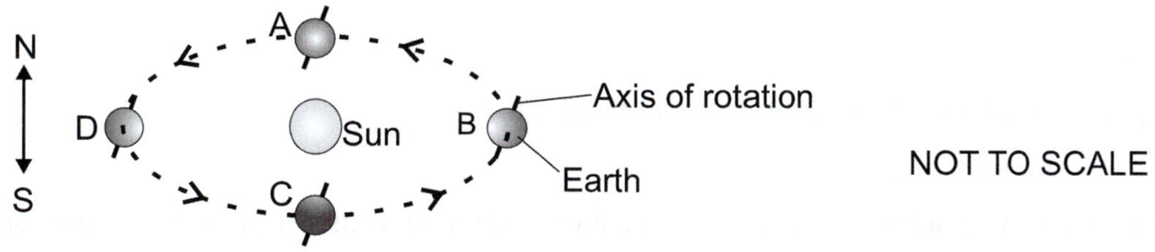


(a) In the diagram above, identify which position of the Earth, A-D, represents summer in the northern hemisphere.

*(1 mark)*

(b) Identify which position of the Earth, A-D, represents winter in the northern hemisphere.

*(1 mark)*

3 A rover of mass 500 kg weighs less on Mars than it does on the Earth.

(a) Explain why this is the case.

*(1 mark)*

(b) Calculate the weight of the rover on Mars. On Mars, $g = 3.7$ N/kg.

*(2 marks)*

# Summary Questions

Section P6 only has five pages of information — not much really, considering it deals with the whole Solar System. It's amazing just how many people go their whole lives and never really know the answers to all those burning questions, like what is gravity? Or why are the days longer in summer than in winter? Make sure you learn all the burning answers now...

- Try these questions and tick off each one when you get it right.
- When you've done all the questions for a topic and are completely happy with it, tick it off.

## Gravity and the Solar System (p.136-p.137) ☐

1) True or false? There is always a gravitational force between any two objects with mass. ☐
2) Why do objects on Earth have a weight? ☐
3) What is weight measured in? What is mass measured in? ☐
4) What is the value for the gravitational field strength, g, on Earth? ☐
5) What is at the centre of our Solar System? ☐
6) How are all the planets kept in orbit around the Sun? ☐

## The Movement of the Earth (p.138-p.139) ☐

7) Why are days longer than nights in summer? ☐
8) Give two reasons why it's (supposedly) hotter in Britain in summer than winter. ☐
9) When it's summer in the northern hemisphere, what season is it in the southern hemisphere? ☐
10) Why does the Sun appear to move across the sky? ☐
11) In which season does the Sun get highest in the sky? ☐
12) Why do stars appear to move in circles over several hours? ☐
13) What is a lunar eclipse? ☐

## Satellites (p.140) ☐

14) What is a satellite? ☐
15) How long does it take for the Moon to orbit the Earth? ☐
16) What are artificial satellites? ☐
17) Give two reasons why scientists might use probes, rather than astronauts, to explore space. ☐
18) Describe two advantages of scientists exploring space. ☐

# Answers

## Section B1 — Cells, Nutrients and Healthy Living

### Page 20 — Warm-Up Questions

1) Any three from: e.g. nucleus — this controls what the cell does / cytoplasm — this is where most chemical reactions happen / cell surface membrane — this holds the cell together and controls what goes in and out / mitochondria — this is where most of the reactions for aerobic respiration take place.
2) A tissue is made from a group of similar cells, while an organ is made from a group of different tissues working together.
3) Place the sample in the middle of a clean microscope slide, then use a pipette to add a drop of water or a stain to the sample. Finally, put a clean coverslip over the top.
4) E.g. carbohydrates and lipids (fats and oils)
5) E.g. vegetables / fruit / cereals
6) E.g. osteoporosis / rickets
7) E.g. obesity / high blood pressure / heart disease
8) Shake the food sample with ethanol for about a minute until it dissolves, then pour the solution into water. If there are any lipids present, they will show up as a milky emulsion.
9) It means that the drug can have an effect on the brain that makes a person feel a really strong craving to keep taking it.
10) It washes off the micro-organisms that cling to your skin when you touch things, which reduces the chance that they will get into your body and make you ill.

### Pages 20-21 — Practice Questions

1 (a) (i) Nucleus (1 mark)
  (ii) Vacuole (1 mark)
  (iii) Mitochondria (1 mark)
  (iv) Cell surface membrane (1 mark)
 (b) Any two from: cell wall (1 mark), vacuole (1 mark), chloroplasts (1 mark).
 (c) Nucleus (1 mark)
 (d) Respiration (1 mark)

2 (a) **A cell** (1 mark) is the simplest building block of organisms. Several of these can come together to make up **a tissue** (1 mark) and several of these can work together to make **an organ** (1 mark).
 (b) A group of organs which work together (1 mark).

3 (a) Recreational drugs are used for enjoyment (1 mark), whereas medical drugs are used to improve health in some way (1 mark).
 (b) (i) E.g. caffeine / nicotine / cannabis/marijuana / speed / ecstasy (1 mark)
  (ii) E.g. aspirin / antibiotics / codeine / tramadol (1 mark)
 (c) E.g. it decreases brain activity / it slows down responses (1 mark).

4 (a) (i) The mirror (1 mark).
  (ii) Because it can damage your eyes (1 mark).
 (b) (i) E.g. switch the objective lens to one that is higher powered (1 mark) and then refocus the microscope (1 mark).
  (ii) Because the cells have been stained (e.g. with eosin Y) (1 mark).
 (c) total magnification = eyepiece lens magnification × objective lens magnification
 = 10 × 10 (1 mark) = × 100 (1 mark)

## Section B2 — Breathing and Reproduction

### Page 30 — Warm-Up Questions

1) During an asthma attack, the muscles around a person's bronchioles contract, and the lining of the airways becomes inflamed and fluid builds up, all of which narrow the airways and makes it difficult to breathe.
2) Sperm — they are made in the testes.
3) The placenta allows the blood of the fetus to get close to the blood of the mother so that substances like oxygen, food and waste products can be exchanged.
4) If the mother smokes, harmful chemicals from the cigarette smoke that enter her blood can cross the placenta. This can slow down the development of the fetus and cause a low birth weight.
5) To prepare it to receive a fertilised egg.
6) So the seeds can grow into new plants without too much competition from the parent plant and from each other.

### Pages 30-31 — Practice Questions

1 (a) 28 days (1 mark)
 (b) Vagina (1 mark)
 (c) (i) Fallopian tube / oviduct (1 mark)
  (ii) When the nuclei of the egg and sperm join (1 mark)
 (d) 39 weeks (1 mark)

2 (a)

| name of organ | letter |
|---|---|
| sperm duct | B |
| penis | C |
| prostate gland | A |
| testis | D |

(2 marks for all four correct, otherwise 1 mark for at least two correct)

(b) Urethra (1 mark)

3 (a) E.g. brightly coloured petals/scented flowers to attract the bees / nectar to feed/attract the bees / sticky stigma to take the pollen off the bees (2 marks — 1 mark for a correct feature and 1 mark for a correct explanation).

(b) (i) The apple will fall from the tree and roll away from it (1 mark).

(ii) The apple will be eaten by birds, and the seeds will eventually be released in their droppings away from the original tree (1 mark).

4 (a) E

(b) When you breathe in, the diaphragm contracts and moves down (1 mark) and the ribs move upwards and outwards (1 mark). This increases the volume of the chest cavity (1 mark), which decreases the pressure and causes air to rush into the lungs (1 mark).

## Section B3 — Photosynthesis and Respiration

### Page 39 — Warm-Up Questions

1) Water, light, carbon dioxide and chlorophyll.
2) The green bit, because that's the part which contains chlorophyll, so that's the part which photosynthesises. Photosynthesis produces glucose, which is stored as starch.
3) When plants and animals carry out aerobic respiration, they take in oxygen and release carbon dioxide. When plants photosynthesise, they do the opposite — they release oxygen and take in carbon dioxide. So plants help to stop the carbon dioxide levels from getting too high and make sure there's plenty of oxygen.
4) To release energy, which is used for all the chemical reactions that keep organisms alive.
5) Aerobic respiration
6) glucose $\rightarrow$ carbon dioxide + alcohol/ethanol

### Pages 39-40 — Practice Questions

1 (a) (i) Anaerobic respiration (1 mark)

(ii) glucose $\rightarrow$ lactic acid (1 mark)

(b) E.g. aerobic respiration produces a large amount of energy, whereas anaerobic respiration produces a small amount. / The products of aerobic respiration are carbon dioxide and water, whereas the products of anaerobic respiration are lactic acid (in muscles) or carbon dioxide and alcohol/ethanol (in plants and yeast) (1 mark).

2 (a) (i) Photosynthesis produces glucose, which plants use to increase their biomass / grow (1 mark). The faster the rate of photosynthesis, the faster sugar is formed and the faster the plant can grow (1 mark).

(ii) It is likely to increase (1 mark) because an increased rate of photosynthesis will lead to more oxygen/bubbles of gas being released in a given time (1 mark).

(b) (i) E.g. temperature / amount of carbon dioxide (1 mark)

(ii) E.g. measure the rate of photosynthesis / amount of oxygen produced with the current level of light (1 mark). Then measure the rate of photosynthesis / amount of oxygen produced with a brighter / closer light and compare the two results (1 mark).

3 (a) Carbon dioxide (1 mark)

(b) Alcohol / ethanol (1 mark)

(c) E.g. she could have added a layer of oil on top of the yeast mixture to stop oxygen getting in (1 mark).

(d) (i) The amount of sugar in boiling tube A (1 mark).

(ii) Any two from: e.g. the temperature of the water bath / the length of time the bubbles were counted for / the amount of yeast (2 marks).

(e) It might have increased (1 mark) because there would have been more sugar available for the yeast to use for respiration/fermentation (1 mark), leading to a higher rate of respiration/fermentation and more carbon dioxide/bubbles being produced (1 mark).

(f) E.g. bread / wine / beer (1 mark)

## Section B4 — Interdependence and Populations

### Page 42 — Revision Task Question

a) Fewer otters means more pike, which will eat more water beetles.

b) E.g. more pike could lead to fewer perch, which could mean fewer water beetles get eaten.

### Page 45 — Warm-Up Questions

1) They all depend on each other to survive.
2) They show which organisms feed on each other.

3) a) A top carnivore is an organism that is not eaten by anything else.
   b) A primary consumer is an organism that eats producers.
   c) A producer is an organism which uses the Sun's energy to make its own food.
4) Any two from: e.g. using pitfall traps / using sweep nets / using pond nets / using quadrats
5) E.g. a quadrat
6) Using resources so the needs of the growing population can be met without destroying things for future generations.

### Page 45 — Practice Question

1 (a) geese / lemmings (1 mark)
  (b) (i) Any two from: e.g. the number of plants may (suddenly) decrease / the number of owls may (suddenly) increase / the number of jaegers may (suddenly) increase / the number of Arctic foxes may (suddenly) increase.
  (Maximum 2 marks.)
  (ii) The number of Arctic foxes may also decrease (1 mark), as they have fewer food sources available (1 mark).
  (c) Yes, because more owls means fewer lemmings (1 mark). Therefore, jaegers and Arctic foxes would become more dependent on geese as a food source (1 mark).

## Section B5 — Variation and Classification

### Page 50 — Warm-Up Questions

1) The two classes of variation are continuous and discontinuous variation. Continuous variation means a variable can vary over a range of values, but variables that vary discontinuously can only take certain values.
2) False

*The different kingdoms are plants, animals, fungi, bacteria and protists. Mammals, fish and birds are different types of vertebrates.*

3) A feature that can be used to classify an organism into a taxonomic group.
4) Protists and fungi
5) Plants and fungi

### Page 50 — Practice Questions

1 (a) Because there can be variation within a species (1 mark).
  (b) Discontinuous (1 mark) because the ears can only be straight or floppy (1 mark).
2 (a) E.g. they will both lay eggs on land (1 mark) and they will both be cold-blooded (1 mark).
  (b) E.g. to protect the animal from predators (1 mark).
  (c) (i) E.g. the turtle has flatter limbs than the tortoise (1 mark). / The turtle has a smaller shell than the tortoise (1 mark).
  (ii) E.g. flatter limbs may help the turtle swim (1 mark). / A smaller shell may mean the turtle can move more freely in the water (because it isn't as heavy) (1 mark).

## Section C1 — States of Matter

### Page 55 — Warm-Up Questions

1) Solid
2) Gas
3) False

*Particles gain energy when they're heated, so they move around more.*

4) Changing state directly from solid to gas.
5) They move about randomly in all directions until they are evenly spread out.

### Page 55 — Practice Question

1 (a) Solids usually have a **high** (1 mark) density and are **difficult** (1 mark) to compress.
  (b) E.g.

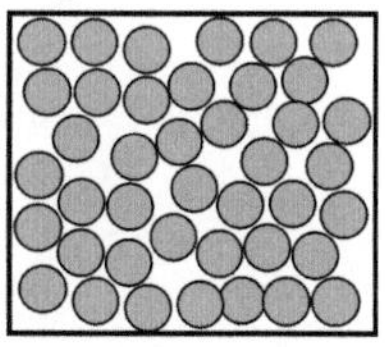

(1 mark)

  (c) It has changed into a gas / it has boiled/evaporated (1 mark).
  (d) Condensing/condensation (1 mark)

*When the water in the air (a gas) comes into contact with the cold kitchen window, it cools down and turns from a gas into a liquid (water droplets) — the process of a gas turning into a liquid is called condensation.*

  (e) No — freezing the water is a change of state, and particles never change during a change of state, all that changes is their arrangement and their energy (1 mark).

## Section C2 — Atoms, Elements, Molecules and Compounds

### Page 64 — Warm-Up Questions

1) An element is a substance that contains only one type of atom.
2) In a compound, atoms of different elements are chemically joined together. In a mixture, the elements are simply mixed together, not chemically joined.
3) Iron, nickel and cobalt.
4) a) metals
   b) non-metals
   c) non-metals
5) Solids or gases

### Pages 64-65 — Practice Questions

1 (a) A (1 mark)

*Careful here — C is a mixture of an element and a compound, not a mixture of two compounds.*

(b) B (1 mark)

(c) D (1 mark)

*$H_2O$ has two atoms of hydrogen and 1 atom of oxygen in each molecule. D is the only diagram that shows 2 of one type of atom and 1 of another.*

2 Sulfur can be found on the **right** (1 mark)-hand side of the periodic table. It has a **brittle** (1 mark) consistency and a **dull** (1 mark) yellow surface. It is a **poor** conductor of heat (1 mark).

3 (a) (i) Na / Ca / Cu (1 mark)

(ii) C / He (1 mark)

(iii) He (1 mark)

*Don't be put off by questions that are based on the periodic table — you just need to look at the information given in the diagram and use it to answer the questions. E.g. in this question, it's more about knowing which sides of the table metals and non-metals are on rather than actually using the table.*

(b) (i) Helium (1 mark)

(ii) Copper (1 mark)

4 (a) (i) Fe (1 mark)

(ii) S (1 mark)

(b) Iron powder (1 mark) because iron is magnetic and sulfur isn't (1 mark).

(c) During the chemical reaction, iron and sulfur atoms joined together (1 mark), which formed a new substance / iron sulfide (1 mark). This new substance / iron sulfide had different properties to iron and sulfur, and wasn't magnetic, so didn't move towards the magnet (1 mark).

## Section C3 — Purity, Mixtures and Separating Mixtures

### Page 72 — Warm-Up Questions

1) Mixtures, unlike compounds, are not chemically joined up.
2) Nitrogen
3) a) Lots of salts
   b) Some salts
   c) No salts at all
4) The particles get further apart. This increases its volume and decreases its density.

### Page 72 — Practice Questions

1 (a) (i) (Simple) distillation (1 mark)

(ii) When the ink is heated the water evaporates off as a gas (1 mark). The water is then cooled, condensed and collected (1 mark), leaving the solid part of the ink behind (1 mark).

(b) E.g. Calvin could measure the boiling point of the water he has collected (1 mark). If the water is pure, it will boil at exactly 100 °C / the boiling point of pure water (1 mark).

2 (a) He should put the paper in a beaker with a little solvent at the bottom (1 mark).

(b) The solvent seeps up the paper, carrying the dyes from the food colouring with it (1 mark). Different dyes are carried by the solvent through the paper at different speeds, so some move further up the paper than others (1 mark). Two factors that affect how far each dye travels are e.g. how soluble the dye is in the solvent (1 mark) and how attracted it is to the filter paper (1 mark).

## Section C4 — Combustion and Thermal Decomposition

### Page 79 — Warm-Up Questions

1) 92 g + 142 g = 234 g

*The total mass after a reaction is always the same as the total mass before the reaction.*

2) A medium blue flame.
3) Magnesium oxide
4) It will relight a glowing splint.
5) Carbon monoxide
6) E.g. global warming may increase melting of polar ice caps, causing sea levels to rise.
7) Blue

## Page 79 — Practice Questions

1 (a) Thermal decomposition (1 mark).

(b) The air hole is fully open (1 mark).

(c) It will have gone cloudy (1 mark) because the gas is carbon dioxide, and carbon dioxide turns limewater cloudy (1 mark).

(d) copper(II) carbonate ⟶ copper(II) oxide + carbon dioxide (1 mark)

2 (a) (i) Fuel, heat and oxygen (1 mark).

(ii) Carbon dioxide and water (vapour) (1 mark).

(b) Sulfur dioxide is released (1 mark). When sulfur dioxide mixes with clouds it forms dilute sulfuric acid, which then falls as acid rain (1 mark).

(c) E.g. carbon dioxide traps heat from the Sun in the Earth's atmosphere, which helps to keep the Earth warm (1 mark). The increased level of carbon dioxide in the atmosphere from hydrocarbon combustion can result in the Earth's temperature gradually increasing/global warming (1 mark).

# Section C5 — Oxidation Reactions, Acids and Alkalis

## Page 89 — Warm-Up Questions

1) Acids have a pH below 7, alkalis have a pH above 7.
2) A salt, water and carbon dioxide.
3) Sulfuric acid
4) In agriculture, to neutralise acidic soil.

## Pages 89-90 — Practice Questions

1 (a) (i) Any one of: lemon juice, wine, milk (1 mark)

(ii) Sodium hydroxide solution (1 mark)

(b) Any one of: lemon juice, wine, milk (1 mark), because these are acids and sodium hydroxide solution is an alkali (1 mark).

2 (a) The nail in test tube B is exposed to more air than the nail in test tube A (1 mark), so there would be more oxygen available for the rusting reaction to take place (1 mark).

(b) E.g. she could use boiled water rather than tap water. / She could coat the nail with plastic/another metal/oil/grease before putting it in the test tube. (1 mark)

3 (a) He could remove a small sample of the reaction mixture and check with, e.g. Universal Indicator paper (1 mark) that the pH is 7/neutral (1 mark).

(b) acid + alkali ⟶ salt + water (1 mark)

(c) Nitric acid (1 mark)

4 Potassium oxide (1 mark) — it reacts with acids but not alkalis, so it must be alkaline (as indicated by the litmus paper) (1 mark).

5 (a) Sodium sulfate (1 mark)

(b) (i) pH 3 (1 mark)

(ii) 7.5 $cm^3$ (1 mark for an answer between 7.2 $cm^3$ and 7.7 $cm^3$)

# Section P1 — Energy and Resources

## Page 98 — Warm-Up Questions

1) Chemical, nuclear, gravitational potential, internal, kinetic, elastic
2) Energy can never be created nor destroyed — it's only ever transferred from one store to another.
3) The Sun
4) E.g. for hot water in homes / for heating homes / for cooking food (using a gas oven or hob)
5) Lots of small wave-powered turbines are set up around the coast. As waves come into the shore they create an up and down motion that turns the turbines. This drives a generator, which generates electricity.
6) E.g. wind turbines can spoil a nice view. / Hydroelectric power schemes can mean that valleys need to be flooded, which can destroy habitats for wildlife.

## Pages 98-99 — Practice Questions

1 (a) Energy is stored inside the **battery** (1 mark) in its **chemical** (1 mark) energy store.

(b)

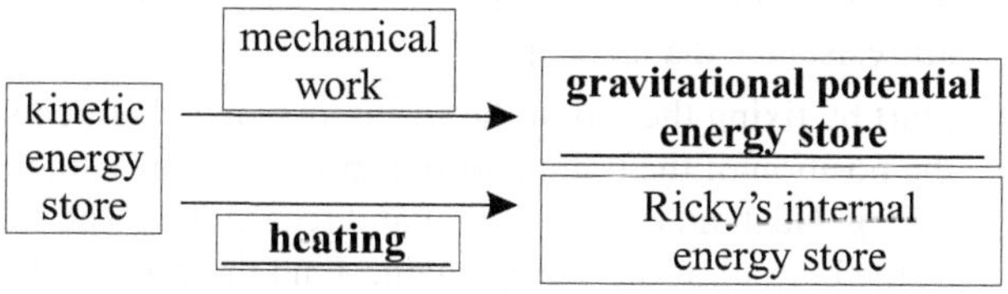


(2 marks)

2 (a) A non-renewable energy resource is one that will run out/cannot be replenished within a lifetime (1 mark).

(b) Any two from: coal / oil / nuclear fuel (2 marks)

3 (a)

| Scenario | Energy store transferred from | Useful energy store transferred to |
|---|---|---|
| Coal being used to cook food on a barbecue | **Chemical energy store of the coal** | Internal energy store of the food |
| A stretched rubber band on a catapult being released | **Elastic energy store of the rubber band** | **Kinetic energy store of the rubber band** |

(3 marks)

(b) The amount of energy that goes into an energy transfer is more than the useful energy that comes out (1 mark), because some energy is always dissipated/wasted during the transfer (1 mark).

4 (a) Hydroelectric power (1 mark)
(b) E.g. wave (1 mark), tidal (1 mark)
(c) Any two from: e.g. renewable energy resources don't run out, unlike non-renewable energy resources. / Renewable energy resources are generally less damaging to the environment than non-renewable energy resources. / Once the equipment has been set up, renewable energy resources can have lower running costs than non-renewable energy resources (2 marks).

## Section P2 — Speed and Forces

### Page 108 — Warm-Up Questions

1) speed = distance ÷ time
2) Your speed relative to the car driving in the opposite direction is much higher than your speed relative to a car travelling in the same direction.
3) Newtons (N)
4)

*Arrows should be the same size and pointing in opposite directions (the forces should be balanced for an object travelling at a steady speed).*

5) E.g. friction and air resistance.
6) E.g. friction allows things to stop, start and slow down. / Friction allows things to grip to a surface.
7) The larger the canopy area of the parachute, the larger the air resistance that acts upon it.
8) Start by fixing the top of the spring in place, then record the position of the bottom of the spring (e.g. by using a ruler). Next, attach the weight and record the position of the bottom of the spring again. Find the extension by subtracting the position without the weight from the position with the weight.

### Pages 108-109 — Practice Questions

1 (a) (i) The driving force is less than the air resistance / the air resistance is greater than the driving force (1 mark).
(ii) The driving force is greater than the air resistance / the air resistance is less than the driving force (1 mark).
(iii) The driving force is equal to the air resistance (1 mark).
(b) The car must be changing direction (1 mark).
*Unbalanced forces either change the speed or direction of an object. In this case, the speed is staying the same, so the direction must be changing.*
(c) E.g. it limits the top speed of the car (1 mark) and it wastes fuel/energy (1 mark).
(d) They may stretch/extend them (1 mark) or squash/compress them (1 mark).

2 (a) 600 + 725 = 1325 km/h (1 mark)
*The aircraft are travelling in the opposite direction to each other, so add their speeds.*
(b) Subtract the speed of one aircraft from the speed of the other aircraft (1 mark).

3 (a) distance = 200 cm ÷ 100 = 2 m (1 mark)
speed = distance ÷ time = 2 m ÷ 0.60 s (1 mark)
= 3.3 m/s (1 mark)
(b) (i) Random error (1 mark)
(ii) Repeat the experiment three times for each height (1 mark) and use these results to calculate a mean time for each height (1 mark).
(c) Unbalanced, because the ball begins to speed up (1 mark).
(d) The values for time will be larger / for speed will be smaller (1 mark). This is because a larger air resistance will act on the ball and parachute compared to just the ball (1 mark) and so the ball will take longer to fall to the ground / will fall to the ground at a slower speed (1 mark).

### Page 110 — Summary Questions

2) speed = distance ÷ time, so
time = distance ÷ speed = 150 m ÷ 3 m/s = 50 s
3) 15 minutes = 0.25 hours
speed = distance ÷ time, so
distance = speed × time = 40 mph × 0.25 h = 10 miles.
5) 23 km/h – 15 km/h = 8 km/h
16) extension = position with weight – position without weight = 11.4 cm – 10.2 cm = 1.2 cm

## Section P3 — Pressure and Density

### Page 115 — Warm-Up Questions

1) $N/m^2$ and $N/cm^2$
2) Weigh the object using a Newton meter to find the force. Calculate the area of the face of the object that is in contact with the floor, then divide the force by the area to calculate the pressure.
3) It increases.
4) $kg/m^3$ and $g/cm^3$
5) Find the mass of the object using a mass balance. Calculate the volume of the object, then divide the mass by the volume to calculate the density.

### Page 115 — Practice Questions

1 (a) (i) Mass of liquid = 190 – 70 (1 mark)
= 120 g (1 mark)
(ii) Density = mass ÷ volume
= 120 g ÷ 100 $cm^3$ (1 mark)
= 1.2 $g/cm^3$ (1 mark)

(b) The second liquid floats because it has a lower density than the first liquid (1 mark).

2 (a) E.g. Martin's mother's weight is spread over a much smaller area when her weight's on her heels (1 mark) so the pressure she exerts on the floor is higher (1 mark).

(b) (i) Pressure = force ÷ area (1 mark)

(ii) Pressure = 600 N ÷ 0.0002 $m^2$ (1 mark)
= 3 000 000 N/$m^2$ (1 mark)

## Page 116 — Summary Questions

3) Pressure = force ÷ area
= 200 N ÷ 2 $m^2$ = 100 N/$m^2$

4) Pressure = force ÷ area
Area = force ÷ pressure
= 1.2 N ÷ 0.6 N/$cm^2$ = 2 $cm^2$

10) Volume = 10 cm × 10 cm × 3 cm = 300 $cm^3$
Density = mass ÷ volume
= 1050 g ÷ 300 $cm^3$ = 3.5 g/$cm^3$

12) Mass of liquid = 350 g – 100 g = 250 g
Density = mass ÷ volume
= 250 g ÷ 200 $cm^3$ = 1.25 g/$cm^3$

# Section P4 — Sound and Light

## Page 124 — Warm-Up Questions

1) A vacuum.
2) The height of a sound wave.
3) The frequency of the sound / the number of vibrations per second.
4) Light.

## Pages 124-125 — Practice Questions

1 (a)

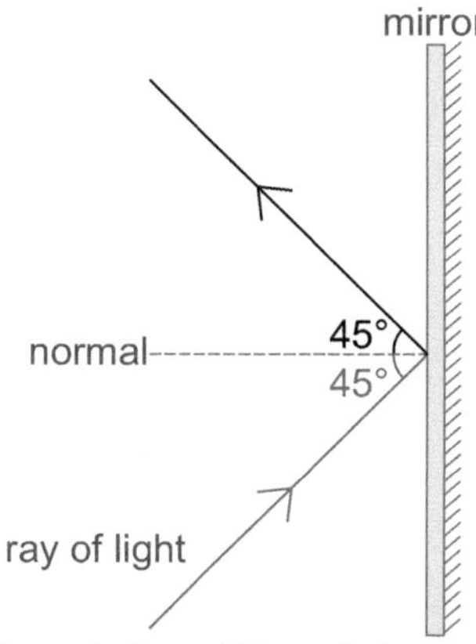


(1 mark for a 45° angle between the normal and the reflected ray, 1 mark for an arrow on the reflected ray to show that it's moving away from the mirror.)

*The angle doesn't have to be labelled to get the first mark here, as long as it's 45°.*

(b) (i) A spectrum of colours (1 mark).

(ii) Each of the different colours that make up white light has a different frequency (1 mark). When white light is shone at a prism, the different frequencies are refracted by different amounts (1 mark) causing the light to disperse (1 mark).

(c) (i) Towards the normal (1 mark).

(ii) E.g.

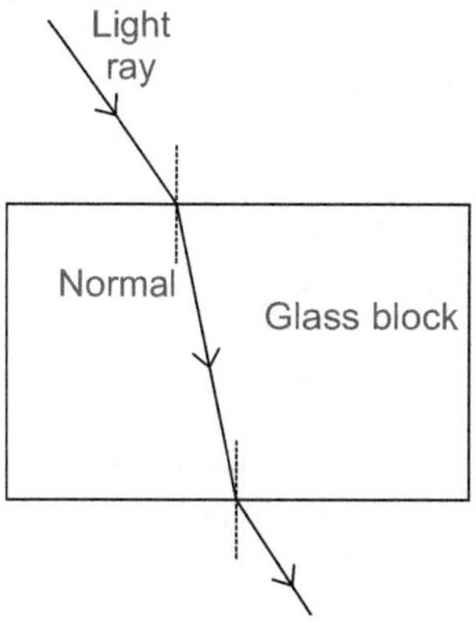


(1 mark for light hitting the glass at an angle to the normal, 1 mark for light bending away from the normal as it leaves the glass block.)

2 (a) 250 ÷ 0.78 = 320.5 (1 mark).

(b) m/s (1 mark).

3 (a) Sound wave B (1 mark).

(b) Sound wave C (1 mark).

(c) The sound would be louder (1 mark).

(d) The sound will have a lower pitch (1 mark).

# Section P5 — Circuits and Magnets

## Page 133 — Warm-Up Questions

1) Electric current is the flow of charge around a circuit.
2) A material that doesn't easily allow electric charges to pass through it, e.g. wood or plastic.
3) Current
4) (a) 

(b) 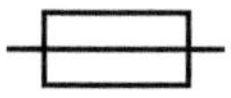

(c) 

5) E.g. because in a parallel circuit, some bulbs can be on while other bulbs are off (unlike in a series circuit, where all the bulbs are either on or off).
6) A region where magnetic materials experience a force.

## Pages 133-134 — Practice Questions

1 (a) Parallel (1 mark).

(b) (i) Nothing — it would stay on (1 mark).

(ii) It would go off (1 mark).

(c) Bulb A will stay on because the electricity is still flowing through it / the circuit is still complete (1 mark). Bulb B will go off because there is no electricity flowing through it / the circuit is broken (1 mark) because wood does not conduct electricity well/is an electrical insulator (1 mark).

2

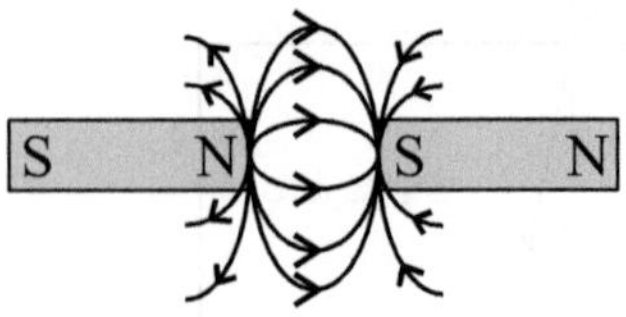


Field lines should point away from any North pole(s) and towards any South pole(s).
(2 marks available — 1 mark for correct diagram and 1 mark for correct reason.)

3 (a) Any one of: increase the number of coils in the wire / increase the current (by adding another cell) (1 mark).

(b) The compass will align itself to the electromagnet's magnetic field (1 mark), pointing directly towards/ away from the iron bar (1 mark).

*Remember — a compass needle always points from N to S along the field lines of a magnetic field. At the end of a coil of wire, the field lines point directly into or out of the coil of wire. You can't tell which end is North and which is South here, so you get the mark whether you've said it points into or out of the iron bar.*

(c) E.g. lifting magnets in scrap yards / showers (as part of a relay circuit) (1 mark).

4 (a) current through resistor
= current through cell – current through bulb
= 1.90 A – 0.60 A = 1.30 A (1 mark).

(b) It will decrease the current flowing through the bulb as the number of components in the circuit has increased (1 mark). More components increase the resistance and reduce the current (1 mark).

## Page 135 — Summary Question

11) 3 A

# Section P6 — Space

## Page 141 — Warm-Up Questions

1) Weight = mass × gravitational field strength / W = m × g

2) A solar eclipse is when the Moon passes between the Sun and the Earth, blocking the Sun's light from reaching Earth.

3) Any four from: e.g. communication / navigation / monitoring the weather / observing the Earth / exploring the solar system.

## Page 141 — Practice Questions

1 (a) B (1 mark) because as the Earth spins, part of it will face the Sun, which is day, and then turn away from it, which is night (1 mark).

(b) 24 (1 mark)

(c) 365 ¼ (1 mark)

2 (a) D (1 mark)

(b) B (1 mark)

3 (a) The strength of gravity on Mars is weaker than it is on Earth (1 mark).

(b) weight = mass × gravitational field strength
= 500 kg × 3.7 N/kg (1 mark)
= 1850 N (1 mark)

# Glossary

We've gathered up some of the most important words you need to know here, so you can remind yourself what they're all about. Words in the definitions that are underlined have their own entry.

**Accurate result**
A result that is very close to the true answer.

**Acid**
A substance that will neutralise a base to form a salt and water.

**Acid rain**
Acidic rain formed when pollutants such as sulfur dioxide mix with clouds.

**Aerobic respiration**
Respiration using oxygen. Carbon dioxide and water are produced in this reaction.

**Air resistance (or drag)**
Air pushing back against you when you move through it.

**Alkali**
A base that will dissolve in water.

**Alveoli**
Small air sacs in the lungs where gas exchange takes place.

**Ammeter**
An instrument used to measure current — must be connected in series.

**Amniotic sac**
Fluid filled sac attached to the placenta, which protects a fetus from knocks and bumps.

**Amphibian**
A vertebrate that lays eggs in water, has smooth skin and is cold-blooded (e.g. a frog).

**Amplitude (of a sound)**
A measure of the loudness of sound.

**Anaerobic respiration**
Respiration without oxygen. In animals, lactic acid is produced in this reaction. In plants and yeast, carbon dioxide and alcohol (ethanol) are produced in this reaction.

**Anhydrous**
A substance that doesn't contain any water.

**Anomalous result**
A result that doesn't seem to fit with the rest of the data.

**Anther**
A male part of a flower, which contains pollen grains.

**Arachnid**
An arthropod that has 8 legs, a 2-part body and no antennae (e.g. a spider).

**Arthropod**
An invertebrate that has many pairs of jointed legs, a body that is divided into segments, and a hard exoskeleton (e.g. an insect).

**Asthma**
A condition where the airways of a person narrow when the lungs are irritated. This leads to difficulty breathing.

**Atom**
A tiny particle that makes up all matter.

**Auditory range**
The range of frequencies that humans, or other animals, can hear. Different types of animal have different auditory ranges.

**Bacteria**
Single-celled micro-organisms that can cause disease. They do not have a nucleus.

**Balanced diet**
A diet which contains the right amount of carbohydrates, proteins, lipids, vitamins, minerals, fibre and water.

**Balanced forces**
Forces that are equal in size but opposite in direction, producing no change in movement.

**Base**
A substance that will neutralise an acid to form a salt and water.

**Benedict's test**
A chemical test for sugar.

**Biomass**
Organic matter that stores the Sun's energy.

**Biuret test**
A chemical test for proteins.

**Boiling**
The change in state of a liquid to a gas, when the liquid is heated to its boiling point.

**Braking distance**
The distance a vehicle travels after the brakes are applied until it comes to a complete stop.

**Breathing**
The process of getting air in and out of the lungs.

**Carpel**
The female part of a flower (consists of the stigma, style and ovary).

**Categoric data**
Data that comes in distinct categories, e.g. nutrients, metals.

**Cell (biology)**
The fundamental unit of all living things.

**Cell surface membrane**
The thin skin around a cell that holds it together and controls what goes in and out.

**Cell wall**
A rigid outer coating surrounding some types of cell. It supports the cell.

**Chemical energy store**
The energy stored in an object that can be released by a chemical reaction.

**Chemical reaction**
A chemical process that involves chemicals combining together or splitting apart to form new substances.

**Chlorophyll**
A green chemical found in the chloroplasts of plant cells.

# Glossary

### Chloroplast
The part of a plant cell where photosynthesis takes place. Contains lots of chlorophyll.

### Chromatography
A method used to separate out the different coloured solutes in a solution.

### Circuit diagram
A simplified diagram of a real electrical circuit which shows all the components as symbols.

### Climate change
A change in things like temperature or weather patterns in a part of the world or across the whole world. E.g. global warming is a type of climate change.

### Combustion
When a substance reacts with oxygen to release energy. Combustion is also called burning.

### Compass
A navigational tool containing a bar magnet (its needle) that aligns with the Earth's magnetic field.

### Compound
A substance formed when atoms from different elements join together.

### Condensing
The change in state of a gas to a liquid.

### Conductor (electrical)
A component or material that allows electrical charge to pass through it easily.

### Conductor (thermal)
A material that allows heat to pass through it easily.

### Continuous data
Numerical data that can have any value within a range, e.g. length or temperature.

### Continuous variation
When a feature of an organism can take any value at all within a certain range.

### Control variable
A variable in an experiment that is kept the same.

### Current (electric)
The flow of charge around a circuit.

### Cytoplasm
The jelly-like substance inside a cell where most of its chemical reactions happen.

### Decibel
A unit used to measure loudness.

### Density
A measure of the 'compactness' of a substance.

### Dependent variable
The variable in an experiment that is measured.

### Diagnostic feature
A feature of an organism that is used to classify different species.

### Diaphragm
A muscle involved in breathing. It moves up when it relaxes and down when it contracts.

### Diffusion
When particles spread out, moving from an area of higher concentration to an area of lower concentration.

### Discontinuous variation
When a feature of an organism can only take certain values.

### Discrete (discontinuous) data
Numerical data that can be counted in chunks, where there's no in-between value, e.g. number of people.

### Dispersion (light)
The separation of white light into a spectrum of different colours, due to different frequencies in the light being refracted by different amounts.

### Dissipated energy
The energy wasted during an energy transfer (the energy not transferred to useful energy stores).

### Dissolving
The process by which a solid mixes with a liquid to form a solution.

### Distillation (fractional)
A method for separating a mixture of liquids according to their boiling points.

### Distillation (simple)
A method for separating a solvent from a solution.

### Drug
A substance that affects the way the body works. It can be medical (used to improve health) or recreational (used for enjoyment).

### Ecosystem
All the living organisms in one area, plus their habitat.

### Elastic energy store
Anything that has been deformed (stretched or squashed) has energy in its elastic energy store.

### Electromagnet
A magnet whose magnetic field can be turned on and off with an electric current.

### Electron
A small, negatively charged particle.

### Element
A substance that contains only one type of atom.

### Embryo
The name given to a developing baby from the time it is a ball of cells until it is a fetus (around 9 weeks).

### Emphysema
A disease which can be caused by smoking. It can result in difficulty breathing due to the destruction of alveoli.

### Emulsion test
A chemical test for lipids.

### Evaporating
The gradual change in state of a liquid to a gas.

### Expiration
Breathing out.

### Fair test
A controlled experiment where the only thing that changes is the independent variable.

### Fallopian tube (oviduct)
The part of the female reproductive system that carries an egg from one of the ovaries to the uterus. It is where fertilisation happens.

# Glossary

### Fermentation
When anaerobic respiration produces alcohol (ethanol) from glucose. The fermentation of yeast is used to make products such as bread, wine and beer.

### Fertilisation
The fusion of male and female sex cells during sexual reproduction.

### Fetus
The name given to a developing baby from around 9 weeks after fertilisation.

### Food chain
A sequence of organisms showing what is eaten by what.

### Food web
A network of interlinked food chains.

### Force
A push or a pull that occurs when two objects interact.

### Force diagram
A simplified diagram which uses arrows to represent the size and direction of all the different forces acting on an object.

### Fossil fuel
The fossil fuels are coal, oil and natural gas. They're non-renewable energy resources.

### Freezing
The change in state of a liquid to a solid.

### Frequency (of sound)
A measure of the pitch of sound. It is the number of complete waves to pass a point per second.

### Friction
The force that tries to stop objects sliding past each other.

### Frictional force
A resisting force that acts on a moving object, e.g. friction and air resistance. These forces always act in the opposite direction to the movement of the object.

### Fungi
Organisms that can't move around, and don't make their own food.

### Gamete
Another word for a sex cell.

### Gas exchange
The process where oxygen enters the blood from the air and carbon dioxide leaves the blood. Takes place in the lungs.

### Gas pressure
The pushing force exerted on the walls of a container as a result of gas particles colliding with the container walls.

### Global warming
The increase in the temperature of the Earth.

### Glucose
A sugar produced during photosynthesis and used in respiration.

### Gravitational potential energy store
Any object in a gravitational field has energy in this store.

### Gravity
A force of attraction that exists between all objects with mass.

### Greenhouse gas
A gas (e.g. carbon dioxide) that traps heat from the Sun in the Earth's atmosphere.

### Habitat
The place where an organism lives (e.g. a freshwater pond or hedgerow).

### Hazard
Something that has the potential to cause harm (e.g. fire, electricity, etc).

### Hertz
A unit used to measure the frequency of sound.

### Hydrated
A substance containing water.

### Hydrocarbon
A fuel containing only hydrogen and carbon.

### Hypothesis
A possible explanation for a scientific observation.

### Independent variable
The variable in an experiment that is changed.

### Indicator
Something that changes colour depending on whether it is in an acid or in an alkali.

### Insect
An arthropod that has 6 legs, a 3-part body and antennae (e.g. a fly).

### Inspiration
Breathing in.

### Insulator (electrical)
A material that doesn't allow electrical charge to easily pass through it.

### Insulator (thermal)
A material that doesn't allow heat to pass through it easily.

### Intercostal muscles
Muscles located between the ribs that are involved in breathing.

### Interdependence
Where, in an ecosystem, each organism depends on other organisms in order to survive.

### Internal energy store
All objects have some energy in this store. The hotter the object, the more energy it has in this store. It can also be called a heat or thermal energy store.

### Invertebrate
An animal that has no backbone.

### Iodine test
A chemical test for starch.

### Kinetic energy store
Anything that's moving has energy in this store.

### Kingdom
The name given to each of the five taxonomic groups that all living things are divided into (plants, animals, fungi, bacteria and protists).

### Law of conservation of energy
Energy can never be created nor destroyed — it's only ever transferred from one form to another.

# Glossary

### Limestone
A naturally-occurring rock mainly formed of calcium carbonate.

### Limewater
A colourless solution that goes cloudy when carbon dioxide is bubbled through it.

### Lunar eclipse
When the Earth passes between the Sun and the Moon, stopping the Sun's light from reaching the Moon.

### Magnetic field
A region where magnetic materials experience a force.

### Magnetic field lines
Lines used to show the size and direction of a magnetic field around an object.

### Magnification
How many times bigger a microscope image is compared to the real object.

### Malleability
A property of a material that describes how easily it can be shaped.

### Mammal
A vertebrate that gives birth to live young, suckles young on milk, has fur or hair, has lungs and is warm-blooded.

### Mean (average)
A measure of average found by adding up all the data and dividing by the number of values there are.

### Median (average)
The middle value in a set of data when the data is in numerical order.

### Medium
A substance through which waves (such as light and sound) can travel.

### Melting
The change in state of a solid to a liquid.

### Menstrual cycle
A monthly sequence of events that occurs in females from the age of puberty. It involves preparing the uterus to receive a fertilised egg.

### Mitochondria
The parts of a cell where the reactions for aerobic respiration take place.

### Mixture
Two or more different substances that are mixed up but aren't chemically joined.

### Mode (average)
The most common value in a set of data.

### Model
A simple description or picture of something that happens in real life.

### Molecule
Two or more atoms joined together.

### Multicellular organism
An organism that is made up of more than one cell.

### Neutralisation
When an acid reacts with an alkali to produce a neutral solution of salt and water.

### Newton
The unit for force.

### Non-renewable energy resource
An energy resource that will run out one day.

### Nuclear energy store
Atomic nuclei have energy in this store. It is released in nuclear reactions.

### Nucleus (biology)
The part of a cell that controls what the cell does.

### Organ
A group of different tissues that work together to perform a function.

### Organ system
A group of different organs that work together to perform a function.

### Organism
Any living thing.

### Ovary
The part of the female reproductive system which produces eggs.

### Ovule
Found in the ovary of a flower. Contains the female sex cell.

### Ovum
Another word for an egg cell (a female sex cell).

### Oxidation
When a substance reacts and combines with oxygen.

### Particle model
All materials are made up of particles, which behave differently depending on whether they are in a solid, liquid or gas.

### Peak flow meter
A small device used to assess a person's vital capacity.

### Peer-review
The process in which scientists check the results and explanations of an investigation before they are published.

### Periodic table
A table of all the elements we have discovered, arranged so that elements with similar properties are in the same columns.

### Periscope
A device that uses mirrors to let you see around an obstacle.

### pH scale
A scale used to measure the strength of acids and alkalis.

### Photosynthesis
A chemical process which takes place in every green plant and in other photosynthetic organisms. Light is used to convert carbon dioxide and water into glucose and oxygen.

### Photosynthetic organism
Any organism that can carry out photosynthesis.

### Pitfall trap
Steep-sided container with a partially open top that is sunk into the ground. It is used to collect organisms when investigating populations.

# Glossary

**Placenta**
An organ that attaches to the wall of the uterus shortly after fertilisation. It allows the blood of the fetus and the mother to get very close together.

**Pollen grain**
Found in the anther of a flower. Produces the male sex cell.

**Pollen tube**
A structure that grows out of a pollen grain down into an ovary following pollination.

**Pollination**
Pollen grains being transferred from a stamen to a stigma.

**Population**
How many individuals of a particular species there are in a certain place.

**Precise result**
When all the data is close to the mean.

**Prediction**
A statement based on a hypothesis that can be tested.

**Pressure**
A ratio of force over area acting at an angle of 90° to the area.

**Primary consumer**
An animal that eats producers.

**Probe (space)**
An unmanned spacecraft.

**Producer**
An organism that uses the Sun's energy to make its own food.

**Product**
A substance that is formed in a chemical reaction.

**Prostate gland**
Part of the male reproductive system. It produces the liquid that's added to sperm to make semen.

**Protist**
A single-celled organism that has a nucleus.

**Pure substance**
A substance made up of only one type of particle.

**Quadrat**
A square frame enclosing a known area, used to estimate population size.

**Random error**
A small difference in the results of an experiment caused by things like human error in measuring.

**Range**
The difference between the smallest and largest values in a set of data.

**Reactant**
A substance that reacts in a chemical reaction.

**Refraction**
The bending of a wave (e.g. light) as it travels from one medium to another.

**Relative motion**
The speed at which two objects are moving together or apart.

**Relay**
A type of switch including an electromagnet used as a link between two circuits.

**Reliable result**
A result that is repeatable and reproducible.

**Renewable energy resource**
An energy resource that can be replaced in a person's lifetime. It won't run out.

**Repeatable result**
A result that will come out the same if the experiment is repeated by the same person using the same method and equipment.

**Reproducible result**
A result that will come out the same if someone different does the experiment, or a slightly different method or piece of equipment is used.

**Reptile**
A vertebrate that lays eggs on land, has dry scales and is cold-blooded (e.g. a lizard).

**Resistance**
Anything in a circuit that slows down the flow of current.

**Respiration**
The process of releasing energy from glucose (a sugar). Happens in every cell of every living organism.

**Risk**
The chance that a hazard will cause harm.

**Satellite**
Something that orbits a planet.

**Secondary consumer**
An animal that eats primary consumers.

**Seed**
The result of reproduction of a flowering plant. It develops from an ovule.

**SI unit**
A unit of measurement used by scientists all over the world.

**Solar eclipse**
When the Moon passes between the Sun and Earth, stopping the Sun's light from reaching Earth.

**Soluble**
If a substance is soluble, this means it will dissolve in a certain solvent.

**Solute**
A solid that is dissolved in a solvent to form a solution.

**Solution**
A mixture of a solute and solvent that does not separate out.

**Solvent**
The liquid that a solute dissolves into to form a solution.

**Spectrum**
The rainbow effect created when white light gets split up.

**Speed**
Distance travelled in a certain amount of time.

**Sperm**
A male sex cell used in animal reproduction.

**Sperm duct**
A tube in the male reproductive system that carries sperm from a testis towards the urethra.

# Glossary

**Stain (microscope)**
A dye used on a microscope slide to make it easier to see certain parts of the object you are viewing.

**Stamen**
The male part of a flower (consists of an anther and a filament).

**Stigma**
One of the female parts of a flower. The stigma is the surface that pollen grains attach to before developing a pollen tube at the start of plant fertilisation.

**Stopping distance**
The distance covered in the time between a driver first spotting a hazard and the vehicle coming to a complete stop. It's the sum of the thinking distance and the braking distance.

**Subliming**
The change in state of a substance directly from a solid to a gas.

**Sustainable development**
Managing the way resources are used, so that the needs of a growing human population can be met without harming the environment.

**System**
An object or group of objects that you're looking at.

**Systematic error**
An error that is consistently made every time throughout an experiment.

**Tertiary consumer**
An animal that eats secondary consumers.

**Testis**
The part of the male reproductive system which produces sperm.

**Theory**
A hypothesis which has been accepted by the scientific community because there is good evidence to back it up.

**Thermal decomposition**
When a substance breaks down into two or more new substances when heated.

**Thinking distance**
The distance a vehicle travels during a driver's reaction time (the time between them spotting a hazard and applying the brakes).

**Tissue**
A group of similar cells.

**Top carnivore**
An animal that is not eaten by anything else.

**Translucent**
A material that absorbs some light and scatters some light.

**Transparent**
A material that doesn't absorb light — the light is transmitted through the material.

**Umbilical cord**
A structure that attaches a fetus to the placenta.

**Unbalanced forces**
Forces that produce a change in the speed and/or the direction of an object.

**Unicellular organism**
A single-celled organism (e.g. Euglena).

**Urethra**
Part of the male reproductive system which carries sperm through the penis during ejaculation. (Urine also passes through the urethra to exit the body.)

**Uterus (womb)**
The part of the female reproductive system in which a baby grows.

**Vacuole**
The part of a plant cell that is filled with cell sap (a weak solution of sugar and salts).

**Vacuum**
A place where there is nothing at all (i.e. no particles or air).

**Valid result**
A result that is reliable and answers the original question.

**Variable**
A factor in an investigation that can change or be changed (e.g. temperature or concentration).

**Variation**
Differences between organisms — either between organisms of different species, or between organisms of the same species.

**Vertebrate**
An animal that has a backbone.

**Virus**
A micro-organism that invades cells and causes disease.

**Vital capacity**
A measure of lung function. It is the total amount of air that a person can breathe out after taking their biggest breath in.

**Weight**
The force acting on an object caused by the pull of gravity.

**Zygote**
A fertilised egg cell.

# Index

# Index

# Index

# Reference Sheet

## The Periodic Table

| Periods | Group 1 | Group 2 | | | | | | | | | | | Group 3 | Group 4 | Group 5 | Group 6 | Group 7 | Group 0 |
|---|---|---|---|---|---|---|---|---|---|---|---|---|---|---|---|---|---|---|
| 1 | | | | | | | | 1 H Hydrogen 1 | | | | | | | | | | 4 He Helium 2 |
| 2 | 7 Li Lithium 3 | 9 Be Beryllium 4 | | | | | | | | | | | 11 B Boron 5 | 12 C Carbon 6 | 14 N Nitrogen 7 | 16 O Oxygen 8 | 19 F Fluorine 9 | 20 Ne Neon 10 |
| 3 | 23 Na Sodium 11 | 24 Mg Magnesium 12 | | | | | | | | | | | 27 Al Aluminium 13 | 28 Si Silicon 14 | 31 P Phosphorus 15 | 32 S Sulfur 16 | 35.5 Cl Chlorine 17 | 40 Ar Argon 18 |
| 4 | 39 K Potassium 19 | 40 Ca Calcium 20 | 45 Sc Scandium 21 | 48 Ti Titanium 22 | 51 V Vanadium 23 | 52 Cr Chromium 24 | 55 Mn Manganese 25 | 56 Fe Iron 26 | 59 Co Cobalt 27 | 59 Ni Nickel 28 | 63.5 Cu Copper 29 | 65 Zn Zinc 30 | 70 Ga Gallium 31 | 73 Ge Germanium 32 | 75 As Arsenic 33 | 79 Se Selenium 34 | 80 Br Bromine 35 | 84 Kr Krypton 36 |
| 5 | 86 Rb Rubidium 37 | 88 Sr Strontium 38 | 89 Y Yttrium 39 | 91 Zr Zirconium 40 | 93 Nb Niobium 41 | 96 Mo Molybdenum 42 | 99 Tc Technetium 43 | 101 Ru Ruthenium 44 | 103 Rh Rhodium 45 | 106 Pd Palladium 46 | 108 Ag Silver 47 | 112 Cd Cadmium 48 | 115 In Indium 49 | 119 Sn Tin 50 | 122 Sb Antimony 51 | 128 Te Tellurium 52 | 127 I Iodine 53 | 131 Xe Xenon 54 |
| 6 | 133 Cs Caesium 55 | 137 Ba Barium 56 | 57-71 Lanthanides | 179 Hf Hafnium 72 | 181 Ta Tantalum 73 | 184 W Tungsten 74 | 186 Re Rhenium 75 | 190 Os Osmium 76 | 192 Ir Iridium 77 | 195 Pt Platinum 78 | 197 Au Gold 79 | 201 Hg Mercury 80 | 204 Tl Thallium 81 | 207 Pb Lead 82 | 209 Bi Bismuth 83 | 210 Po Polonium 84 | 210 At Astatine 85 | 222 Rn Radon 86 |
| 7 | 223 Fr Francium 87 | 226 Ra Radium 88 | 89-103 Actinides | | | | | | | | | | | | | | | |

metals | non-metals | separates metals from non-metals

## Formula Triangles

If you've got any formula that's in the form "A = B × C" or "A = B ÷ C", you can put it into a formula triangle to help you rearrange it. You do this using two easy rules:

1) If the formula is "A = B × C" then A goes on the top and B × C goes on the bottom.
2) If the formula is "A = B ÷ C" then B must go on the top (because that's the only way it'll give "B divided by something") — and so pretty obviously A and C must go on the bottom.

**Example**

How to use them: Cover up the thing you want to find and write down what's left showing. So to find t from this one, cover up t and you get d/s left showing, so "t = d/s".

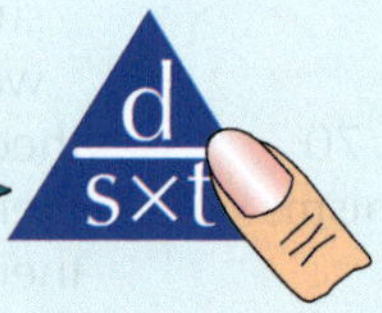


## Useful Physics Formulae

| Quantity | Symbol | Units | Formula |
|---|---|---|---|
| Speed | s | m/s, mph, km/h | speed = distance ÷ time, s = d/t |
| Pressure | P | N/m², N/cm² | pressure = force ÷ area, P = F/A |
| Density | D | g/cm³, kg/m³ | density = mass ÷ volume, D = m/V |
| Weight | W | N | weight = mass × gravitational field strength, W = m × g |